REFLECTIVE FACULTY EVALUATION

John A. Centra

REFLECTIVE FACULTY EVALUATION

Enhancing Teaching and Determining Faculty Effectiveness

Jossey-Bass Publishers · San Francisco

Substantial discounts on bulk quantities of Jossey-Bass books are available to corporations, professional associations, and other organizations. For details and discount information, contact the special sales department at Jossey-Bass Inc., Publishers. (415) 433-1740; Fax (415) 433-0499.

For sales outside the United States, contact Maxwell Macmillan International Publishing Group, 866 Third Avenue, New York, New York 10022.

Manufactured in the United States of America

The paper used in this book is acid-free and meets the State of California requirements for recycled paper (50 percent recycled waste, including 10 percent postconsumer waste), which are the strictest guidelines for recycled paper currently in use in the United States.

10% POST CONSUMER WASTE

The ink in this book is either soy- or vegetable-based and during the printing process emits fewer than half the volatile organic compounds (VOCs) emitted by petroleum-based ink.

Credits are on page 245.

Library of Congress Cataloging-in-Publication Data

Centra, John A.
   Reflective faculty evaluation : enhancing teaching and determining faculty effectiveness / John A. Centra — 1st ed.
      p.   cm.—(The Jossey-Bass higher and adult education series)
   Includes bibliographical references (p.   ) and index.
   ISBN 1-55542-579-8
   1. College teachers—Rating of. 2. Student evaluation of teachers.   I. Title.   II. Series.
LB2333.C456   1993
378.1'22—dc20   93-19504
                                                                          CIP

FIRST EDITION
HB Printing   10 9 8 7 6 5 4 3 2 1   *Code 9378*

The Jossey-Bass
Higher and Adult Education Series

*To my parents and teachers,
from whom I learned
when to judge and,
more importantly,
when not to judge*

CONTENTS

Tables, Figures, and Exhibits xi

Preface xiii

The Author xix

1. The Role of Evaluation in Developing
  Teaching Effectiveness 1

2. Approaches to Teaching and Implications
  for Evaluation 20

3. Student Evaluations of Teaching:
  What Research Tells Us 47

4. Using Student Evaluations:
  Guidelines and Benefits 80

5. Teachers' Self-Reports and Portfolios 94

6. Critical Roles of Colleagues and
    Department Chairs   115

7. Determining Effectiveness in Research
    and Service   135

8. Legal Considerations in Faculty Evaluation   158

9. Closing Reflections on Determining
    Faculty Effectiveness   173

    Resource A: Available Student
    Rating Instruments   179

    Resource B: Sample Forms for Classroom
    Observation and Colleague Evaluation   205

    References   217

    Index   237

TABLES, FIGURES, AND EXHIBITS

Tables

3.1. Reliability of Student Evaluation Instruments: Examples from Two Instruments   59

3.2. Student Ratings of Instruction and Courses in Different Disciplines—Four-Year College (Highest)   68

3.3. Student Ratings of Instruction and Courses in Different Disciplines—Four-Year College (Middle)   69

3.4. Student Ratings of Instruction and Courses in Different Disciplines—Four-Year College (Lowest)   69

3.5. Disciplinary Comparisons on Other SIR Scales   70

5.1. Correlations Among Raters for Motivational Skills, Interpersonal Skills, Intellectual Skills, and Total Teaching   108

5.2. Correlations Among Raters for Scores in College Service, Community Service, Credentials, and Professional Activities   108

7.1. Types of Publications Considered Important for Gaining Tenure, by Type of Institution   137

7.2.   Average Number of Publications by Full-Time
       Faculty Members, 1986 and 1987, by Discipline,
       at Four-Year Institutions   144

Figure

1.1.   The NVHM Model for Change   15

Exhibit

3.1.   Examples of Items Used in Multisection Validity
       Studies, Categorized into Dimensions   55

PREFACE

*W*hen I wrote *Determining Faculty Effectiveness* in 1979, the need to find solid ways to evaluate and improve faculty members' performance was considerable. It still is. Good teachers still need more frequent recognition of their efforts; poor or beginning teachers still need to know how and what to improve; and publication—not necessarily good research—continues to drive promotions at many institutions. Evaluation—good evaluation, that is—addresses all these concerns.

Background

We have learned much since 1979. New research findings have been published and new approaches to evaluation developed. In this book, I present the latest findings and approaches and discuss current issues: a more complete definition of scholarship that includes teaching and public service; the need for better use of and guidelines for student evaluations; better ways to involve colleagues in evaluating and improving teaching; proper use of self-reports and portfolios; varieties of effective teaching; and legal considerations in faculty evaluation.

Certain basic principles about faculty evaluation that I discussed in 1979 still apply. One of these is the difference between evaluation for improvement (formative evaluation) and evaluation for decision making (summative evaluation). While these are separate and sometimes conflicting types of evaluation, they can also complement each other. A second basic principle is that the quality of evaluation, whatever its purpose, is higher if multiple sources of information are used. For example, formative evaluation is more likely to lead to improvements if a teacher is given confirming evidence from more than one source. Moreover, not all sources are valued by each teacher. In Chapter One, I introduce four conditions that must be fulfilled if teaching is to improve through formative evaluation. In the later chapters, I expand on them.

I have titled this book *Reflective Faculty Evaluation* because reflection is important for both teaching performance and the evaluation of teaching performance. Self-reflection is critical in improving any professional practice, including college teaching. When students or colleagues submit formative evaluations, for example, teachers should reflect on the information and how it relates to their intentions for a course before taking action. They should be open to suggestions that may challenge what they have been doing and how effective they have been. Reflection should also be part of a self-report or portfolio; mere description is not sufficient. True professionals in any field are constantly thinking about what they are doing and how they can improve. Similarly, formative evaluation is likely to be of higher quality if the people doing the evaluations reflect about what they want to convey. Students and colleagues should think carefully about the judgments and suggestions they make and the effect those will have on a teacher's performance. Haphazard feedback based on poor information does not deserve to be taken seriously.

The title of the book also refers to the summative decision process. Administrators and other professionals who help make tenure and promotion decisions should also deliberate before taking action. They should carefully consider the information they receive about candidates, taking into account all areas of their performance over time. Evaluators should guard against a tendency to think only about what the person has done lately: that diminishes both the importance and the memory of earlier accomplishments. They should keep in mind the individual faculty members' progress as they develop different areas of expertise during their careers.

Although the lecture method is by far the dominant method of instruction in colleges and universities, research has demonstrated its limitations, particularly when higher levels of learning are called for. Given its limited impact, many educators are encouraging alternative methods that feature active learning, as they should be. But unfortunately, many evaluation forms and evaluators still focus on traditional methods of teaching. It is a matter of the proverbial tail wagging the dog: teaching methods should not be dictated by evaluation methods. After discussing the varieties of teaching that are in at least some small way being used by college teachers, I suggest ways to determine the effectiveness of the alternative approaches.

Audience

Faculty members, administrators, and faculty development specialists will all, I believe, find the book useful. All three groups want to improve teaching; and evaluation information, *if properly used,* can help. Administrators want to make fair and legally sound decisions; *Reflective Faculty Evaluation* should help them in that, too, as it should faculty members who are interested in making a strong case for promotion or tenure. The teaching portfolio has developed into a structured approach for faculty to report on their own growth and accomplishments. The portfolio can also be used constructively in posttenure review.

I examine the strengths and limitations of the various procedures used in evaluation, with an emphasis on the research findings. The discussions are nontechnical and easily understood.

The book does not provide a specific system of assessment that colleges and universities can simply adopt. They will, however, find guidelines, general principles, research evidence, and ideas to consider as they develop their own approaches. Circumstances and institutional cultures differ, as do the individuals who will be affected by any evaluation system; the individuals should therefore have some involvement in the design of the system.

Overview of the Contents

Seven of the nine chapters deal largely with the evaluation and improvement of teaching. And rightly so, I believe, given the complexity of teaching and the renewed interest in acknowledging its importance. Chapter One sets the stage. Teaching and scholarship must be balanced, and good teaching must be recognized if its status is to improve. Ph.D. programs should pay more attention to preparing their graduates for teaching. Chapter One discusses all these needs and the role that evaluation can play in dealing with them. The major focus of the chapter is on how evaluation can lead to teaching improvement. I propose a model of evaluative procedures that, if properly followed, can significantly enhance improvement. This NVHM model is referred to in later chapters of the book that discuss student, colleague, and self-evaluations of teaching.

Chapter Two presents a brief history of teaching methods and summarizes the various approaches currently used in college classrooms. Evaluators of teaching should be sensitive to the different goals and procedures that a teacher may employ. The perennial question, What is good teaching? and the need to maintain ethics in teaching are also discussed.

Because of the wide use of student evaluations of teaching and the importance given to them, two chapters are devoted to the topic. In Chapter Three, I present the history of student evaluations and review the extensive research findings on them. Most of the findings support the use of student evaluations, although readers will also learn about their limitations.

Chapter Four continues the subject with a discussion of the benefits of using student evaluations for formative and summative purposes. The chapter concludes with twelve guidelines for the proper use of student evaluations.

The potential of various kinds of self-reports, including the teaching portfolio, is discussed in Chapter Five. A study I conducted on the use of the portfolio at one college is described and the implications of the findings are summarized. The chapter concludes with a discussion of the ways in which a teacher's own classroom research can lead to improvement in teaching.

For evaluation to truly affect teaching, colleagues and chairs must be involved. Chapter Six describes how some institutions have successfully involved colleagues in formative and summative evaluation. One approach, ad hoc committees on teaching, seems especially promising; information about an individual's performance from a number of sources is combined, and a reasonable procedure is provided for colleagues' evaluations of the information. The chapter concludes with guidelines for colleagues and chairs to follow in their evalutions.

Research has been broadly defined to mean faculty activities that advance knowledge and the arts. Some people have defined it even more broadly to include teaching and public service. Chapter Seven discusses these conceptions of research and scholarship. Also included in the chapter is a discussion of the relationship between a person's performance as a researcher and as a teacher; the trend toward heavier emphasis on quality over quantity in evaluation of research performance; the wide variations in research patterns by discipline; and the role of ethical norms in performance evaluation. Public service includes a wide range of faculty activities that, as I argue in Chapter Seven, need to be evaluated and given proper recognition in performance reviews.

The current legal climate is described in Chapter Eight. The purpose of the chapter is not to make an instant legal expert of every faculty member or administrator who reads it but rather to provide enough information so that flagrant violations of individual rights are avoided when evaluation systems are designed and judgments made. The importance of obtaining legal counsel early on is also emphasized, and other guidelines and recommendations for institutions are offered.

The final chapter, Chapter Nine, includes a brief discussion of the use of measures of student learning in formative and summative evaluation. I also provide criteria for judging the quality of teacher-made examinations and other assessment practices. Some final thoughts round out the text.

Acknowledgments

Many colleagues and students contributed to this book, either directly by reviewing chapters or indirectly by discussing the issues with me over the years. Those who contributed indirectly include the many researchers and teachers with an interest in the field. William McKeachie, who has written so extensively on this topic, provided a very helpful review of the first draft. The comments of a second, anonymous reviewer were useful, too. Various colleagues brought their special expertise on the topic to their review of individual chapters: Philip Abrami on student evaluations, Richard Crockett on legal considerations, and Joseph Shedd on colleague evaluations. I am grateful for the diligence and care shown by Olympia Lira in helping to prepare the manuscript, and for the assistance of graduate students Mardy Eimers, Madeline Moed, and Carol Van Der Karr.

The college experiences of my three daughters, Cathy, Liza, and Joan, undoubtedly influenced the writing of parts of the book. And not least, I thank my wife, Nancy Centra, for her encouragement and—because she is herself a masterful teacher—her insightful comments during the lengthy gestation of the work.

Syracuse, New York   John A. Centra
August 1993

THE AUTHOR

John A. Centra is professor and chair of the Higher Education Program at Syracuse University. He received his B.A. degree (1954) in social sciences from the State University of New York, Albany, his M.A. degree (1957) in personnel psychology from Columbia University, and his Ph.D. degree (1965) in counseling psychology from Michigan State University.

Centra spent seventeen years as a research psychologist at the Educational Testing Service, where he conducted studies on college teaching, faculty development, the effects of colleges on students, and other topics. He has been at Syracuse University since 1985, where, in addition to performing teaching, dissertation advising, research, and department-chair duties, he has served on tenure and promotion committees and on university committees on instruction and the assessment of learning. He has given talks and workshops or consulted at more than one hundred colleges and universities. Centra has given presentations at numerous national and international conferences, and has taught in Europe and Asia. He received the 1993 American Educational Research Association W. J. McKeachie career achievement award from the Special Interest Group on Faculty Evaluation and Development.

He is author of *Determining Faculty Effectiveness* (1979) and more than seventy-five published articles, monographs, and books. Among these are *Women, Men and the Doctorate* (1974), *Maintaining Faculty Vitality Through Faculty Development* (1985), *Assessing General Education* (1988), *College Teaching: An Art or a Science?* (1990), and *The Use of the Portfolio and Student Evaluations in Summative Evaluations* (1993).

REFLECTIVE FACULTY EVALUATION

Chapter 1

The Role of Evaluation
in Developing Teaching Effectiveness

*P*oor evaluation, whether of students or of faculty, renders an unfair judgment and fails to reveal shortcomings in performance. Good evaluation, on the other hand, provides decision makers with the information necessary for informed choices, and teachers with useful feedback for improvement.

Faculty members' performance falls into three primary areas: teaching, research, and service. Although the relative importance of each varies greatly from institution to institution depending on its mission, teaching and research performance are generally the most critical in faculty tenure and promotion decisions. Many faculty members and administrators believe it is far easier to evaluate the quality of research than of teaching. It is true that measures used for teaching performance have not seemed as precise as those used for research. It is also likely that faculty members vary more in their scholarly performance than in their teaching performance. And the variation is greater from faculty member to faculty member at a given institution as well as from year to year for individuals. For example, faculty members who publish or receive grants produce more research in some years than in others, while their teaching performance remains more constant. Nevertheless, significant fluctuations in

1

teaching do occur, and certainly teachers differ from each other in commitment and performance. Better ways are needed to assess performance, so that both individuals and institutions can improve and recognize good teaching. Also needed are broader definitions of scholarship and creative endeavor, so that their links with teaching can be recognized and encouraged.

In this book, I discuss new approaches to evaluating college teaching. The sources of information remain the same as those I discussed in my earlier *Determining Faculty Performance* (1979)—evaluations by students, colleagues and chairs, faculty development specialists, and self-reports. What is new are the ways in which these sources can be tapped to provide a more complete picture of an individual's teaching performance and its many complexities. This more complete picture results from *continuous and reflective documentation of information* from all sources, so that evaluators do not base their decisions simply on what comes first to mind.

Most of the book deals with the evaluation of teaching, because teaching is complex and often undervalued. Scholarship, in its many forms, is also discussed. Teaching, scholarship, and service are overlapping activities for many faculty members. In fact, some writers argue that teaching and service are forms of scholarship (Boyer, 1990; Lynton and Elman, 1987). Evaluation of an individual's performance should take this overlap into account and attempt to determine how one activity contributes to the other. Moreover, faculty members may emphasize different activities at different stages of their careers (Baldwin, 1990); their performance in each will therefore fluctuate over time. Researchers who turn their talents to public service or to teaching are one example. Evaluators should not be surprised by these shifts, and, in fact, should expect them as part of normal faculty career development.

Service—to the institution, community, and profession—is generally given much less consideration in personnel decisions than are research and teaching and is seldom the focus of faculty development activities (Centra, 1979). But at some institutions, and in departments that prepare students for professions, service is valued and rewarded. Evaluation of research and service is discussed in Chapter Seven.

Balancing Teaching and Scholarship

The conflict between teaching and research has plagued a large segment of American higher education since the research function was first brought to American universities from Germany in the late 1800s. The basic conflict, between what many faculty members find rewarding and what they believe their institutions reward, remains today. Consider the following results from three recent studies:

1. A survey of more than 35,000 faculty members found that being a good teacher was an essential goal for 98 percent of them, yet only 10 percent believed their institutions rewarded good teaching. This same survey found that almost 80 percent of university faculty members said that conducting research was the highest priority at their institutions; about 33 percent at four-year colleges and only 11 percent at two-year colleges said so (Higher Education Research Institute, 1991).

2. In a study of forty-seven research and doctorate-granting institutions, faculty members, chairs, deans, and other administrators were queried about the relative importance of research and undergraduate teaching on their campuses. While all the groups affirmed that research and undergraduate teaching were of equal importance to them, they thought their universities placed greater emphasis on research. Furthermore, faculty members believed that administrators favored research, whereas administrators said they weighted teaching more heavily (Gray, Froh, and Diamond, 1992).

3. The 1989 National Survey of Faculty by the Carnegie Foundation for the Advancement of Teaching revealed sizable differences of opinion by type of institution and by discipline. The need to publish to achieve tenure was considered to be most critical at research and doctorate-granting institutions (where 75 percent of the faculty strongly agreed that it was necessary); it was also more critical in the natural and social sciences than in other fields. But only 4 percent of two-year college faculties and 24 percent of liberal arts college faculties reported that publishing was necessary for tenure (Boyer, 1990).

What some survey results reflect is the friction between personal values and institutional culture at many universities. They also reflect a basic misunderstanding between faculty members and administrators: either the administrators are not making their priorities about the importance of teaching known or they are not backing up beliefs with action. Although personnel decisions emanate from the department level, administrators can establish policies and allocate budgets to promote effective teaching (Seldin and Associates, 1990). Supporting faculty or instructional development centers (see Centra, 1978a, and Weimer, 1990, for a description of possible programs), providing top-notch classroom facilities, endorsing broader definitions of scholarship, and favoring promotions for strong teachers with modest research records are just a few of the ways in which administrators can alter the institutional culture. At some institutions, changing the student culture may also be needed to change the institutional culture. A student body that places excessive value on social life and is interested only in learning skills that will be useful in getting jobs presents more of a challenge than many faculty members are able or willing to meet. Changing the student culture is not easily done. In an effort to do so, one institution has introduced a "compact" that students sign at entrance, pledging their commitment to academic values and individual effort in their course work.

Finally, at comprehensive colleges and universities, faculty members hired in the 1960s and early 1970s were often told that research was not important for advancement. But faculty hired thereafter were given a new message: research was indeed valued, although teaching competence was also expected. The shifting missions and curricula of these institutions (many of which were teachers colleges) resulted not only in different criteria for determining faculty effectiveness but in conflicting faculty subcultures within the institutions.

At institutions where research is not emphasized (most two-year colleges and many liberal arts colleges), faculty members' doubts about adequate recognition of teaching, as revealed in the surveys discussed earlier, probably result from their lack of confidence in evaluation procedures. Most institutions are probably doing a better job today than they did ten or twenty years ago, but there is still much room for improvement.

Formative and Summative Evaluations

Formative and summative evaluations, which were first applied to program evaluation, have become familiar and useful in faculty evaluation. Formative evaluation is used to improve teaching performance; the information is given to teachers, whether it is obtained from students, colleagues, or faculty development specialists, and is meant to bring about positive changes. In contrast, summative evaluation is used to make personnel decisions—to hire, promote, grant tenure, or give a merit raise. The key word in both definitions is *use*—not intended use but actual use. Thus, evaluation results that are intended to be used formatively but are actually used summatively should not be thought of as formative. Formative evaluations should be used only as an aid to improvement; any other use at the same time alters the effects on the teacher, and the role of the evaluator. People involved in formative evaluation—whether chairs, colleagues, or faculty development specialists—will not be as effective in helping teachers if they are also making summative judgments based on the information obtained. The reason has more to do with the teachers than with the evaluators: teachers will not be as open to discussing weaknesses or seeking advice from people who will also judge them.

Some methods of evaluation were first used for formative purposes but were later adopted for summative purposes. Student evaluations are an example. After faculty members and administrators on many campuses decided that student evaluations were both valid and nonthreatening, they endorsed them for use in personnel decisions. Once this was done, systematic and controlled procedures for collecting the information, and standards for making judgments were needed. Indeed, if these results are to be used for personnel decisions, care must be taken to minimize bias and "contamination" (see the Guidelines for Student Evaluations in Chapter Four).

If possible, it makes sense to use evaluation procedures formatively before adopting them summatively. In this way, teachers become acquainted with the procedures and the criteria to be used, and have the opportunity to improve their performance before being judged.

Some people have suggested that "informative feedback"

may be a better term than "formative evaluation." Many teachers have become accustomed to evaluations that are judgmental only and might therefore be more comfortable with the notion of feedback, in spite of the term's mechanistic tone. But although informative feedback may sound less threatening, the terms *formative* and *summative* emphasize the critical connection between the two: that people have the opportunity to improve on the criteria they will eventually be judged on. Moreover, whether the term used is *formative evaluation* or *informative feedback,* what is important is the kind of criticism given. Criticism should be constructive, not destructive. Destructive criticism highlights psychological and personal attributes that lead to failures or weaknesses (Boice, 1992). As such, it is a personal attack that makes the person angry, tense, and resistant to change. Constructive criticism recognizes strengths as well as weaknesses, and offers suggestions for change in behaviors or procedures.

In this book, I discuss the application of evaluation information for both formative and summative purposes. Having information for these uses is the major reason institutions and individuals invest the time and effort needed to obtain it, but a third reason should be kept in mind: accountability to the consumer. Legislators, parents, and students want evidence that institutions are providing the best instruction possible. The popularity of various annual reviews of colleges, such as *U.S. News and World Report*'s annual review of the "best" colleges, attests to the consumer's desire for information. Unfortunately, the criteria used for these evaluations—such as institution-reported retention rates and faculty-to-student ratios—are at best proxy measures of teaching and learning. Some institutions, in an effort to demonstrate their concern for quality instruction, have established mandatory student evaluations of teaching performance and annual teacher-of-the-year awards. Such practices may appeal to the various public constituencies, but a wider array of evaluation and improvement practices such as those discussed in this book are likely to have a greater impact on the quality of teaching.

Criteria and Standards

Put simply, criteria define what aspects of a performance will be evaluated; standards define the desired level of achievement. Teaching and scholarship are two major areas of faculty evaluation. For teaching, research suggests that establishing rapport with students, organizing the subject matter in a course, and receiving high evaluations from students on "teaching effectiveness" are possible criteria for assessment. For scholarship, publishing articles in a refereed journal is an example of a criterion for evaluation. Many debates revolve around determining what an acceptable level of teaching effectiveness is, or how many articles per year are sufficient, and quality. Though there may not be complete agreement about all the criteria to be used, there is even less agreement about what constitutes excellent, good, or unacceptable performance.

Standards are frequently determined comparatively. For example, professor A is in the top 10 percent of teachers at one institution on a global evaluation item. On occasion, standards are determined in an absolute way. For instance, in the evaluation of scholarship, faculty members in a particular college are expected to produce two published articles in a refereed journal per year. The increased use of portfolios or dossiers provides another standard: the individual's own teaching philosophy, expectations, and reflections. Portfolio statements should address the following issues: What criteria does the teacher endorse? What kind of personal standards does that individual set? Are these worthwhile? Does the portfolio include either evidence that the teacher has met the standards or other examples of success? (See Chapter Five for a discussion of portfolios and their evaluation; Chapter Eight includes a discussion of the application of criteria and standards in legal cases.)

Relative judgments can damage collegiality and cooperation, especially when the comparison group is small and faculty members are competing against each other for promotions or raises. Some management experts, W. Edwards Deming (1982) most notably, argue that relative judgments and merit ratings damage teamwork and nourish rivalries, while at the same time adversely affecting quality. Deming's quality-management principles emphasize a collaborative role for managers; he asserts that their job is to enlist the help of employees in continuously improving the overall system. His ideas are credited with helping Japan develop the production force to become a major economic power. Total Quality Management (TQM), a system for creating organizationwide participation in planning and improvement, is an extension of these principles. Yet many companies have evaluation systems that emphasize relative merit ratings: managers must rate 10 percent of their employees as exemplary and eligible for the highest bonuses or raises, and another 10 percent as failures and subject to dismissal. Our culture, with its grading system in schools and colleges, has encouraged managers to think in this way. Deming and others argue that quality and productivity have suffered because of these traditional measurement and reward systems. What is needed, they say, is a work environment that is more conducive to change, where managers help employees improve both the environment and their own performance, and where teamwork is encouraged.

Such principles can be readily translated to the academic environment. Collaboration among faculty members strengthens both teaching and research. Chairs and deans often strive to improve the work environment and individual performance. Tenure and promotion decisions must be made, however, and for these, summative evaluation information from the many sources I discuss in this book provide a complete and I hope convergent view of performance. Evaluation for merit increases is another story, because giving such increases is in itself a controversial practice. Merit increases to base salary may not only fail to provide the incentive needed but also discourage collaboration and other practices that improve the overall quality of teaching, research, and service at an institution. This clearly is a dilemma for institutions. If not giving merit increases means that some faculty members receive lower salaries than they should in the competitive academic market, those teachers will look elsewhere. Giving merit increases may not only decrease cooperation but cause people who feel they were unfairly overlooked to do only a minimal amount of work. Several models and formulas exist for converting faculty-performance ratings into merit increases (Centra, 1979, pp. 166–170; Camp, Gibbs, and Masters, 1988). They generally depend on quantitative ratings of each area of an individual's performance and frequently do not give deserved attention to qualitative indicators. Moreover, if fine distinctions are made, so that one professor receives only slightly less money than another, it hardly seems worth the effort made or the hard feelings of those who feel slighted. In short, if merit increases are given, they should be large enough to be meaningful, and based on valid and significant differences in performance.

Improving Teaching Through
Formative Evaluation: A Model

Formative evaluation does not always lead to improvement in teaching. In fact, truly significant improvement is likely to take place only if the evaluation fulfills four conditions. These conditions constitute a model for improving teaching through formative evaluation. They apply to each source of evaluation (including students and colleagues and self-reports). I discuss their use with each source in later chapters of this book.

The four conditions can be named (1) new knowledge, (2) value, (3) how to change, and (4) motivation, or NVHM. Through formative evaluation the teachers must first learn something new about their teaching performance (new knowledge). Second, they must value the information; this generally means they must have confidence in the source and in the evaluation process (value). Third, teachers must understand how to make the changes called for (how to change). And finally, teachers must be motivated to make the changes (motivation). Let us examine each condition more closely.

New Knowledge

Whether a teacher gains any new knowledge from an evaluation depends on his or her perceptiveness and the source of the evaluation. Students, colleagues, chairs, and faculty development specialists can all provide evaluation information; each also provides a different perspective and different kinds of information. Students, for example, observe the teacher over an extended period of time and can report on how different course elements influence their learning. Colleagues and chairs may provide a new perspective on course content or assignments. Faculty development specialists, because of their own training and knowledge, can offer information on everything from the syllabus to classroom techniques to the final-examination questions. Successively less new information can be gained with continued use of each source. For example, if student evaluations are collected year after year, and particularly if the same form for them is used, teachers can be expected to learn less from the student viewpoint after several years than they did during the first year or two. Self-evaluations provide the least new information because teachers often simply confirm their own views, which are often misconceptions. Self-evaluations are usually assessments of one's own performance in various categories, with numerical self-rating scales often being used to obtain the information. Self-reflection, on the other hand, can be more useful. Self-reflection requires a great deal of thought about what one is doing and which practices might be improved. Schön (1983) has discussed the importance of reflective practice for professionals; I elaborate on the use of self-reflection with portfolios and self-reports in Chapter Five.

Value

Unless teachers believe that the information they receive has value and that the source is to be respected, they may simply dismiss it. Teachers differ in how they view each source, but in general they probably value the opinions of faculty development specialists, chairs, and colleagues more highly than those of students. Of course, this also depends on the basis for the evaluations. An evaluation by a faculty development specialist who has not observed a class, for example, will not be considered so helpful as that of one who has. Although students are the instructor's most constant observers, some faculty members believe they do not have the maturity and knowledge needed to make valid or useful evaluations. Moreover, if they are harsh or overcritical, student evaluations may increase anxieties to a point where the teacher becomes defensive and rejects any suggestion for change. In any situation, anxious individuals become less creative, more rigid, and perform at a lower level than usual (McKeachie, 1982). Hence, the impact of student evaluation on teaching practices is often modest (see Chapter Four). Whatever the source, the evaluation must be a balance between challenge and support or it will be perceived as a threat and provoke the same anxious and self-defeating reaction.

Colleagues and administrators who can be most effective in

bringing about teaching improvements have skills that have grown out of their own past experiences, often as teachers. Yet their knowledge may be intuitive and difficult for them to convey. Schön (1983) has discussed how professionals learn to solve problems and make judgments through reflection-in-action: "When we go about the spontaneous, intuitive performance of the actions of everyday life, we show ourselves to be knowledgeable in a special way. Often we cannot say what it is that we know" (p. 49).

Reflection, thus, is as important for evaluators as for those being evaluated. Evaluators need to draw on their past experiences and tacit knowledge in developing the strengths of individual teachers.

How to Change

Failure to understand how to change is probably what most frequently prevents significant improvement. Most information, whether from students or from colleagues, is long on judgment and short on helpful advice. The typical student evaluation form, for example, rates course organization but offers few suggestions for change (except, perhaps, to make the course objectives clearer). Many changes in teaching practices are what one writer described as "tinkering," minor course and instructional adjustments (Stevens, 1988). Much formative evaluation leads to tinkering because those are the kinds of suggestions that are usually offered, especially with student evaluations. Knowledgeable faculty development specialists, and perhaps a handful of colleagues, can be more helpful in bringing about extensive changes and innovations. Faculty development or instructional improvement programs have the greatest potential to help individuals significantly change their teaching. A survey done in the mid 1980s found that about 28 percent of the colleges studied had a center for or director of faculty development (Erickson, 1986). A survey I conducted in the mid 1970s of 756 two- and four-year institutions (Centra, 1978a) found a similar number of development units, with almost half of all institutions employing people who, if they did not direct units, had administrative duties that included coordinating faculty development activities. The titles given to most units contain the words "development," "excellence," or "effectiveness" rather than "improvement" or "clinic," which would imply that the units serve only faculty members who have problems or need to improve. Thus, typical titles are Center for Teaching Excellence, or Center for Teaching Effectiveness and Student Learning. My survey revealed that faculty development specialists relied heavy on formative evaluations in their individual consultations with teachers. Weimer (1990) and Eble and McKeachie (1985) provide recommendations for organizing and operating instructional development units. As Weimer points out, no one approach is right for all institutions; the institution's culture and goals should determine what is right for it. Eble and McKeachie found that administrative support was critical to success.

Motivation

There are two types of motivating forces: intrinsic and extrinsic. Either one can influence teachers to seek feedback or to change following formative evaluation. Deci (1975, p. 125) defined intrinsic motivation as the underlying need for "a sense of competence and self-determination." Deci and Ryan (1985, p. 29) later added: "To be truly intrinsically motivated, a person must feel free from pressures, such as rewards or contingencies." When a person is intrinsically motivated, external rewards such as salary increments, promotions, or recognition are not necessary; the rewards are inherent in the activity itself. Extrinsic motivation, by contrast, depends on such rewards. Hackman and Oldham (1980) and Hackman and Lawler (1970) identified three critical features of intrinsic motivation:

> *Experiencing Meaningfulness of Work:* The individual experiences the job as meaningful and challenging, and sees that it affects the lives of others; the individual has the skills needed to meet the challenge.
> *Experiencing Responsibility for Work Outcomes:* The individual feels responsible for the effects of his work and autonomous in its performance.
> *Knowledge of Results:* The individual receives continual informal feedback about her job performance and not only

learns how she is doing but experiences pleasure in doing the job.

Understanding what motivates faculty intrinsically is critical to improving teaching performance. Extrinsic rewards are clearly limited as a source of motivation. Full professors with tenure no longer look to promotions as rewards; the limited amount of money that many institutions are able to offer as merit increases is not likely to motivate very many teachers. Teacher-of-the-year financial awards are probably equally ineffective: the few given out have little effect on the many faculty members who are not sure how to compete for such prizes. The effect of annual teaching awards in raising standards or teachers' performance is more cosmetic than actual, particularly for those who most need to improve. Moreover, most teaching-award winners and other exemplary teachers are likely to have been motivated by intrinsic rather than an extrinsic factors. Merit raises and teacher-of-the-year awards do, however, have symbolic value: they signal the institution's appreciation of teaching. Nevertheless, they should be accompanied by other teaching-improvement programs if institutions want to demonstrate a true commitment to excellence in teaching (see below).

Another problem with extrinsic rewards is that they can decrease intrinsic motivation. This is especially true if the reward is given in a controlling way, for example, by imposing a minimum number of publications needed for promotion, which could diminish intrinsic satisfaction in doing research (Deci and Ryan, 1985). Another example would be when individuals were already highly motivated intrinsically to do what they do and the extrinsic rewards, such as salary increases, cannot be continued (Lepper, 1978). McKeachie (1979a) points out that high salaries do not guarantee motivation, but low salaries cause dissatisfaction and a corrosion of the faculty's commitment to excellence. And extrinsic rewards may promote only those activities that are valued by an institution; for instance, at many institutions, they reflect an emphasis on research over teaching. The reality is that young faculty members who are intrinsically motivated to teach rather than publish will have difficulty receiving tenure at research-oriented institutions, unless they are also able to meet publication requirements.

Thus, as we have already discussed, institutions need to change both their culture and their reward system. In addition, they should develop intrinsic motivation to teach effectively in as many of the following ways as they can:

1. Help new faculty develop the skills needed to meet the challenge of teaching. New faculty or, for that matter, experienced faculty who are overwhelmed by teaching will derive little sense of competence or reinforcement because they will be doing their jobs poorly.
2. For the same reasons, help graduate students receive training and mentoring in teaching (see following discussion).
3. Help provide continuous feedback, using methods such as those discussed in this book, to reinforce competent practices or to reveal weaknesses. Evaluation, however, must not be overly harsh or it will discourage teaching innovations and otherwise degrade the sense of self-determination.
4. Make available proper classroom facilities and the necessary teaching-support materials.
5. Help teachers feel challenged and renewed through such practices as altering course schedules, encouraging team teaching and interdisciplinary courses, and promoting faculty exchanges with other colleges. Offer teachers opportunities to teach small classes so that they can see the effects of their instruction on individual students.
6. Encourage curricular innovations.
7. Facilitate informal discussions and seminars on teaching among the faculty.

Significance of the Model

Improvement in teaching can, of course, take place without formative evaluation. Workshops and training sessions are just two examples of practices that are not dependent on individual evaluations. But when formative evaluation is used, I believe that the greatest change will take place when it fulfills all four of the conditions just discussed. This does not mean that improvements will not occur if only two or three conditions are fulfilled; however, in those in-

Figure 1.1. The NVHM Model for Change.

(N)	(V)	(H)	(M)

New   +   Value   +   How to   + Motivation = Maximum
knowledge   change   change

stances, the changes are not likely to be so dramatic. The model can best be understood as a linear progression of the four conditions, with a final return loop, as illustrated in Figure 1.1. The loop signifies that motivation not only affects the improvements but also may cause teachers to seek additional new knowledge about their instructional effectiveness.

Studies of the effects of student evaluations on changes in instruction have partially tested the model (Centra, 1979). For example, formative evaluation conducted by a knowledgeable faculty development specialist would probably meet at least the first three conditions and therefore have significant impact. By contrast, self-evaluation alone, which is unlikely to meet at least two of the conditions, would probably have only minor impact. The model also helps explain why some faculty members change their behavior, while others exposed to the same evaluation information do not. Individual differences, which affect the fulfillment of one or more of the conditions, would affect the outcomes of formative evaluation for each.

Role of Evaluation
in the Preparation of College Teachers

The teaching assistantship in graduate school is typically the first teaching experience for college teachers. During this time, neophyte teachers want to know how they are doing, as do beginners in most endeavors. The following comment from a first-year teaching assistant (TA) is not unusual: "The feedback from the evaluations we got, yeah, it is . . . really important. Because otherwise it's like teaching in a vacuum; it's not really teaching then because you don't know what's getting through to your students. Yeah, it's really important to get that feedback" (Peverly, 1992, p. 106).

The TA is referring to student evaluations in this case, but evaluations from department supervisors and feedback from peers are at least equally important. Evaluation is a critical part of the TA training programs that many universities have initiated in recent years. Continual evaluation from a variety of sources, including video feedback, is used in many of the programs. An example is Syracuse University's program, which was established in 1987 and has become a model for TA training. Under the auspices of the graduate school, the program begins with a fifteen-day summer orientation session. During this time, TAs from foreign countries are tested on their English-language skills and receive an introduction to the university and American higher education. International students who are deficient in spoken English skills either are not assigned teaching duties or are required to take intensive language instruction. All TAs attend sessions for six days that deal with such topics as your first class, using media, leading a discussion, lecturing, evaluating students, and dealing with problems. Micro teaching sessions, in which TAs each teach a brief lesson in their discipline and receive critiques on their performances, are especially helpful. The program ends with three days of seminars and discussions within the departments. A variety of social events are included during the two weeks. Although the Syracuse summer orientation program was effective in introducing students to the university and to teaching, it was later decided that a longer period of time and more involvement by each department would have greater impact on the TAs' development (Peverly, 1992). With this in mind, the graduate school obtained external funding to extend training throughout the entire graduate school experience and involved selected department faculty as teaching mentors (Teaching Assistant Program of the Graduate School, 1991). The mentors are trained to better supervise and evaluate TAs acquiring their first teaching experience. After their first year or two, TAs are formally evaluated by their mentors and, if qualified, receive appointments as teaching associates. As associates, they independently teach a section of a course under the supervision of their mentor and begin to fulfill the requirements of the Certificate in University Teaching, which is awarded following a series of classroom visits and a final assessment by the teaching mentor. Micro teaching workshops and other seminars, together with the development of a teaching portfolio, are part of the preparation for the certificate (see Chapter Five for a description of the portfolio, as used in the Syracuse program). During this time, the TAs continue to be socialized as future faculty members, taking part in various department meetings and social gatherings.

Many elements of the Syracuse program are supported by past research on TA training. Micro teaching, feedback based on videotapes, peer feedback, and critiques from trained classroom observers have all been effective in improving TA performance (Abbott, Wulff, and Kati Szego, 1989; Carroll, 1980). The relationship between the mentor or supervising professor and the TA is especially important. A study by Wilson and Stearns (1985) concluded that both TAs and mentors preferred an open and participatory relationship, although both also saw the need for closer attention to the TAs' teaching than was given. Unfortunately, supervising professors generally discuss subject matter rather than "how-to-teach" questions with their TAs (Wilson and Stearns, 1985; Peverly, 1992). Furthermore, they should provide guidance in teaching methodology yet allow TAs freedom to develop their own teaching styles. The following comment by a TA illustrates this point: "My supervisor helped me a lot, but I can't be her. One day she helped me plan a lesson. She came in and sat the next day to observe me. . . . She likes to be in control most of the time [but] we differ in our approach to teaching" (Peverly, 1992, p. 83).

Credit Courses in College Teaching

Many universities have begun to offer credit courses in college teaching for graduate students, with formative evaluation often an important part of the course experience. In one university, a science professor offers a how-to-teach course for science students, but more typically, someone from psychology, education, or the faculty development center offers a general course.

Before teaching such a course myself, I collected syllabi from instructors around the country. Some of the best practices I found were the following:

1. Videotaping students as they employ different teaching methods, then critiquing their performance
2. Using case studies and vignettes to apply concepts and principles and to analyze complex teaching situations
3. Having students maintain course logs that include reflections on their own presentations and growth during the course, as well as comments on class discussions, readings, and other assignments
4. Having students observe exemplary teachers, then using written descriptions of the observations in class as a basis for discussions on different successful teaching styles
5. Having students read about and discuss student learning styles and the nature of human learning
6. Teaching students what a course syllabus should contain
7. Suggesting ways to evaluate one's own instruction and student learning in a course

Special TA training programs or credit courses on college teaching are supplements to the Ph.D. degree. A handful of institutions offer the Doctor of Arts (D.A.) degree as an alternative to the Ph.D., for students interested in preparing more formally for undergraduate teaching (Dressel, 1982). Although the D.A. degree has existed for more than twenty years, it is unlikely to be adopted widely because it has not gained the respect among faculty and administrators that the Ph.D. has. Training students in teaching as part of Ph.D. programs—giving them the skills to monitor and reflect on their own performance and growth after they enter the profession—is a more realistic goal. Graduate students should also learn more about the "history, organization, and culture of American higher education," as the Study Group on the Conditions of Excellence in American Higher Education suggested (1984, p. 65). This would help them make informed choices about the kinds of institution they would prefer to join as faculty members. They should also be better equipped to play a constructive role in institutional decision making.

Summary

Evaluation can play an important role in developing teaching effectiveness. This chapter presents a model including four conditions that if fulfilled, greatly enhance teaching through formative evaluation. The model can also be used for further research on instruction. The four conditions are new knowledge, value, how to change, and motivation. In the following chapters, the fulfillment of the four conditions is discussed as they apply to self-evaluations, student evaluations, and evaluations by colleagues and chairs.

The need to give equal weight in evaluations to teaching and research is also discussed in this chapter. At most research universities, teaching receives a low priority, in spite of lip service paid to its importance. And at institutions where research is not emphasized, many faculty members do not have confidence in the methods used to evaluate teaching. Evaluation of research and public service is discussed further in Chapter Seven.

The relationship between the formative (instructional improvement) and summative (personnel decision-making) uses of evaluation is also analyzed here. Evaluative information is collected and used differently for each. Evaluation procedures that were first used for teaching improvement (for example, student evaluations), in many instances, have subsequently been adopted for summative use.

The differences between criteria and standards, as well as the effects of relative judgments and merit increases on collegiality, are described as well. Criteria define what aspects of a performance will be evaluated; standards define the desired level of achievement. Although there may not be complete agreement on which criteria to use, there is often even less agreement on what constitutes excellent, good, or unacceptable performance.

In Chapter Two, we look at a variety of effective teaching practices and evaluation procedures.

Chapter 2

Approaches to Teaching
and Implications for Evaluation

Although a variety of instructional approaches are available to college teachers, the lecture is as dominant today as it was in earlier times. This chapter provides a historical perspective on the evolution of teaching and its evaluation over the centuries. An array of alternatives to the lecture is then presented, concentrating on three active learning methods and teaching evaluation with each. Questions on ethics and norms are also discussed: What do most faculty members identify as improper teaching activities? Should institutions consider adopting a code of teaching responsibility? Finally, various points of views on good teaching are presented: Is it a science or an art? How do the different views affect evaluation?

Historical Perspective

Two of the greatest teachers of the world lived centuries ago. Although they employed very different teaching styles, both, ironically, were put to death for being too effective. In 399 B.C., the first was given a cup of hemlock to drink after an Athenian jury found him guilty of "corrupting youth" with his ideas on logic, morals, and education. Four hundred years later, the second man was crucified in Jerusalem. These two great teachers, Socrates and Jesus, had one other thing in common: both lived in relative poverty, as have so many teachers throughout the centuries.

The different teaching styles these two men used are still widely practiced. Socrates' dialectical exchange with his students, now known as the Socratic method, continues to be used in college classrooms, particularly at law schools. Based on the premise that students learn to think by being actively engaged in questioning and problem solving, the Socratic method was probably the first cognitive approach to teaching. Jesus' compelling lectures, known for their content and delivery, inspired a multitude of followers and ultimately an entire religious movement. The lecture method has become almost synonymous with college teaching. Students in medieval European universities were lectured to because the teacher possessed one of the few copies of the text. These classes were less lectures than readings, and students took notes religiously. Even the eventual availability of books, however, did not curtail the use of the lecture method.

The lecture method was used by many college teachers in colonial America because of the scarcity of books, but the recitation was the more typical mode of instruction (Brubacher and Rudy, 1976). Using a citation from a textbook or a previous lecture as a base, teachers questioned individual students vigorously. At its best, the recitation was a highly developed Socratic dialogue between teacher and student and helped train the student in comprehension and analysis. At its worst—which it was, most of the time—it emphasized and rewarded rote memory: students were expected to recite Latin, Greek, or other prose passages verbatim. As one student said, the tutor heard his class rather than taught it. The better students, in fact, realizing that they learned little from this method, frequently boycotted such classes.

Another method of instruction practiced in colonial colleges was syllogistic disputation, which had first been used in medieval universities and required an effective command of Latin. The teacher would select a thesis which the student was required to defend or deny in Latin.

> In the first part of his response he explained the terms of the thesis and cleared them of any ambiguity. After

making clear the issue he set forth his affirmation or
denial in a series of Aristotelian syllogisms. When he
finished, the other students were allowed to object, but
their objections had to be couched in Latin syllogisms. After the objections had been stated it was the
respondent's turn to rebut them in further syllogisms.
And so the disputation continued until the respondent
or objectors had been silenced. At this point, the tutor,
who had been acting as a moderator, stepped in to
summarize the arguments and state his own point of
view [Brubacher and Rudy, 1976, p. 93].

Evaluation during the colonial era took place at the end of
the academic year, when a committee of trustees and the college
president observed as the teacher asked students questions based on
the year's recitations and disputations. This exercise was neither a
test of the student's knowledge nor of the teacher's effectiveness,
because, according to Smallwood (cited in Rudolph, 1977, p. 146),
teachers simply asked their students easy or leading questions.

By the mid 1800s, written examinations had largely replaced
oral examinations. The exams were generally given at the end of the
sophomore and senior years, and unlike the practice in the oral
tests, all students were given the same questions (Brubacher and
Rudy, 1976). But because teachers graded the tests related to their
own courses, the examination results were hardly objective measures of teaching effectiveness, just as the final grades an instructor
gives today are not. In 1869, in his inaugural address as president
of Harvard, Charles Eliot decried the fact that the teaching and
examining functions resided in the same person. Thus, even at that
time, college administrators wished for measures of student learning that teachers could not manipulate and that therefore would
represent objective assessments of teacher effectiveness.

The typical eighteenth-century Yale student spent twelve to
fifteen hours per week in recitations, five to ten hours in lectures,
and two to four hours in disputations (Brubacher and Rudy, 1976).
Each method was supposed to train students' mental faculties as
well as store their minds with knowledge—the discipline and fur-
niture of the mind, as the famous Yale Report of 1828 called it.

Although conservative in their recommendation that Latin, Greek, and other traditional subjects remain the focus of the curriculum, Yale faculty members and administrators argued in that report that active teaching methods were more effective than passive methods such as lectures.

A few decades later, two active approaches to teaching, the seminar and the laboratory, were imported from Germany to the United States; an altered role for the lecture was also introduced. According to the new German model, the lecture was less a reading and more a means for instructors to inform students about the latest research—as it drew its subject matter from many sources—and to motivate students through the professors' enthusiasm for their specialties (Brubacher and Rudy, 1976). These are still the major strengths of the lecture method. Moreover, lectures can be delivered to large groups and are therefore more cost effective than small group methods. Further, many students enjoy learning by listening, and many professors find lecturing to be a familiar and comfortable method of instruction. Nevertheless, study after study has demonstrated that student assimilation of lecture content lessens dramatically after the first 15 minutes or so. One study delivered to a large audience noted that 10 percent of the students showed signs of inattention within 15 minutes, about 33 percent were inattentive within 18 minutes, and within 35 minutes the entire audience ceased to pay full attention (Verner and Dickinson, 1967). Even medical students, who are generally highly motivated to learn, lost concentration after 15 minutes (Stuart and Rutherford, 1978). McLeish (1968) analyzed student lecture notes and found that they referred to only 20 percent of the material delivered during a 45-minute interval, and that there was a sharp decrease in note taking after the first 15 minutes. McKeachie (1986) concluded that the lecture method was as effective as other teaching methods when measures of knowledge were examined but was inferior when measures of knowledge transfer to new situations, attitude change, problem solving, or critical thinking were studied.

In spite of the limitations of the lecture, it is the primary or only method used by more than 80 percent of college teachers (Thielens, 1987; Blackburn, Pellino, Boberg, and O'Connell, 1980). Most classroom observation questionnaires and student evaluation forms reflect this extensive use in the kinds of questions they ask: How well does the teacher communicate? How well organized was the teacher (were lectures outlined clearly)? How enthusiastic was the teacher? Was the pace of lectures too fast or too slow? And so forth. It would indeed be unfortunate if such evaluation questions dictated the teaching method that teachers choose. Given the limited impact of the lecture by itself, alternate methods should be encouraged and more flexible evaluation criteria should be used.

Alternatives to the Lecture

Active learning as an alternative to the lecture is not a new idea. As the ancient Chinese proverb runs,

> I hear and I forget,
> I see and I remember,
> I do and I understand.

In 1828, the Yale Report called for more active learning, and the call has been echoed in recent studies in the United States. The *Involvement in Learning* report, issued in 1984, for example, urged faculty to use active instruction methods in their courses (Study Group, 1984). An educators' conference at Wingspread, Wisconsin, in 1986 resulted in the "Inventories of Good Practice in Undergraduate Education" which have been widely discussed by college faculties (Chickering and Gamson, 1987). The inventory groups teaching activities into seven areas, each representing a "Good Practice." Among the ten activities included in the good practice of active learning are the following:

> I give my students concrete, real-life situations to analyze.
> I use simulations, role playing, or labs in my classes.
> I ask my students to undertake research or independent study.
> I ask my students to present their work to the class.

The six other good practices are (1) encouraging student-faculty contact, (2) encouraging cooperation among students, (3) giving prompt feedback, (4) emphasizing time on task (making sure students spend the time necessary to prepare for class and complete assignments), (5) communicating high expectations, and (6) respecting diverse talents and ways of learning. Faculty members' responses to the seventy activities listed in the inventory have been the basis for discussions in department meetings and faculty development workshops, and a publication describing applications of the seven principles has been edited by Chickering and Gamson (1991). (Copies of the inventory are available from The Johnson Foundation, Inc., P.O. Box 17305, Milwaukee, Wisconsin 53217.)

If active learning occurs when students participate in the teaching process, passive learning takes place when they simply listen or receive knowledge. Paulo Freire (1971) refers to passive learning as "banking," with students storing knowledge (deposits) made by teachers (bankers). "The students are not called upon to know, but to memorize the contents narrated by the teacher" (p. 68). Freire prefers an approach where the teacher's and students' roles merge, where they think and search for knowledge together. Belenky, Clinchy, Goldberger, and Tarule (1986) call this connected teaching, likening the teacher to a midwife rather than a banker. A midwife-teacher draws the students' knowledge out and assimilates their feelings about the subject matter. The material is not seen only through the teacher's eyes, as it is in most traditional learning situations (p. 224). Although Belenky, Clinchy, Goldberger, and Tarule discuss connected teaching as a model especially appropriate in helping women develop, there is no reason why it would not also be of help to men. The concept may, however, be much easier for humanities and social science teachers to employ than for natural science teachers; it is also easier to use with small classes.

Methods of instruction can be placed on a continuum of passive to active learning. At the passive end are lectures; here, students have little or no active involvement, while the teacher is very active. At the opposite end of the continuum, active learning might be represented by independent study; here, students take the greatest responsibility for their own learning, while the instructor becomes a facilitator of the process. Methods of instruction can also be grouped by format or approach, based on the same passive-to-active criteria, as follows:

1.   The didactic or lecture approach
2.   The Socratic or interactive approach
3.   The facilitative approach

    Individualized instruction is based primarily on the facilitative approach and has been espoused especially for older students (Hiemstra and Sisco, 1990).

    A variety of teaching methods are described in the next section to illustrate some of the ways in which teachers can perform effectively in the classroom. An understanding of this variety is necessary for better evaluation. Evaluation should be tied to the teacher's appropriate role in each case; if that role is to facilitate learning, then the teacher's ability to dispense information (which would be important in the didactic approach) should not be a focus of the evaluation.

Active Learning Methods

The following list gives a continuum of teaching methods, starting with those that promote passive learning and continuing with those that promote increasingly more active learning. The methods listed are by format, as described in the previous section.

Mainly Didactic

Lecture
Lecture with slides, transparencies, or other visuals
Active modification to the lecture
Lecture and discussion

Mainly Interactive

Seminars, recitations
Laboratories
Case studies, simulation, games, debates, role playing
Cooperative learning, collaborative learning

Mainly Facilitative

Peer teaching
Computer-assisted instruction

Personalized System of Instruction (PSI)
Individualized instruction (for example, contract learning)
Independent study, internships

There is some evidence that the different methods are effective in attaining different learning objectives, although the research is not complete, particularly in the college setting (Gagne and Dick, 1983). Using Bloom's cognitive levels from the *Taxonomy of Educational Objectives* (1956), it is possible to match the most appropriate teaching method with the desired level of learning. Weston and Cranston (1986) suggested a set of matches, which I have added to and modified as follows:

Bloom Cognitive Level	*Most Appropriate Teaching Method*
Knowledge and Comprehension (Learning facts, principles, or theories; understanding of and ability to explain concepts)	Lecture, lecture with visuals, programmed instruction, PSI, readings
Application (Ability to apply correctly the learned information)	Lecture and discussion, seminars, active modifications to the lecture, computer-assisted instruction, simulations, case studies, games, field experience, laboratory, independent study, individualized instruction
Analysis and Synthesis (Ability to break down subject content into constituent parts and synthesize it into a unified whole)	Seminar discussions, independent group projects, collaborative or cooperative learning, simulation, independent study, laboratory
Evaluation (Ability to judge the importance or value of the learned information)	Independent study, group projects, collaborative or cooperative learning, field experience, laboratory

Obviously, some of the methods are repeated; these are effective in attaining more than one level of learning. But in general, higher levels of learning require more active student involvement in the learning process.

A full description of these methods, together with some research evidence on their effectiveness in higher education, can be found in a number of books and monographs (for example, Bonwell and Eison, 1991; McKeachie, Pintrich, Lin, and Smith, 1986). Three of the methods—active modifications to the lecture, collaborative learning, and PSI—will be briefly described in the next section, and we will see how an effective evaluation of a course and a teacher that use these methods might be conducted.

Active Modifications to the Lecture

Because it is cost effective for large classes and can present students with a great deal of information in a short span of time, the lecture method will continue to be widely used. The lecture can, however, be modified or supplemented to engage students in their own learning. One university tried to do this by equipping a new large classroom with electric panels at each desk that allowed the teacher to receive instant responses from students to questions the teacher raised. The experiment was not popular with professors, and the room is currently being used as a traditional lecture hall, the panels disconnected. Many other approaches to modifying lectures that are free of gadgetry have had more success (Bonwell and Eison, 1991; Weimer, 1987). One modification is the "feedback lecture": the teacher lectures briefly (fifteen to twenty minutes), and students then work in pairs and discuss a question related to the material presented (Osterman, 1984); a second minilecture based on the student discussions concludes the period. Professors also give students a study guide that provides readings, sample test questions (pre- and post-tests), and an outline of lecture notes.

Frederick (1987) described a number of modifications to the lecture format that promote active learning in large classes. Three are summarized as follows:

1. A problem-solving lecture begins with a minilecture that posits a problem or issue that the students then work on in small groups.
2. An interactive lecture begins with the students telling all they know or think they know about a particular topic; ideas are written on the board and the teacher builds a lecture around them, correcting any misconceptions.
3. A modification of the recitation or disputation method used in colonial colleges begins with a reading of a passage in the text to engage students' analytical and critical skills.

Collaborative Learning

Collaborative learning is rooted in the ideas of the philosopher John Dewey, the cognitive psychologists Jean Piaget and L. S. Vygotsky, and the social psychologist Kurt Lewin (MacGregor, 1990). In varying ways they all argued that learning was student centered, experience based, and social in nature. They saw the teacher's role as creating a context for learning rather than transmitting knowledge. Lewin, best known for his small group theory, also laid the foundation for the branch of collaborative learning known as cooperative learning. His disciples have been especially successful in developing cooperative learning at the elementary and secondary school levels, but the principle of cooperative as opposed to competitive learning can be equally effective in college classrooms. Collaborative learning has been growing in use in American college classrooms since the mid 1970s. Though there are several variations on the general theme, basically, collaborative learning involves students working with other students in common inquiry and conversation, thereby developing their social and intellectual skills (MacGregor, 1990). Teachers design the learning experiences and work together with students in a mutual search for understanding. Consider the following examples of collaborative learning by MacGregor (1990). The first example is drawn from a biology class, the second from a writing class, where the use of collaborative learning, according to Bruffee (1985) seems especially appropriate.

Having read a chapter on the origins of life in their introductory biology textbook, students arrive at class and pick up worksheets. They gather around the teacher, who, using the phospholipids in egg yolk to mix oil and water, is demonstrating hydrophobic and hydrophilic characteristics of phospholipid molecules. Then, dividing in groups of three or four, the students start on the worksheet problems. They diagram possible arrangements of phospholipids in the "primordial soup" that might have led to the first cell membranes, and then they speculate on the sources of these molecules. The teacher circulates, observing the groups and posing questions occasionally if a group appears completely stalled. The class period ends with groups sharing answers to the questions and posing additional ones of their own: fodder for the following day's discussion [p. 19].

In a writing class organized thematically around American social history, students are working in groups to plan, draft, and polish papers. They begin by reading a brochure and viewing a video on Irish immigration to the Five Points section of New York City in the 1850s. First in small groups and then in large ones, the students discuss the content and deepen their understanding of it by creating questions for each other and answering them. Working alternately in small groups and as a whole class with the teacher, the students move through a process of brainstorming possible paper topics, which range from stereotypes and prejudice then and now to how American values were played out in the immigrant experience in New York. The students and teacher, again working in small and in large groups, move to narrowing the list to several workable topics, discussing various rhetorical structures to achieve different goals in writing on the topics. Later, the students go to a writing lab, where they work individually at word processors, and circulate to read each other's material

and try out ideas. After several group work sessions on
each draft, papers begin to emerge [MacGregor, 1990,
p. 20].

In college mathematics, Treisman (1985) experimented with
teaching minority students calculus by dividing them into small
groups of students who worked together to solve calculus problems.
Observing the success that Asian-American students had in learning
calculus this way at the University of California, Berkeley, Treisman redesigned courses around calculus problems that the students
could work on in this way. They no longer passively listened to
lectures, watched instructors solve problems, or spent hours in
remedial courses that stressed math fundamentals; instead, they
were motivated to learn the course skills by solving the problems
themselves. Treisman's collaborative model has been adopted by a
number of college mathematics departments.

How should a collaborative learning course and the teacher's
effectiveness in it be evaluated? Weiner (1986) claimed that evaluators must first consider the quality of the task set by the teacher.
"Is it clearly worded and unambiguous? Does it split the exercise
into workable segments? Do students know what to do and how to
do it? Is the task pertinent to the students' needs, goals, and abilities? Does the exercise move toward consensus? Do the questions
students deal with stimulate critical thinking? And, perhaps, most
important of all, does it call on what students can be expected to
know in a way that will lead them together beyond what they already know—is the task difficult enough to challenge but not too
difficult to stonewall conversations?" (p. 57).

According to Weiner, evaluators should next consider the
teacher's classroom management. How well does the teacher organize and facilitate group work? Closely associated is a third consideration: the teacher's behavior during group work. Evaluators may
mistakenly believe that the teacher should offer comments to each
group during its discussions; on the contrary, the teacher should
leave the groups alone, so that students can gain confidence and
independence in their own knowledge.

The final two considerations are especially important. As the
student groups present their reports, the teacher must synthesize

them in a way in which the class can discuss their similarities and differences; the goal is to reconcile differences and assimilate the various perspectives into a larger vision (Bruffee, 1982, cited by Weiner). The teacher's final task is to compare the students' findings with those of the community of scholars and peers. Research in the discipline, and books and articles written on the problem at hand are used as a basis for comparison with the students' perspective. Evaluators need to judge the teacher's knowledge of relevant content in the discipline, as well as the teacher's ability to discuss with the students the similarities and differences between their conclusions and those of scholars.

For evaluators or colleagues to make these judgments, they must have at least a general awareness of how collaborative learning works. They should meet with the instructor before the class to learn about the particular problem that will be used, and the objectives for that class and for the course overall. Preferably, more than one session should be observed.

Personalized System of Instruction (PSI)

The personalized system of instruction (PSI), or the Keller method (after the psychologist who designed it), employs five unique practices:

1. The teacher divides the course into units and creates a printed study guide of it for students.
2. Students master a unit (as demonstrated by their performance on a test) before moving on to the next unit.
3. Students proceed at their own pace, with some completing course requirements much sooner than others.
4. Student tutors evaluate their peers' performance and offer support or remedial work to those having difficulty.
5. The teacher gives noncompulsory lectures to help motivate students (McKeachie, Pintrich, Lin, and Smith, 1986, p. 122; Keller, 1968).

Studies have shown that students generally gain basic knowledge and skills very well through this approach, probably because the frequent testing motivates them to study (Kulik, Kulik, and Cohen, 1979). PSI has been used largely in introductory or first-level courses, and instructors who have used it on an ongoing basis usually modify the amount of self-pacing, the role of the student tutors, and other features (Lloyd and Lloyd, 1986).

The instructor's most important tasks with PSI are to create and organize the course units, write the study guide and examination questions, oversee the tutors' crucial work, and deliver a few lectures. Because the lectures are sporadic and not a critical part of the course, they should not be given heavy emphasis in the evaluation. Student rating forms that focus on lecture and communication skills would therefore have only minor relevance. In contrast, the organization of the units and the study guides, the quality and variety of the tests (which should include objective, essay, and oral tests), and the type of interaction among students, tutors, and the instructor should be emphasized. Some of these qualities could be evaluated by the students in the course, while colleagues and department chairs could assess others, especially if they are familiar with the PSI format and philosophy. Student learning could also be reviewed. The retention of students in the course, the percentage of them successfully completing each unit, and the number of units completed are criteria of interest, as are the level of course objectives and the test questions used. Tests that examine recall rather than comprehension, analysis, and other higher-level abilities examine learning at the lowest level of the Bloom taxonomy (Bloom, 1956); such tests would not reflect all the intended objectives of such a course.

Ethics and Norms of Teaching

John Dewey, an early leader of the American Association of University Professors (AAUP), believed strongly that the academic profession would benefit from a code of professional responsibility (Dill, 1982). Academic freedom for faculty members, an early concern of the AAUP, was highlighted in the well-known Statement on Academic Freedom and Tenure issued in 1940. But it was not until 1966 that the AAUP issued its Statement on Professional Ethics, which reaffirmed the profession's vow to state the truth and promote knowledge (Schurr, 1982).

1. The professor, guided by a deep conviction of the worth and dignity of the advancement of knowledge, recognizes the special responsibilities placed upon him . . . to seek and to state the truth as he sees it.
2. As a teacher, the professor encourages the . . . pursuit of learning in his students.
3. As a colleague, the professor has obligations that derive from common membership in the community of scholars.

These very general descriptions hardly represent a fully developed professional code of ethics. Schurr doubts that a list of specifications and requirements adequate for a complete code of ethics could or should be developed. Callahan (1982) points out that the only detailed professional code of ethics in this country is that of the American Bar Association and states: "Such a code did not work well for lawyers, and there is no need to believe that a similarly detailed code would work any better for academics" (p. 343).

While a code of ethics per se does not exist, academic scholars have long adhered to a set of norms for preferred and prohibited behaviors in performing scholarly work. The sociologist Robert Merton (1973) defined four norms of science which informally guide the actions of academic scholars. These four norms—Communality, Disinterestedness, Organized Skepticism, and Universalism—are discussed more fully in Chapter Seven of this book, which deals with research and scholarship. According to Merton, the academic profession regulates itself by rewarding individuals who adhere to the norms and reprimanding those who do not. How well the profession regulates itself in scientific and scholarly inquiry can certainly be questioned. And when it comes to teaching, behavioral norms and ethical considerations have rarely been addressed in any systematic way. Good teaching and its evaluation, Scriven (1982) argued, requires attention to the quality of what is taught, the quantity of what is learned, and the propriety of the process. The third consideration involves ethics and norms.

One recent study attempted to investigate the normative

structure of undergraduate teaching by creating an inventory of 126 teaching behaviors that was presented to a sample of faculty members from a variety of institutions (Braxton, Bayer, and Finkelstein, 1992). The faculty members responded to each behavior by indicating whether it was an example of

1. Appropriate behavior, to be encouraged
2. Discretionary behavior, neither particularly appropriate nor inappropriate, and requiring no reaction
3. Mildly inappropriate, generally to be ignored
4. Inappropriate behavior, to be dealt with informally by colleagues or administrators
5. Very inappropriate behavior, requiring formal administrative intervention

Twenty-five behaviors had means of 4.00 or higher and might therefore represent improper behavior in teaching. A factor analysis of these twenty-five behaviors revealed four behavior patterns. The factor representing the highest level of impropriety, *moral turpitude,* included such acts as the instructor's attending class while intoxicated, having a sexual relationship with or making suggestive comments to a student enrolled in a course, and setting course standards so high that most students received failing grades. Of the 126 behaviors listed, intoxication in class and inappropriate sexual behavior were those most frequently judged to require administrative intervention. A second factor, *particularistic grading,* included allowing friendship with students or their personal characteristics to affect grades; a call for regulation of these behaviors is similar to Merton's universalism, according to which scholarship must be judged by its merits rather than the personal qualities of researchers. Another improper act that was included in this factor was reading identifiable student course evaluations before awarding final grades; the likelihood that grades would be affected apparently caused faculty members to judge this to be a highly improper activity.

Interpersonal disregard, the third factor, included behaviors that reflected an instructor's poor regard for others, such as making condescending or critical remarks to a student in class, frequently using profanity, routinely being late for class, frequently failing to keep office hours, and making negative comments about colleagues in the presence of students.

The fourth behavior pattern reflects poor instructional planning: *inadequate planning*. Instructor behavior deemed improper included changing the location or time of class meetings without consulting students, failing to prepare a course outline or syllabus, consistently failing to prepare for class, and refusing to advise student departmental majors.

Most of the 126 behaviors listed were seen by faculty as "discretionary" or "mildly inappropriate": not taking class roll, allowing a few students to dominate class discussions, or not returning graded tests promptly to students, are some examples. Many such activities are poor teaching practices and should be taken into account in evaluations. But highly improper practices such as those cited earlier deserve special attention. Braxton, Bayer, and Finkelstein's list does not exhaust the possibilities of improper teaching behaviors. Whether the identification of these is proof that behavioral norms or a code of ethics exists among college teachers is open to question.

One university's academic council approved a code of teaching responsibility for use in making salary, promotion, and tenure decisions (Olson, 1977). Some of the provisions in the code were the following:

1. Stating, in writing or orally, course objectives and grading procedures at the beginning of the term and then following through on them
2. Meeting class at the scheduled or agreed-upon time
3. Returning graded materials soon enough that they are useful in student learning
4. Scheduling office hours and being available during those hours

In their book discussing ethical issues in psychology, Keith-Spiegel and Koocher (1985) offer teaching guidelines that are appropriate to all fields. They include the following suggestions (p. 379):

- Course materials should be carefully prepared and include recent, important work in the topic being taught.
- When lecturing on sensitive or controversial material, the professor should prepare the students in advance, the presentations should be objective and well-balanced, and the choice of content should be pedagogically justifiable. Professors should not present their own values or opinions in a way that could be mistaken for established fact.
- Descriptions of academic courses or other educational programs should accurately reflect the experience students will receive and the obligations they will incur.

Most faculty members are responsible teachers and would have little difficulty meeting most of the standards of a reasonable code of ethics. Considering the need for a code at individual campuses might be desirable; it would be applied in personnel decisions and rewards would be withheld when violations occurred. Students and colleagues could provide reliable information about instructor behavior.

The Science and Art of Teaching

In his well-known book *The Art of Teaching,* Highet (1959) argues that teaching is an art, not a science. Teaching, he proposes, involves emotions that cannot be systematically appraised and employed; moreover, a "scientific relationship between humans, whether it be in teaching, marriage or friendship, will be inadequate and as cold as a chess problem" (p. vii). For Highet, teaching is like painting a picture or composing music.

Is teaching an art? Does good teaching require the creative skill that fine art requires? Is a person born with the skills needed to be a good teacher, so that they are simply revealed through practice? If so, it is unlikely that we can do very much to develop teachers or systematically assess their performance. Whether good teaching is an art, or a skill that can be learned is not a trivial question. In fact, it forms the cornerstone for evaluating and improving teachers' performance.

The knowledge acquired through careful observation over

the years supports the premise that teaching is as much a science as an art. Studies have identified characteristics of good teaching. This is not to say that there is no room left for variations or individual expression; creativity, individuality, and other qualities are equally important. Gage (1978) sees teaching as a practical art that calls for "intuition, creativity, improvisation, and expressiveness"; as such, it leaves room for "departure from rules, formulas, and algorithms" (p. 15). Axelrod (1973) describes teaching as an improvisational art, and says that like artists in other spheres, teachers need to develop their own individual styles.

Gage argues that the art of teaching has a scientific basis. A science, he believes, requires rigorous laws that yield predictability and control. Research on teaching at the elementary and secondary levels (which Gage largely draws on to reach his conclusion) has not demonstrated such predictability. Because of the complexity of teaching, "any singly significant variable in teacher behavior should have only a low correlation (ranging from $\pm$ .1 to about $\pm$ .4) with student achievement or attitude" (Gage, 1978, p. 26). The same can be said about behaviors of college teachers, which correlate in a similar range with course achievement when student ratings are used to assess or describe instructional variables (Centra, 1977b; Cohen, 1981).

In research on teaching, it is apparent that the laws or theories relating any two variables need to be modified to include other variables as well. These interactions do not occur only in research on teaching, they also appear in the natural sciences when real-life rather than laboratory phenomena are studied (Gage, 1978). Therefore, the fact that research on teaching has not produced *highly* predictable results does not in itself negate the scientific basis of teaching. Other practical fields and professions have a scientific basis but also require artistry to achieve the best results. Gage mentions medicine and engineering as examples. Practice in both fields requires knowledge of much science, but "Artistry enters into knowing when to follow the implications of the laws, generalizations, and trends, and especially, when not to, and how to combine two or more laws or trends in solving a problem" (Gage, 1978, p. 18). It seems that college teachers need to be aware not only of the scientific basis of teaching but also of when and how to build on it.

Qualities of Good Teaching

Although he proclaims teaching to be an art, Highet (1959) goes on to describe the qualities and abilities needed. The qualities include knowledge of one's subject, a sense of humor, and enjoyment of students; the abilities include memory and willpower. Highet even specifies crucial practices, such as preparing course and class outlines or finding other ways of providing structure. Many of these abilities and practices can be observed and evaluated and seem teachable; as such, they seem less like artistic abilities than Highet claims.

Many characteristics of good teaching are open to evaluation. A synthesis of thirty-one studies in which students and faculty members specified the characteristics important to good teaching revealed extensive similarities from study to study, as well as from group to group (Feldman, 1988). Students and faculty members at the same institutions (two-year and four-year colleges) were asked to describe attitudes or practices they believed to be important; some studies asked respondents to characterize "best" or "ideal" teachers. Students and faculty members gave high rankings to the following factors:

Sensitivity to and concern with class level and progress
Preparation and organization of the course
Knowledge of the subject
Enthusiasm (for the subject or for teaching)
Clarity and understandability
Availability and helpfulness
Fairness
Impartiality in evaluation of students
Quality of examinations

Students' responses showed a somewhat greater emphasis on stimulation of interest and speaking skills. Faculty placed greater importance on being intellectually challenging, encouraging independent thought, and motivating students to do their best. Both groups also mentioned concern and respect for students; the nature and value of course material; the quality and frequency of feedback to students; and openness to opinions of others, along with encouragement of questions and discussion. All in all, Feldman's synthesis indicates that faculty and students are very similar in their views of what constitutes good teaching and good teachers (see also Marques, Lane, and Dorfman, 1979).

Other studies have focused on a smaller number of characteristics of excellence that were agreed on by students and faculty alike. Sherman and others (1987) identify the following five characteristics, some of which echo those noted in Feldman's review.

1. Enthusiasm (high energy level; pleasure in teaching; love of the subject; deep interest in the subject; vocal delivery that is lively and varied)
2. Clarity (clear explanation of concepts; comprehensibility; systematic presentation of material with summaries of major premises)
3. Preparation and organization (detailed course outlines; established course objectives; good preparation for each class session; good definition of evaluation procedures)
4. Stimulation (stimulation of interest, thoughtfulness, and intellectual curiosity in students; ability to motivate students)
5. Knowledge (grasp of subject matter; ability to make interrelationships of knowledge areas clear).

Lowman (1984) proposed a two-dimensional model of effective college teaching. The first dimension he terms *intellectual excitement*. It encompasses both what is taught (clarity of explanation) and how it is taught (public-speaking virtuosity). Skills necessary for clear communication include mastery and accuracy of content; the ability to analyze, integrate, apply, and evaluate information; and the ability to organize the subject matter. Public-speaking virtuosity requires what Lowman calls teacher-as-performer skills, such as the ability to use voice, gestures, and movement to stimulate emotions; a strong sense of timing; and the ability to focus energy into a teaching performance. Lowman terms the second dimension *interper-*

sonal rapport. It encompasses the teacher's awareness of interpersonal phenomena and the communication skills that increase the students' motivation, enjoyment, and independent learning. According to Lowman's model, a teacher with good skills in interpersonal rapport is extremely warm and open, encourages students to ask questions and express their views, is sensitive to how students feel about the material or its presentation, and encourages students to be creative and independent in dealing with the material. According to Lowman, to be outstanding, teachers must excel in one of the model's two dimensions and be at least competent in the other.

For the most part, Lowman's model and many of the characteristics of effective teaching identified in the studies reviewed by Feldman (1988) and others presuppose a lecture or lecture-discussion method. This is not surprising. When people are asked to identify characteristics of good teaching (or good teachers), they think about what most teachers do—lecture. Their responses, therefore, really address the characteristics of effective didactic teaching.

Furthermore, good teaching is more complicated than any list of qualities or characteristics can suggest. First, some characteristics are more easily measured than others and so may be given more weight than they deserve. Second, teachers display different strengths, and a good teacher may be strong in many of the identified characteristics but not in all of them. The ultimate outcome of good teaching—good learning—can be achieved through a variety of approaches. For example, one teacher may not organize the course or each session as well as could be hoped, but his or her motivational skills, enthusiasm, communication skills, positive attitude toward the students, and other characteristics may more than make up for the deficiency.

Various studies have supported the thesis that effective teaching may vary, not only by individual style but also, to some extent, by academic discipline, academic level, and individual student. For example, effective graduate teaching is not necessarily the same as effective undergraduate teaching. Murray (1985) compared student-ratings data on teachers who were teaching both graduate and undergraduate courses and obtained generally low correlations; in other words, teachers who do well at one level do not necessarily do well at the other. Shulman's (1986, 1989) research on differences in teaching per academic discipline suggests that teachers in the various disciplines explain key concepts in different ways and with varying success.

In his study of college humanities teachers, Axelrod (1973) identified two types of subject matter–centered instructors, two types of student-centered instructors, and a third type of instructor—whom he found to be the most common—instructor-centered instructors. Subject-matter enthusiasts believe that the teacher's task is to cover a well-defined set of topics systematically and precisely, while the student's is to master the course content through traditional assignments and study methods. Instructor-centered instructors prefer to put their own interpretations on the subject matter and are therefore more intellectual and individualistic in selecting both what to cover and how to cover it. Student-centered instructors, the least common type, are primarily concerned with the students' cognitive or personal development. They use analysis, problem-solving techniques, and other active learning methods to help students correctly approach and understand the material.

Definitions of Effective Teaching

Because definitions of effective teaching are often so broadly stated, they are extremely difficult to apply in evaluation. A committee that I served on at Syracuse University took on the task of providing guidelines to deans and department chairs for the evaluation of teaching performance (Centra, Froh, Gray, and Lambert, 1987). We decided to include a definition of good teaching that would provoke little disagreement: "Effective teaching produces beneficial and purposeful student learning through the use of appropriate procedures" (p. 5).

The definition identifies both the outcomes of effective teaching—student learning—and the process—what teachers do—as important. Student learning at the college level is difficult to measure systematically in a way that allows comparisons between teachers (see Centra, 1979, and Chapter Nine of this book). Our monograph focused heavily on appropriate procedures, or the process of teaching, by discussing six of the qualities mentioned earlier in this chapter that characterize effective teaching:

- Good organization of subject matter and course
- Effective communication
- Knowledge of and enthusiasm for the subject matter and teaching
- Positive attitude toward students
- Fairness in examinations and grading
- Flexibility in approaches to teaching [Centra, Froh, Gray, and Lambert, 1987, p. 5]

The first five qualities, for the most part, relate to didactic teaching; the sixth encourages teachers to use a variety of teaching methods. "Appropriate student learning outcomes" was added as a seventh important quality, though we realized that isolating the effects of teaching on learning is not easily done. Information and judgments from a variety of people (oneself, students and alumni, colleagues, various administrators), as I discuss in the remaining chapters of this book, were also briefly mentioned in our monograph, for together they provide the most comprehensive basis for summative and formative evaluations.

Finally, definitions of teaching effectiveness depend on the individual's explicit or implicit theory of how students learn. Appropriate teaching behaviors are those that facilitate student learning in accordance with the theory. Fuhrmann and Grasha (1983) identify three teaching approaches that are based on three different learning theories.

First is the behaviorist approach, a very systematic method of teaching. According to this theory, "effective teaching is demonstrated when the instructor can write objectives relevant to the course content, specify classroom procedures (for example, pacing, reinforcements) and student behaviors needed to teach and learn such objectives, and show that students have achieved the objectives after exposure to the instruction" (Fuhrmann and Grasha, 1983, p. 287).

The behaviorist approach is prevalent in college teaching and in teacher evaluation, although many teachers may not realize that they hold this view. An example of its use in evaluation is the student rating forms that ask if course objectives were made clear, if there was agreement between objectives and course content, and if the instructor accomplished the objectives. These teachers see their task as constructing an environment that promotes learning; Axelrod (1973) identified them as instructor-centered, the most common of his types.

Lecture-based courses employ the behaviorist approach in varying degrees. The list of qualities that we produced at Syracuse was based largely on a behaviorist approach.

A second approach, based on cognitive theories of learning, emphasizes how teachers can make students more effective problem-solvers and critical thinkers. "Effective teaching is demonstrated when instructors use classroom procedures that are compatible with a student's cognitive characteristics, can organize and present information to promote problem solving and original thinking on issues, and can show that students are able to become more productive thinkers and problem-solvers" (Fuhrmann and Grasha, 1983, pp. 287–288).

Collaborative learning is one current application of cognitive theories of learning. Together with other small group instructional methods, collaborative learning, as discussed earlier in this chapter, hopes to develop students' problem-solving skills by actively involving the students.

A third approach, based on humanistic theories of learning, promotes self-initiated learning, or learning through self-discovery. "Humanistic teaching is effective when teachers can demonstrate that students have acquired content that is relevant to their goals and needs, that they can appreciate and understand the thoughts and feelings of others better, and that they are able to recognize their feelings about the content" (Fuhrmann and Grasha, 1983, p. 288). Teachers should be a model of the behaviors and values that they hope students will develop; they must become learners along with the students rather than take on the role of expert. Freire's (1971) ideas, and the connected-teaching method advocated by Belenky, Clinchy, Goldberger, and Tarule (1986), discussed earlier in this chapter, are humanistic theories of learning.

There are surely other theories that propose how students learn and how teachers should teach, although the three just discussed probably encompass most viewpoints. Certainly the views of Highet, Gage, Axelrod, and Freire contain one or more of the three approaches. Most teachers are not aware that they subscribe to a specific theory, and in fact many may apply different theories at different times or even within the same course or class period. What is important is that people have different assumptions about how students learn best and how teachers should teach; these assumptions form the basis of each person's definition of good teaching. Fuhrmann and Grasha (1983) argue that helping teachers clarify their assumptions, decide which to keep, and gain new insights are the first steps in improving instruction. In evaluating teaching, it is important to understand teachers' assumptions and definitions of good teaching. It is also important to know what they expect students to learn in a course. This information should be part of the personal statement or reflections included in a portfolio or dossier (see Chapter Five). Evaluation can then focus on how consistent the assumptions are with the teacher's behavior and how successful he or she is in implementing them. Evaluation systems can and should be designed to reflect the varieties of successful teaching.

Summary

The brief history of teaching given in this chapter describes how more active forms of student learning were gradually included. In the latter part of the nineteenth century, college teachers began using the seminar and the laboratory, while more recently other interactive approaches, such as case studies and collaborative learning, have been adopted. Courses in which students have the greatest responsibility for their own learning and in which teachers act as facilitators have also become more frequent in the past few decades. Still, traditional lectures dominate, and most evaluation procedures assume a lecture-based or lecture-and-discussion method of teaching. Study after study has shown that student assimilation of lecture content diminishes dramatically after the first fifteen minutes or so. Teachers might therefore combine brief lectures with active learning exercises during a class section. Moreover, alternatives and modifications to the lecture need to be encouraged along with appropriate methods for evaluating them. Evaluations should gauge effectiveness no matter what the instruction method used.

This chapter also discusses ethics in teaching and suggests

that institutions consider establishing a reasonable code of teaching responsibility. The code could define both deviant behaviors and behaviors that reflect responsible teaching. Students and colleagues could provide reliable information to evaluate instructor behavior based on the code.

Definitions of effective teaching and the assumptions or theories they are based on are summarized in this chapter. Like many other fields and professions, teaching seems to have a scientific basis but requires artistry to achieve the greatest effect. Much agreement exists about the characteristics of good teaching. Some, such as clarity in presentation, are associated with didactic teaching. Others, such as course planning, enthusiasm, knowledge of the subject, and positive attitudes toward students should be present in both didactic and active approaches to teaching. Whether they realize it or not, most teachers have a theory about how learning takes place and teach accordingly. The most prevalent theory is the behaviorist. Cognitive and humanistic theories of learning are also widely held. For both formative and summative evaluation, it is important to understand a teacher's implicit theory of instruction. The teaching portfolio or dossier is an opportunity for teachers to reflect on what they do, why they do it, and how successful they have been.

In Chapter Three, we examine the research on student evaluations.

Chapter 3

Student Evaluations
of Teaching:
What Research Tells Us

*R*are is the American college or university that does not currently use student evaluations of teaching in one way or another. At some schools, instructors voluntarily use a questionnaire or collect students' written suggestions for course improvement. At others, a mandated system includes student ratings, and the information can affect tenure, promotion, and even merit-pay decisions. The steady increase in the use of student evaluations over the past twenty-five years was probably caused by growing awareness of a need for better evaluation, for both formative and summative purposes. Moreover, a steady flow of research has generally supported the reliability, validity, and utility of student evaluations.

Yet they also have their critics. As one researcher noted, opinions about student evaluations vary, from "reliable, valid and useful" to "unreliable, invalid, and useless" (Aleamoni, 1981). The late Kenneth Eble noted, "No corner of the university . . . lacks faculty members who fulminate against student evaluations, with little or no examination of [the] research" (1983). This chapter examines that research, both the supportive evidence on and the limitations of student evaluations. One limitation, as pointed out in Chapter Two, is that the typical student rating form is devised to reflect effectiveness in lectures, lecture and discussion, and other teacher-centered methods. Unless modified, the typical form does not rate student-centered or active approaches to learning such as collaborative learning. The usefulness of the forms is also limited by the ways in which they are collected and interpreted. A survey of evaluation writers and researchers by Franklin and Theall (1989) indicated that the psychometric properties of student evaluations are less at issue than are the data collection and interpretation procedures. Anecdotes about misuse abound: the teacher or the department head who altered answer sheets before turning them in; administrators who made major tenure, promotion, or salary decisions based on minor differences in student evaluation scores; teachers who tried to bias the ratings by comments they made as they distributed the forms in class; teachers who collected student evaluations to use for self-improvement but then never used the information or misinterpreted it.

What is needed at this time is a greater awareness of the research evidence on student evaluations and better use of the evaluations.

Franklin and Theall's (1989) study clearly demonstrates the need for greater awareness of the research evidence on student evaluations. Some 670 college faculty members and administrators at three colleges were tested on their knowledge of and attitudes toward student evaluations. The questions reflected research findings (for example, are student evaluations valid?) or opinions (for example, do students have a right and responsibility to rate instruction?). The scores at all institutions were similar and indicated a lack of knowledge about much of the research. An equally important finding was that attitudes and knowledge were related: respondents who knew more about the research also had more favorable attitudes about the use and potential of student evaluations.

This chapter begins with a history of student evaluations. We then review the major research findings, while Chapter Four (following) offers guidelines for the proper use of the evaluations. The research summary relies heavily on key studies, previous reviews, and meta-analyses of specific issues. Given more than 1,500 journal articles and papers referenced in the ERIC system since 1966 (when ERIC began), it is virtually impossible not to be selective. The chapter ends with a discussion of the various instruments available for obtaining evaluation information from students.

History and Background

The first formal student evaluations of teachers probably took place in the universities of medieval Europe. Teachers taught by reading to students from one of the few existing copies of the text, and they were expected to adhere to a strict schedule of topics (Rashdall, 1936). Students evaluated teachers in two ways. First, a committee of students appointed by the rector made sure they covered each topic by the date specified in advance; any irregularities were reported to the rector, who fined the professor for each day he (in those days, always a "he") had fallen behind. Second, students paid fees directly to each teacher (called the *collecta*). Teachers' salaries, therefore, were determined by the number of students attending their classes (Rashdall, 1936). Today's student rating questionnaires seem tame by comparison.

The modern era of student evaluations can be broken roughly into four periods: the thirty-year period preceding 1960, the 1960s, the 1970s, and the period from the 1980s to the present. Before 1960, most of the research on student evaluations was conducted by Herman Remmers and his colleagues at Purdue University. The Purdue rating form, published in 1927, was probably the first student evaluation form. Remmers conducted a series of studies with it, investigating such issues as the relationship of students' grades to their ratings of teachers (1930), the reliability of student ratings (1934), and the comparison between alumni and student evaluations (Drucker and Remmers, 1951). Because of his pioneering work, Remmers well deserves the title, the Father of Student Evaluation Research (Marsh, 1987).

Although Remmers and other researchers, such as E. R. Guthrie (1954) at the University of Washington, promoted their use, student evaluations were rarely used in colleges and universities until the 1960s. The student protests that rocked so many campuses in the last half of the decade were in reaction not only to the Vietnam War and related national policies but also to policies in effect on their campuses. An irrelevant curriculum and uninspired teachers were among frequently heard student complaints. Increasingly, students saw themselves as consumers. They demanded a voice in governance; they wanted to improve the education they were receiving. Evaluating their courses and teachers was one way to make their voices heard. At many large universities, students administered their own rating systems—often haphazardly—and published the results. More often, institutions began to develop their own student evaluation systems, which faculty members could use if they wished.

As a staff member in the Office of Institutional Research at Michigan State University in 1964, I was given the task of developing a student evaluation form that the faculty could use for instructional improvement. The university was acting in response to the student government's proposal to implement a rating program. Remmers's early work was very helpful to me at that time. The form I helped develop, the Student Instructional Rating Report, included an open-ended comment section, which was retained by the faculty member, and a second section that was machine scored. Like forms at many other universities, it has been modified many times in subsequent years.

In the 1960s, faculty members usually volunteered to administer the forms in their courses themselves, so that they might make necessary improvements on their own. Administrative use of the results was infrequent because few institutions had centrally administered student rating systems.

Interest in pertinent issues—the validity of the ratings, in particular—inspired a new wave of research and the 1970s became the golden age of research on student evaluations. Well-designed studies investigated questions of bias, validity (Do student evaluations really measure teaching effectiveness?), and utility (Can they help improve instruction?). The generally favorable findings helped support the use of the evaluations for tenure and promotion decisions as well as for instructional improvement. During the 1970s, more and more institutions adopted them, with a majority reporting their use by the end of the decade (Centra, 1979). Department heads ranked student evaluations among the top three sources of information on teaching effectiveness (colleagues and department heads were the other two) and, moreover, believed them to be the most important source (Centra, 1977a).

The fourth period, from the early 1980s to the present, has included the continuing refinement of the research findings, and a series of reviews and meta-analyses has substantiated the findings on important issues. The relationship between student evaluations and student learning in courses, for example, were analyzed across a wide range of studies; taken together, findings create a much more convincing report than the results of only one or two studies. We turn now to a discussion of these studies.

Research Findings: What We Know and Don't Know

Research informs us about what generally happens—it cannot predict what will definitely happen. When dealing with humans, and particularly when studying situations where one human is teaching another, it is unlikely that perfect correlations will be found. There are simply too many variables. Unlike the hard sciences, where, for example, the properties of physical objects are highly predictable and measurement instruments have near-perfect accuracy, human beings are unpredictable and the behavioral measures we use for them are imperfect.

In short, the research on student evaluations, like that on other teacher-evaluation methods, shows significant tendencies but no certainties. An example from another area of evaluation may help make the point. Consider the prediction of college grades based on high school grades: the average correlation between these grades and those received on completion of the freshman year is about .45 (Donlon, 1984). Although this is far from perfect, when used with other predictive measures, it is high enough to help colleges reliably select students for admission. Now consider student evaluations of teachers. As the research discussed in the following section indicates, the correlation between students' evaluations of a teacher's effectiveness and student learning in that teacher's course (in itself another estimate of a teacher's effectiveness) is likewise approximately .45 (Cohen, 1981). Does this warrant the use of student evaluations as a measure of teaching effectiveness to be taken into consideration in tenure decisions? Assuming that past behavior is the best predictor of future behavior, one could argue that a correlation of .45 *is* high enough to warrant their use in this way as at least one measure of future teaching performance.

In the section that follows and in the next chapter, research findings will be examined. First, we will look at the approaches used to obtain student reactions. What is the content of student evaluation instruments? What types of items and item clusters are included? How were the forms developed? How valid are student responses to open-ended questions? What additional approaches can be used to obtain student feedback?

Second, we will examine the critical issues of reliability and validity. To what extent do students in a classroom agree in their ratings? Do the ratings fluctuate over short periods of time? Do student evaluation results resemble other measures of teaching?

Third, we will investigate possible bias. Are there teacher, student, or course characteristics that have undue influence on rating results?

Finally, in Chapter Four, I present an updated review of the research on the usefulness of student evaluations. Which conditions must be fulfilled to lead to improvement in instruction? How much impact do student evaluations have on tenure and promotion decisions?

Student Evaluation Instruments

Most faculty members who collect student evaluations use a questionnaire made available to them by their institutions. Institutions develop their own set of questions or adapt forms used elsewhere. These colleges may either machine-score the forms or allow individual faculty members to hand-score the weighted responses. Some departments prefer to develop and administer their own forms, even though their questions are often very similar to those in the forms developed by the institution. Institutions can also pay a fee to use a system developed at another institution or center. Involving faculty representatives in the decision about which form to use will help ensure the faculty's commitment to its use. Faculty involvement is especially important if the information is being collected primarily for their own use.

Descriptions of the best-known evaluation systems, sample forms, and cost information are provided in the resources section of this book. Some systems feature a computerized catalogue of items from which teachers select items they believe will be most useful. Their selections are added to a few core items, that are not optional, and the computer prints the individualized questionnaire. Purdue's Cafeteria System, and the Instructor and Course Evaluation System (ICES) developed at the University of Illinois, are two well-known computer-catalogued systems (see the resources). The ICES system includes more than four hundred items classified by content and level of specificity. According to analyses by the University of Illinois' Office of Instruction Resources, most teachers select items that assess their course management rather than their teaching skills or personal characteristics (Ory, Brandenburg, and Pieper, 1980). Perhaps teachers select these items because they feel less threatened by this kind of criticism, or perhaps they believe they can more easily modify their course management than their personal characteristics or teaching skills.

Probably the two most widely used commercial forms are the Student Instructional Report (SIR) developed at the Educational Testing Service (ETS) in the early 1970s, and the Instructional Development and Effectiveness Assessment form (IDEA) developed at the Center for Faculty Evaluation and Development at Kansas State University. Because of the extensive use of forms over the years, both have produced tables of comparison data for different class sizes, different subject areas, and so forth. Given the differences found in student evaluations of courses with different characteristics, the comparison data are useful. As with most of the forms available, instructors can add their own items to the SIR and the IDEA forms; the items are then machine-scored for the teacher. Institutions interested in adopting a form should look carefully at the computerized reports produced through their use. The reports should be easy to read and interpret by the teachers or administrators who will use them. Some of the evaluation forms described in the resources are available at no cost.

The University of Washington's Instructional Assessment System (IAS) offers a range of forms for faculty to choose from, depending on the type of course. For example, forms are available for large lecture courses, seminars, problem-solving courses, and other course types.

Many of the items included in student evaluation instruments are similar. When Remmers developed one of the first such instruments, he selected items that experts agreed were most important to teaching and that students were capable of observing and judging. These same principles guided the construction of several current instruments. For example, SIR items were culled from a larger pool after a sample of faculty members indicated which items they believed would be most useful for instructional improvement and most fairly judged by students (Centra, 1972a). Marsh took a similar approach (1982).

Many instruments have subsequently been submitted to factor analysis, resulting in item clusters—or factors—that reflect different dimensions of teaching effectiveness, as judged by students. Similar dimensions emerge, whether the factor analysis is of mean item scores for teachers or individual student ratings (Linn, Centra, and Tucker, 1975). Because much is already known about teaching effectiveness, confirmatory factor analysis is the preferred analysis method; it allows one to determine an expected factor structure before interpreting scores (Centra, 1973c; Marsh, 1987).

Furthermore, because teaching is a complex activity, it makes sense to evaluate it on different dimensions. Consider, for example, two dimensions of teaching: (a) course organization and structure, and (b) teacher interaction with students. A teacher may rate high in one and relatively low in the other but still be effective (just as a person with a high IQ can rate much higher in math than in language skills).

Feldman (1976, 1984) devised a system for categorizing items from many different student evaluation forms. The list, with some later modifications, is presented in Exhibit 3.1. One item per category is provided as an example (see also Abrami and d'Apolonia, 1990). Feldman developed the categories after a review of studies in which students identified the characteristics of superior college teachers. Student evaluation questionnaires yield fewer factors; typically, five or six emerge from factor analyses of the instruments. The factors often combine more than one of Feldman's categories. SIR's course organization and planning factor, for example, con-

**Exhibit 3.1. Examples of Items Used in
Multisection Validity Studies, Categorized into Dimensions.**

1. **Stimulation of Interest**

   The instructor put material across in an interesting way.

2. **Enthusiasm**

   The instructor demonstrated dynamism and enthusiasm for the subject.

3. **Knowledge of the Subject**

   The instructor had a thorough knowledge of the subject matter

4. **Preparation and Organization of the Course**

   Each class period was carefully planned.

5. **Clarity and Understandableness**

   The instructor summarized or emphasized major points in lectures or discussions.

6. **Elocutionary Skills**

   The instructor was clear and audible

7. **Class Level and Progress**

   The instructor seemed to know when students did not understand the material.

8. **Clarity of Course Objectives**

   The instructor's objectives for the course were clear.

9. **Relevance and Value of Course Materials**

   Rate the extent to which the text was a useful part of the course.

10. **Relevance and Usefulness of Supplementary Materials**

    Overall, I would rate the supplementary readings as _____ .

11. **Workload**

    The student had to work hard in the course.

12. **Perceived Outcome**

    The course increased my general knowledge.

Exhibit 3.1. Examples of Items Used in
Multisection Validity Studies, Categorized into Dimensions, Cont'd.

---

13. **Fairness of Evaluation**

Examinations reflected important aspects of the course.

14. **Classroom Management**

The students had a voice in deciding how we did what was done.

15. **Personality Characteristics**

Rate the instructor's sense of proportion and sense of humor.

16. **Feedback**

The instructor made helpful comments on papers or exams.

17. **Encouragement of Discussion and Diversity of Opinions**

In this class, we tried to understand points of view that differed from
our own.

18. **Intellectual Challenge and Encouragement of Independent Thought**

This course challenged me intellectually.

19. **Concern and Respect for Students**

The instructor was friendly.

20. **Availability and Helpfulness**

The instructor was readily available for consultation, by appointment or otherwise.

21. **Overall Course**

Rate the overall effectiveness of the course.

22. **Overall Instructor**

How would you rate your teacher in general?

---

tains both the preparation and organization of the course and clarity of course objectives categories developed by Feldman.

Many factor analyses of student evaluation instruments have
been reported in the literature. Although the specific factors vary,

depending on the items included in each form, many similar factors are identified. Following is a list of commonly identified factors (for examples of items included within each, see Centra, 1979, p. 23):

1. Organization, planning, or structure
2. Teacher-student interaction or rapport (sometimes broken down into two factors, instructor-individual and instructor-group interaction)
3. Clarity, communication skill
4. Work load, course difficulty
5. Grading and examinations, assignments
6. Student learning, student self-ratings of accomplishments or progress

Global or overall ratings of the teacher and the course are also common but they are not separate factors; instead, they generally correlate with several of the factors shown in the list. Student effort or involvement and instructor enthusiasm are two other factors derived from some forms. Student ratings of their own effort or involvement in the course help remind them of their own contribution to learning. Instructor knowledge of the subject matter is not frequently rated because most teachers do not think students can or should judge them in this area.

Some writers have argued that the various factors should receive differential weights for tenure and promotion decisions (Marsh, 1987). How this might be done equitably is uncertain. One possibility, according to Marsh, is to have each instructor determine the weight for each factor; another is to weight the factors according to the research findings on their correlation with student learning. If instructors determined the weights, they would presumably select factors that reflected their particular approach to teaching; however, they could instead select those in which they usually did best. If the factors are weighted according to correlations with learning, some will receive no weight and will be disregarded by teachers. As we will discuss in the next section, the factor or item cluster scores in a form should be taken into account for tenure and promotion as well as for teaching improvement purposes. The development of an equitable and systematic a priori weighting scheme, however, is unlikely.

Reliability and Validity of Student Evaluations

Reliability estimates for student evaluation questionnaires continue to be shown to be good. Although not much has been found about the extent of agreement in student responses since Remmers's early research, much more is now known about the validity and stability of student evaluations.

The relative agreement among students in a class and the stability of ratings over time are the two important gauges of reliability for student evaluations. The extent of agreement within a class can be determined by the intraclass correlation coefficient (Winer, 1962), an index that compares variation in responses within classes to variation across a sample of classes. Students in one class seldom give a teacher exactly the same rating, but ideally the ratings do not vary widely. Reliability estimates range from 0 to 1.00. A .90 reliability is excellent; generally speaking, an acceptable reliability coefficient is above .70.

Reliability is computed for each item on a questionnaire and for factors or scale scores. Of great importance is the number of students rating each course. The reliability coefficient for a single rater, for example, is typically about .20, much too low to be useful. For ten student raters, however, the reliability coefficients are often above .70, and for twenty-five students they are above .90, equivalent to the reliability of the best intelligence tests. Consider the values for SIR (Centra, 1973c) and the Students' Evaluation of Educational Quality form (SEEQ) (Marsh, 1987) shown in Table 3.1.

For tenure and promotion decisions, both the number of students rating the courses and the number of courses rated should be considered. The number of courses needed to give a dependable assessment of a faculty member's ratings was studied by Gilmore, Kane, and Naccarato (1978). Applying generalizability theory to student evaluations, the three researchers concluded that ratings of at least five courses with at least fifteen students rating each one (thus providing a reliable estimate of each) are needed if the rating will be used in administrative decisions. If fewer than fifteen

Table 3.1. Reliability of Student Evaluation Instruments:
Examples from Two Instruments.

	Reliability Coefficients	
	SIR	SEEQ
Number of	One Item	Average
Student Raters	Overall Teacher Rating	for Factors
5	.65	.60
10	.78	.74
25	.90	.90
50	.95	.95

students make the ratings, then more than five courses—preferably ten—should be rated.

In comparing the effects on the ratings of the teacher and of the course, Marsh (1987) concluded that student evaluations of instruction are primarily a judgment of the teacher. In a setting where all students took the same courses, the individual instructor accounted for five to ten times more variance in the ratings than did the course.

But what happens when faculty members are teaching different types of courses, such as both freshman lecture classes and small graduate research seminars? Murray, Ruston, and Paunonen (1990) found that teachers were differently suited to different types of courses. Their sample of forty-six psychology teachers taught six types of courses that varied in the following ways: class size ranged from more than two hundred to fewer than fifteen; method of instruction varied from lecture to lecture-laboratory to lecture-discussion to seminar; students in the courses varied from primarily nonmajors to beginning or advanced majors to graduate students. Instructors who received high ratings in one type of course frequently received low ratings in another. The ratings were more consistent across undergraduate course types (mean r=.66) than across undergraduate and graduate course types (mean r=.15) (p. 254). Furthermore, effective teachers of undergraduate lecture courses tended to be extroverted and sociable, whereas effective teachers of graduate seminars were neither. Thus, compatibility of teachers with course types seems partly determined by personality traits.

This study (Murray, Ruston, and Paunonen, 1990) indicates

that when a teacher is teaching courses that vary considerably in type, the five-course rating minimum that Gilmore, Kane, and Naccarato (1978) suggest be used for administrative decisions should include ratings of the different course types. Because few teachers are likely to be equally effective in all, institutions may want to assign tenured teachers to those in which their ratings indicate that they are most effective. (This assumes, of course, that enough professors will be willing and able to teach large lectures rather than graduate seminars.)

As with any survey, it is also important to have a representative sample of the students in a class. For example, if out of a class of forty-five students only fifteen respond, the results may be reliable but not accurate. This would be especially true if the thirty nonresponding students shared views significantly different from those of the response group. Generally, if two-thirds or more of the students in a class respond, the results are fairly representative.

The reliability of student evaluations can be best illustrated with an adaptation of Lincoln's famous remark about fooling people. We might accurately say that, with student evaluations, instructors may fool all of the students some of the time; they may even fool some of the students all of the time; but they will not fool all of the students all of the time.

Validity

Do student evaluations measure anything other than student satisfaction? Do teachers who are given high student ratings also do well on measurements of student learning? Do student ratings correlate with those of specially trained observers? To determine the relationship between learning and ratings, researchers have used multisection courses with common final exams; mean student ratings in each section are correlated with mean final exam performance. A meta-analysis by Cohen (1981) of forty-one such studies reporting on sixty-eight separate multisection courses concluded that student ratings are a valid index of teacher effectiveness. The average correlation between achievement measures and the students' overall rating of the teacher was .43; with an overall rating of the course, the correlation was .47. The highest correlations were for the rating factors Skill (.50) and Structure (.47). Two items included in these factors were "The instructor teaches near the class level," and "The instructor uses class time well." Correlations in the .45 to .50 range are considered high. For the rapport factor, including items referring to teacher accessibility and warmth, the mean correlation was modest (.31), as it was with Feedback (.31), including such items as "The teacher keeps students aware of progress." The lowest correlation (-.02) was for the factor on course difficulty, which included such items as "The instructor asked for more than students could get done," and "This course required more work than others for comparable credit."

Although the mean correlations were moderately strong for the global ratings and two of the factors, there was great variation among the studies; some had negative or near-zero correlations, while others were above .80. This wide variation caused Dowell and Neal (1982) to conclude: "The evidence suggests that the validity of student ratings is modest at best and quite variable" (p. 59). Dowell and Neal, however, reviewed only six studies, omitting some with the best designs.

Abrami, d'Apolonia, and Cohen (1990) identified four categories of variables that might affect the validity coefficients of multisection ratings and achievement studies (p. 226):

1. *Ratings variables:* the quality of the rating instrument and the manner in which the evaluation takes place, such as timing and anonymity
2. *Achievement variables:* the general structure and quality of the achievement measure and the manner in which it was administered
3. *Explanatory variables:* course, student, or instruction features that may affect either the rating or the achievement measures—such as student ability, subject area of the course, instructor autonomy, or instructional setting differentially
4. *Miscellaneous variables:* methodological and other factors that might affect validity, such as the number of sections and restriction in range of scores for ratings or achievement

Altogether Abrami, d'Apolonia, and Cohen (1990) identified seventy-five study features that could explain the wide variation in the research findings. Some of these, they stated were studied by the primary researchers or past reviewers, but in general, previous analyses did not explore characteristics that could explain their findings. This point is well taken and can be illustrated in a student ratings-to-achievement study I conducted. Student ratings of instruction were correlated with examination performance in seventy-two sections of seven different courses (Centra, 1976). There were between seven and twenty-two sections in each course, taught by forty-five experienced teachers. Students had been randomly assigned to sections in two of the courses. The final examination was the same for each section and was made up by an examination committee rather than the instructor teaching the course. The study found that half the correlations between mean ratings and mean examination scores were .60 or higher. To explore the relationship further, I plotted the mean ratings and achievement scores for twenty-two psychology classes (Centra, 1978b). The twenty-two were taught by nine teachers, with each teaching at least two sections. A plot of these twenty-two sections revealed an unusual feature: for all three sections taught by a certain teacher (teacher X), the student mean ratings were among the highest, but the student test scores were the lowest. In short, the ratings for teacher X did not reflect student learning. For the other eight teachers, the ratings to test score relationship was very much in line.

How then do we explain teacher X, the outlier? As it turns out, although a common final examination was used, all the teachers had had considerable autonomy in choosing the material to emphasize during the course. Most followed the syllabus, but teacher X, an adjunct member of the department, simply did not adequately cover all the syllabus, and the students' performance on the final test reflected this. Despite this failure, teacher X apparently did possess qualities of effective teaching and these were reflected in the student ratings.

This example not only demonstrates why validity coefficients in multisection studies may vary but also illustrates why student evaluations should be used in conjunction with other indicators of teaching effectiveness, including carefully considered estimates of student learning.

One limitation of these studies is that multisection courses are typically freshman or sophomore courses that emphasize lower-level learning, basic knowledge, and skills in a subject area. Teaching behaviors that best accomplish those learning outcomes may not work as well with higher-level outcomes such as critical thinking or synthesis. The relationship of student ratings to achievement, therefore, may not be as strong for teaching behaviors attempting to achieve higher-level outcomes. Of course, some of the different findings in the multisection validity studies could also be due to the different levels of achievement assessed in some courses (category 2—achievement variables—of Abrami, d'Apolonia, and Cohen, 1990). In any event, it is important to consider additional evidence of the validity of student evaluations. We attempt to do this in the sections that follow.

How Student Evaluations Compare with Those of Trained Observers

Murray (1983) found that students' ratings and trained observers' ratings of the same teachers were comparable. He trained observers to report on the teaching behaviors of fifty-four college teachers who had previously obtained high, medium, or low student evaluations. Six to eight observers then spent three separate one-hour class periods noting teaching behaviors so that each teacher was observed for a total of eighteen to twenty-four hours during the semester. According to the observers, teachers who had received high ratings from students did teach differently than teachers who had received average or poor ratings. For example, they reported that highly rated teachers were more likely to repeat difficult ideas (the clarity factor), speak emphatically or expressively (the enthusiasm factor), and be sensitive to student needs (the rapport factor). All told, the three groups of teachers differed on twenty-six individual behaviors. In short, student evaluations seemed to be determined by actual classroom behaviors rather than by pleasing personalities or other invalid indicators. Murray's list of twenty-six specific behaviors can also be used by faculty development specialists to improve teaching. His observation list, coupled with student rating items, provides teachers with a wide array of behavioral reports that might help them improve their performance in many dimensions of teaching.

Comparisons with Alumni Ratings

A commonly heard criticism of student evaluations is that they fail to reflect long-term effects of instruction. Critics argue that demanding teachers who have high expectations for students may not be appreciated until years later, when the students are more mature and can better assess their experiences. The research has not supported this view. An early study by Drucker and Remmers (1951) found positive correlations between ratings by students and by alumni who had been out of college for ten or more years. The correlations ranged from .40 to .68 on such dimensions as presentation of subject matter and attitude toward students. A higher correlation (.75), was reported by Centra (1974) for an overall rating of teachers by students and by alumni who had graduated as many as five years earlier. Both of these studies were cross-sectional— different groups rated the teachers each time. Overall and Marsh (1980) collected ratings from the same students, first at the end of the courses and then at least a year after graduation. For one hundred courses, end-of-course ratings had a .83 correlation with retrospective overall course ratings; for individual items, the correlations were similar.

The three studies indicated good stability in student evaluations. However, the correlations seem to decrease with passing time, suggesting that students' memories of instructors' characteristics fade over time.

Even though the correlations were high, a closer look at some of the ratings indicated noteworthy exceptions. In the Centra (1974) study, one teacher was named a best teacher by forty-four alumni and a worst teacher by four others. When rated by current students, another teacher was given the highest rating by more than half the class and the lowest rating by a small number of the students. But rather than reflecting instability in the ratings, the figures indicate that teachers may have a special appeal or lack of appeal for a minority of students. As some writers have pointed out, teachers are not simply good or bad, they are good or bad in relation to particular students (McKeachie, Lin, and Mann, 1971). Most institutions, however, prefer to reward teachers who are effective with a large proportion of students. Similarly, good teachers attempt to reach as many students as they can.

Possible Biases to Student Evaluations

Many faculty members believe that student evaluations are easily biased by any number of circumstances, although they may not be able to point out those that are most likely to cause bias (Franklin and Theall, 1989). The faculty at a major research university was asked about student bias. Faculty members, in the following percentages, believed these factors would bias student ratings (Marsh, 1987):

Course difficulty	72%
Grading leniency	68%
Instructor popularity	63%
Student interest in subject before course	62%
Course work load	60%
Class size	60%
Student reason for taking the course	55%
Student GPA	53%

Exactly what is bias? One definition is that it is a circumstance that unduly influences a teacher's ratings, although it has nothing to do with the teacher's effectiveness. Consider grading leniency: if instructors who gave students higher grades than they deserved received high ratings regardless of their effectiveness as teachers, this would reflect bias. Some circumstances, however, may really affect both student ratings and teacher effectiveness; the method of teaching is one example. Small discussion classes often receive higher ratings than lecture classes, but it is also likely that in small discussion classes teachers can be more effective because they can more easily involve more students, clarify individual questions, teach to the level of the class, provide useful feedback on assignments, and so forth. Therefore, is one's method of teaching an undue influence? Probably not. Yet it is probably unfair to compare the overall ratings of someone who teaches only small discussion classes with someone who lectures only to classes of seventy students or more. In other words, possible bias should be considered, but the evaluation must also be fair. For personnel decisions it is particularly important to understand how student, course, or teacher characteristics affect student evaluations so that these characteristics can by taken into account when rating results are interpreted. Individually, most characteristics do not have an undue influence, but the combination of several characteristics may. In addition, certain circumstances can apparently cause a biasing effect. In personnel decisions, as mentioned earlier, it is important that ratings of a number of different courses taught by a particular teacher be used in order to reduce the likelihood of bias for or against the teacher.

Research on course characteristics, student characteristics, teacher characteristics, and their possible effect on ratings is reviewed in the following section. Most of the studies are correlational; they show relationships rather than definite cause and effect. In this sense, the studies are not ideal. Experimental designs that isolate the effects of individual characteristics are difficult to carry out, but multivariate studies and the use of path analysis have helped clarify the cause and effect relationship.

Course Characteristics

Course characteristic variables that have been studied include class size, subject matter or discipline of the course, type of course (required or an elective), the time of day it is given, and its level of difficulty.

Class Size. Feldman (1984) reviewed studies of class size and concluded that a small biasing relationship exists, with smaller classes getting higher ratings. In particular, smaller classes get higher ratings in the dimensions of instructional rapport and interaction with students (Marsh, 1987). This makes sense, because such behaviors are expected to be affected by small class size. Studies that included a large number of classes of all sizes reported a U-shaped nonlinear relationship. Centra and Creech (1976), for example, compared almost five thousand classes and found that those with fifteen or fewer students received the highest ratings. Classes with sixteen to thirty-five students and those with more than one hundred ranked next with equivalent ratings. Classes with thirty-five to one hundred students received the lowest ratings. There may be several reasons for the higher ratings of the largest courses. Departments probably assign such courses to teachers who are especially skilled at teaching large groups. Second, because of the large numbers of students involved, teachers may prepare their presentations especially carefully and make liberal use of large-class techniques (for example, audiovisual aids). Finally, many courses of more than one hundred include group seminars, where the teacher or teaching assistants can respond to student questions and discuss course material.

It should be pointed out that ratings fluctuated somewhat between classes of similar size. For example, classes with twenty-two students had a mean rating of 3.78, as did classes with twenty-five students. But classes with twenty-three students had a mean rating of 3.66. Such fluctuations indicate that variables other than class size can affect both the ratings and student learning.

Because of the differences in ratings by class size, both the SIR and IDEA systems make comparison data available. Although the differences are statistically significant, they are not especially large and probably have little practical significance. For example, the SIR comparison data (Education Testing Service, 1990) indicate that classes with 10 to 14 students received a mean overall teacher rating of 4.18 on a five-point scale (1,545 classes; 15,715 students). Classes with more than 35 students received a mean rating of 4.02 (1,358 classes; 46,375 students). This difference of .16 in favor of smaller classes is about 25 percent of a standard deviation, hardly enough to be meaningful. A slightly larger difference occurs in ratings of lecture and discussion classes—.20 in favor of discussions. The difference in ratings of the value of the course was even greater (.28) in favor of the discussion method. Therefore, although class size affects ratings of lecture and discussion classes, the method of teaching is apparently somewhat more important.

Subject matter or discipline. After ranking the ratings of teachers in different disciplines that were presented in eleven studies, Feldman (1978) divided the disciplines into four ranked groups. English, history, the humanities, the arts, and foreign languages were placed in the groups that received high and medium-high ratings. The social sciences, political science, sociology, and anthropology fell in the middle group. Most of the sciences (including physics, chemistry, and geography), mathematics, and engineering fell into the group that received the lowest ratings. A more recent analysis by Cashin (1990), using the vast data pools derived from SIR and IDEA, arrived at similar findings. Cashin considered ratings of both course and instructor effectiveness. Nine disciplines rated high or medium-high in both course and teacher effectiveness: art, communications, fine and applied arts, foreign languages, health professions, home economics, music, secretarial studies, and speech. Eleven disciplines rated low or medium-low in both: accounting, business and management, chemistry, computer and information science, data processing, economics, engineering, mathematics and statistics, philosophy, physical sciences, and physics. The remaining disciplines, including the social sciences, education, nursing, biological sciences, English language and literature, were given medium ratings. Both studies' rankings are summarized in tables 3.2 through 3.4.

Both analyses indicate one consistent finding: classes in mathematics and the natural sciences are likelier to receive low ratings than those in other disciplines. I analyzed disciplinary differences on the five SIR scales reported in the comparison data

Table 3.2. Student Ratings of Instruction and Courses
in Different Disciplines—Four-Year College (Highest).

Feldman Review of Eleven Studies	Cashin Analysis of SIR and IDEA Data
English	Art
History	Communications
The humanities	Fine and applied arts
The arts	Foreign languages
Foreign languages	Health professions
	Home economics
	Music
	Secretarial studies
	Speech

Table 3.3. Student Ratings of Instruction and Courses in Different Disciplines—Four-Year College (Middle).

Feldman Review of Eleven Studies	*Cashin Analysis of SIR and IDEA Data*
Social sciences	Social science fields
Political science	Education
Sociology	Nursing
Anthropology	Biological sciences
	Health professions
	English language
	Literature

Table 3.4. Student Ratings of Instruction and Courses in Different Disciplines—Four-Year College (Lowest).

Feldman Review of Eleven Studies	*Cashin Analysis of SIR and IDEA Data*
Physics	Accounting
Chemistry	Business and management
Geography	Chemistry
Mathematics	Computer and information science
Engineering	Data processing
	Economics
	Engineering
	Mathematics and statistics
	Philosophy
	Physical sciences
	Physics

guide issued in 1990 (Educational Testing Service, 1990). These comparisons, reported in Table 3.5, revealed no differences in ratings of the course organization and planning or tests and exams scales. But ratings of the faculty-student interaction, course difficulty and work load, and communications scales in the natural sciences and mathematics and statistics were low, especially compared with most humanities classes.

These findings suggest that according to student ratings, mathematics and statistics and natural science courses (and the teachers who teach them) tend to be less student oriented, less effec-

Table 3.5. Disciplinary Comparisons on Other SIR Scales.

Scale	
1. Course organization and planning	No difference
2. Faculty-student interaction	Natural sciences and mathematics and statistics about 30 percentile points lower than humanities
3. Course difficulty and work load	Natural sciences and mathematics and statistics about 30 percentile points lower than humanities
4. Communications	Natural sciences and mathematics and statistics slightly (10 to 20 percentile points) lower than humanities
5. Tests and exams	No difference

tive in presentation (they are often lectures), and more difficult and quicker paced.

As far as course difficulty, work load, and effort are concerned, a five-college study I conducted revealed differences in teachers' and students' views (Centra, 1973b). Teachers in the natural sciences thought the level of difficulty and pace of their courses were appropriate; students found the courses difficult and fast paced. Teachers in the natural sciences also thought that students did not put enough effort into their courses; students disagreed.

It is important to stress that the disciplinary ratings do not affect every teacher; certainly many natural science teachers are student oriented and excellent lecturers. The differences discussed here reveal general tendencies; furthermore, they present only the students' view, because they are based on student evaluations.

Some more objective analysis may help explain the differences in the ratings. Cashin (1990) argued that the more quantitative courses receive lower ratings because students' quantitative skills are less well developed than their verbal skills, and because of this, quantitative-based courses are more difficult to teach. Cashin also points out that the low-rated disciplines are generally those in which institutions compete most heavily with business and industry for Ph.D.'s; it is possible that the faculty teaching those courses is less effective as a group than the faculty in other disciplines.

Furthermore, it is true that knowledge is growing more rapidly in the natural sciences than in the humanities. Teachers may therefore feel pressured to cover increasing amounts of material in each course and as a result, students may feel rushed and confused about key material. Moreover, natural science teachers often spend more time doing research and seeking funds than do humanities teachers; their teaching effectiveness may diminish proportionately.

Whatever the reasons, institutions that use ratings for personnel decisions may want to see if their own classes and teachers are rated similarly based on discipline. Comparison data may be accumulated by the college over time, or administrators may want to peruse the national comparative data accumulated for SIR and IDEA. As with class size, the differences between most disciplines are not great; a few did, however, differ by as much as half a standard deviation (about 20 to 30 percentile points in the SIR data, in which scores are assigned percentile equivalents).

Required and Elective Courses. Students tend to give slightly higher ratings to courses in their major field or that they elect to take than they do to required courses (Centra and Creech, 1976). For the former, both the teacher and the courses are rated as more effective or more valuable. Students (and possibly teachers as well) are generally less interested in required courses, which are often introductory or survey courses that meet distribution requirements in a college's general education sequence. Feldman's (1978) review of the research concluded that a small positive relationship (correlations in the .10s and .20s) existed between class ratings and the students' average intrinsic interest in the subject area. Intrinsic interest—or prior subject interest as Marsh (1987) refers to it—correlated by about .40 with students' own evaluations of their learning in the course. Although the students' prior subject interest probably affects course ratings more than it does teacher ratings, some rating systems such as IDEA attempt to take it into account in their instructor reports.

Time of Day Class is Given. Students' time-of-day preferences have no apparent effect on their teacher or course ratings (Feldman,

1978). For the several studies he reviewed, Feldman reported no indication of consistency based on time of day in ratings. Some students and teachers may abhor early morning classes, while others may feel they are at their best at that time; the net effect on the ratings is negligible.

Difficulty Level of the Course. Many teachers believe that courses that are less difficult or have lower work loads are more highly rated by students, but the opposite appears to be more likely. According to numerous studies, the teachers who rated more highly gave more work or were believed to teach more difficult courses (Marsh, 1987). These findings are particularly true within disciplines; between disciplines, perceived difficulty level and ratings do differ, as discussed previously. For example, natural science courses as a group are perceived as more difficult and also tend to receive somewhat lower ratings.

Student Characteristics

Student characteristics studied for possible biasing effects on their ratings include grade point average, academic ability, and age. Research has not shown that these characteristics significantly affect student ratings (Centra and Creech, 1976; McKeachie, 1979). Some teachers believe that more able or mature students provide more valid ratings than do those with lesser abilities or experience. But only when teachers have focused their teaching on the better students in a class were the ratings affected; in such cases, those students gave higher ratings (Elliot, 1950). Thus teachers who direct their efforts at a particular group of students to the obvious exclusion of others can expect varied ratings. Teachers can investigate this issue themselves if they use a rating form that asks students to indicate previous GPA, expected grade, and educational experience. The responses of any of the subgroups can be analyzed by hand or by computer. Classroom research of this kind can help teachers diagnose the level of their teaching. Given the large number of older as well as traditional-age students in many college classrooms today, analyses of responses within classes may suggest to the teacher which, if any, segment is being slighted. If so, adjustments in teaching methods or course design may be needed.

Instructor Characteristics

Instructor characteristics studied for their influence on ratings include personality, academic rank and experience, research productivity, leniency in grading, gender, and race. Finally, the instructor's "seductiveness," or the effect of highly entertaining or expressive personalities on ratings, was examined.

Personality. Individual personality traits can be measured through self-report personality inventories or through the reports of others. Studies that used the first type of measure found generally insignificant correlations between personality traits and ratings (Feldman, 1986). However, in studies of the perceptions of a teacher's students or colleagues, correlations with ratings were moderate to large. One interpretation of this finding is that students are involved in both measures—the teacher's personality and effectiveness—and so the two measures are not independent. This may reflect contamination of the findings, or it may simply be that teachers whom students rated as effective have also projected positive personality traits that students, or colleagues, can identify (but which the individual in question cannot). In that sense, "good teaching" and "good personality" do overlap; still, they are not synonymous.

Academic Rank and Experience. We can draw only limited conclusions about the effect of rank and experience, because studies have been largely cross-sectional rather than longitudinal. Two findings are consistent, however: teaching assistants receive lower global student ratings than ranked teachers (assistant, associate, or full professors), and first-year teachers receive lower ratings than those with more seniority (Centra, 1978b). Both these findings make sense and cannot be seen as a source of bias in ratings. Anecdotal evidence points to the greatest improvement in teacher effectiveness during the first years of teaching.

Research Productivity. Because undergraduate students usually know little about their teachers' scholarly output, we would not expect a biasing effect on ratings based on this factor. But the argument often made is that research increases teaching effectiveness by increasing teachers' awareness and currency in their subject matter. If this were true, we would expect a positive relationship between student ratings of teacher effectiveness and the number of articles produced by faculty members. In contrast, we would expect a negative relationship if highly published faculty members received lower student ratings, because they spent more time on scholarship. Feldman's (1987) meta-analysis based on twenty-nine studies found a correlation of only .12 between ratings and various measures of research productivity. I compared student ratings to the number of articles reported by teachers in the most recent five-year period. I found higher correlations in the social sciences than in the natural sciences and humanities, especially with more experienced faculty members (Centra, 1983). The correlations are, in general, moderate. The lack of a strong relationship indicates that the measures of research productivity typically used in personnel decisions (for example, number of articles, citation counts) cannot be assumed to reflect teaching effectiveness. (See Chapter Seven for a more complete discussion of the relationship between teaching and research.)

Leniency in Grading. Many faculty members believe that students give higher ratings to teachers from whom they have received (or expect to receive) high grades. The research evidence is mixed on this question. A few studies have shown a modest effect, but one could argue that grades should be higher in courses in which students learn more, as should their ratings of the teachers (Marsh, 1987; Centra, 1979; McKeachie, 1979b). The positive correlations could therefore be seen to support the validity of ratings. The few studies that found a leniency-ratings relationship had manipulated student grades in order to determine how such grades affected ratings (for example, Holmes, 1972). But the effect was relatively small and inconsistent. Students typically do not receive grades from teachers until after they have submitted their anonymous ratings; certainly this procedure helps minimize a possible leniency bias. Of course, if teachers believe that their grading policy will affect students' ratings, this belief in itself may cause some to be more lenient.

Gender. Studies of the effects of gender—of both the teachers and the students—have been conducted in simulated settings, or "laboratories," and in actual classrooms. Feldman reviewed both types of studies through meta-analysis. In the laboratory studies, students were shown photographs or videotapes of male and female teachers or were given descriptions of fictitious teachers who differed in gender and other characteristics. Most studies found either no difference or inconsistent differences in the students' ratings of the overall effectiveness of the teachers (Feldman, 1992). In a few studies, male teachers received higher ratings than female teachers. When teacher gender and student gender were studied together, only a small variance was predicted by same gender or opposite gender combinations. Three studies reported that male students gave less favorable ratings to female teachers than did female students (Basow and Silberg, 1987; Kaschak, 1978; Lombardo and Tocci, 1979). In contrast, female students saw no difference in the effectiveness of male and female teachers. The same-gender or different-gender bias, however, was not confirmed in other laboratory studies reviewed by Feldman.

Analysis of actual classroom studies indicates no practical difference in the ratings given to male and female teachers (Feldman, 1993; Stratham, Richardson, and Cook, 1991). In twenty-eight studies, the correlation between gender and overall evaluation of the teacher was found to be only .02, with female teachers favored very slightly. When teachers were compared on the various dimensions, women scored slightly higher on "sensitivity to and concern with class progress" (r=.12) and "usefulness of teaching aids" (r=.22). These findings, though modest, coincide with gender-stereotypic behaviors; women are expected to be more caring and sensitive than men. Whether the female teachers actually exhibited behaviors or whether students merely expected the behaviors because the teachers were female is not known.

In ten classroom-based studies, the gender of both the students and the teachers was taken into consideration. Feldman ranked same-gender and different-gender means of each study. On average, same-gender ratings were highest. Ratings were lower to a similar extent when female students rated male teachers and male students rated female teachers. Thus, the classroom studies do not support the three laboratory studies previously cited.

On the basis of the classroom studies and most of the laboratory studies, students generally do not rate male and female teachers much differently. If a teacher has a class in which most students are of the same gender as the teacher, however, the ratings could be somewhat higher than with a more mixed group.

Race. Is there a same-race or different-race bias in student ratings? Do students who are racially similar to a teacher rate that teacher more highly than those who are not? No studies have been reported that investigate systematic racial bias in student ratings. Based on the gender studies, however, the expectation would be that a class of same-race teacher and students would result in a somewhat higher rating than one where race differs.

"Seductiveness." The question of whether a teacher who is highly entertaining or expressive receives unduly high ratings from students has been examined through a series of so-called educational-seduction studies. In an early study by Naftulin, Ware, and Donnelly (1973), a professional actor delivered a graduate-level lecture that was nonsubstantive and contradictory in content. Dr. Fox—as the actor was named—was nevertheless a very entertaining and expressive lecturer. The high overall ratings that Dr. Fox received supported the researchers' contention that students can be inveigled into thinking that they have learned something even when lecture content is irrelevant and meaningless. The many limitations of this study led to others, in which students were shown videotaped lectures that varied in the extreme in instructor expressiveness and the amount of lecture content. Students then rated the taped lectures and, in many of the studies, also took a test to determine their knowledge of the lecture content. A meta-analysis of these "Dr. Fox" or educational-seduction studies—as they have come to be known—by Abrami, Leventhal, and Perry (1982) concluded that highly expressive lecturers received high scores on global ratings and on items logically related to expressiveness (for example, enthu-

siasm). However, students did not necessarily learn more in such lectures unless the content level was indeed high. In other words, student ratings were much more sensitive to instructor expressiveness or enthusiasm than to the lecture content.

Do these findings indicate that student ratings are unduly affected by expressive instructors? Probably not. First, Abrami, Leventhal, and Perry (1982) mention that, a twenty- to thirty-minute videotaped lecture represents only a minuscule percentage of the actual lecture time in a three-credit course. Second, such extreme manipulativeness is unlikely in real-life teaching situations. Few college teachers provide no content in their courses and instead substitute enthusiasm. For these reasons, generalizations from the laboratory experiments to actual classroom teaching are tenuous. But if we were to generalize, a reasonable lesson from seduction research would be that by teaching more enthusiastically, teachers will receive higher ratings *and* their students will retain more of the course content.

Circumstances Under Which Evaluations Are Made

Circumstances that can bias the results of student evaluations include (a) whether ratings are anonymous, (b) whether students understand the intended use of the evaluations, and (c) whether the instructors are present when they are rated. The research has addressed each of these concerns. What has not been studied at this time is the possible effect on student ratings of the general campus environment or of prevailing student attitudes.

Students who identify themselves in their ratings are expected to be far more generous, especially if the forms are returned to the instructor before final grades. Feldman (1979) reviewed several studies that supported this expectation, although the results were not as clear nor the differences as large as expected. Identification is probably only crucial if students think their grades may be affected or if they have to explain the reasons for their ratings to the teacher.

Students can learn about the intended use of their ratings through oral or written directions. The intended use may be for personnel decisions or for the instructor's self-improvement. In the former instance, students would be expected to be more lenient, while they might be more critical in the latter. This expectation has not been fulfilled, according to most past studies. Centra (1976) experimentally manipulated the written directions to students about the use of the results and found essentially no differences among forty-one classes studied. Similarly, Frankhouser (1984), after randomly dividing eighteen classes into two groups, found no significant differences in the ratings when different oral directions were given to each. Thus, the intended use of the ratings does not appear to affect appreciably how students respond.

When instructors remain in the room while students complete the forms, the ratings are higher than when a neutral observer is present (Feldman, 1979). Even though the differences were not shown to be large, ratings that will be used for tenure or promotion purposes should be administered by a neutral observer; also, students should be anonymous. A few institutions go to the time and expense of typing the comments before giving them to teachers in order to protect the students' identities.

Summary

Although the research is largely supportive of student evaluations, they have been shown to have limitations. Student evaluations do differ somewhat for some course and instructor characteristics, including class size, method of teaching, academic field, prior student interest in the subject, grading leniency, and teacher expressiveness or "seductiveness." At least two of these variables, however, do not meet the definition of bias used in this chapter: an undue influence on the ratings a teacher receives that has no relationship to teaching effectiveness. For example, teaching method can affect both ratings and student achievement; thus it may not represent bias. Even several biasing factors considered together account for only about 15 percent of the variance in student ratings (Marsh, 1987). Although such variance is not excessive, it could alter a close personnel decision. In tenure and promotion decisions, consideration of the ratings of several different courses over several years minimizes the possibility of bias.

The reliability measure of student evaluations, in particular, the relative consistency of ratings and their stability over time, are both good, providing that a sufficient number of students rate a course. The validity of student evaluations, as measured by correlations with student learning or comparisons with ratings by trained observers or alumni, is also acceptable. However, the magnitude of the correlations reported in the studies of validity and bias underscores the need to supplement student evaluation information with other sources when assessing teaching.

The research evaluated in this chapter forms the basis for many of the twelve guidelines for the proper use of student evaluations that I discuss in Chapter Four. Evidence of the utility of student evaluations both for instructional improvement and in personnel decisions is also discussed.

Chapter 4

Using Student Evaluations:
Guidelines and Benefits

*T*his chapter addresses questions about the usefulness of student evaluations for formative and summative purposes. I discuss the four conditions that must be fulfilled for student evaluations to produce significant changes in teaching. Studies of the use of student evaluations in tenure and promotion decisions are briefly summarized, although other chapters in this book examine additional studies in which the evaluations have been used for summative purposes. I close the chapter with twelve guidelines for the proper use of student evaluations, whatever the purpose may be.

How Useful Are Student Evaluations?

Can student evaluations lead to improvement in teaching? What impact do they have on tenure and promotion decisions? Many students doubt that their teacher ratings have much effect. According to a survey of two institutions, students thought that their ratings were not actually used in tenure and promotion decisions, and that most teachers paid little attention to them (Marlin, 1987). Yet more than 70 percent of the chairpersons at both institutions reported that student evaluations had a significant impact on tenure and promotion decisions. In a survey of faculty members at nine campuses of the University of California, 78 percent reported making changes in teaching based on student evaluations (Outcalt, 1980). No doubt the impact of the evaluations on teaching improvement and administrative decisions varies from institution to institution and from instructor to instructor. Nevertheless, the research indicates that student evaluations can be useful for both formative and summative purposes.

Teaching Improvement

As discussed in Chapter One, at least four conditions must be fulfilled for student evaluations to lead to improvement in instruction. First, teachers must learn something new from them. Second, they must value the new information. Third, they must understand how to make improvements. And finally, teachers must be motivated to make the improvements, either intrinsically or extrinsically.

New Knowledge

Comparisons of teachers' self-evaluations and their students' evaluations indicate that many teachers are not aware of how students perceive them (Centra, 1973b; Blackburn and Clark, 1975). I studied more than four hundred teachers who had not collected ratings previously and thus could not be sure how students evaluated them. Teacher self-ratings on specific items and on a global item had correlations of approximately .20 with student evaluations, confirming that many were unaware of their students' perceptions. Marsh (1982) and others found higher correlations (about .45 to .49), but most of the teachers in these samples had seen the results of their student evaluations in previous courses and were therefore less likely to be learning entirely new information. We can expect, therefore, that first-time users and teachers offering a course for the first time are more likely to gain new information. These teachers have greater potential for change.

Value

Not all teachers value student ratings. Although they may be required to collect student ratings, these teachers may question the appropriateness of students' judging them, they may doubt the validity of the evaluations, or they may have other reasons for discrediting the results. It is unlikely that this group, generally a minority, will use rating information to make changes.

How to Change

Even if teachers learn something they did not know previously and believe the information has credibility, they may not know how to make significant changes. The items may not have been specific enough, or the instructor may not know, for example, how to organize the course better if that was an indicated area of weakness. Some kind of assistance, therefore, may be needed, although a significant number should certainly be able to help themselves. Studies have indicated that when a consultant (for example, a faculty development specialist) discusses the results of student evaluations with the teacher, instructional improvement is more dramatic than when the teacher alone interprets the results (Cohen, 1980).

Motivation

Some teachers' need for extrinsic motivation to improve may have been caused by their institution's use of teaching performance in promotion, tenure, or salary decisions. A need for extrinsic motivation might explain why the student ratings of twelve tenured faculty members in one department did not improve over a twelve-year period, while nontenured teachers' ratings increased steadily from the year of first appointment to the year in which they received tenure (Murray, 1984). Nevertheless, some faculty members may improve because, as professionals, they are intrinsically motivated to do so. People may be challenged when they have not met their own standards. A challenge from students may trigger an incongruity in their own standards. In this sense, intrinsic motivation is similar to equilibrium theory, which claims that people change when a condition of imbalance (Heider, 1958) or dissonance (Festinger, 1957) is created within themselves. Thus, teachers may change in ways suggested by student evaluations in order to make their performance conform to their own perceptions.

It is possible, however, that student ratings can lower motivation to improve. According to McKeachie (1979b), low student ratings and critical comments from students can make teachers anxious and discouraged. He argues that this is one reason student ratings fail to improve teaching.

Research Evidence on Teaching Improvement

A frequently employed technique to investigate the effects of student evaluation on instructional practices has been to compare midsemester ratings for groups of teachers. Teachers are generally assigned at random to either a feedback group, which receives the results of the midsemester ratings soon thereafter, or a no-feedback group, which does not receive the results. If the ratings had some effect on teaching practices, we would expect the end-of-semester ratings for the feedback group to be higher than for the no-feedback group. Cohen (1980) conducted a meta-analysis of nineteen such studies and concluded that the feedback group averaged about a third of a standard deviation gain (thirteen percentile points). This was true both for the overall evaluation and for three dimensions. L'Hommedieu, Menges, and Brinko (1988) reached a similar conclusion based on their meta-analysis. A third of a standard deviation gain is modest, but then instructors had only a half-semester to make changes that might be reflected in later ratings. In one study I conducted, instructors whose self-evaluations at midsemester were considerably higher than their student ratings were most likely to change their behavior significantly (Centra, 1973a). This finding in particular supports the need to fulfill condition one mentioned earlier: ratings are most likely to have an effect when instructors learn something new about their teaching. The finding that a difference between self-evaluations and student evaluations was more likely to lead to a change in behavior also supports the intrinsic motivation and imbalance theories just discussed.

In some of the nineteen studies analyzed by Cohen (1980), instructors were given professional consultations on how to improve their teaching based on the student rating information. In these studies, larger gains in subsequent ratings were found than in other studies, indicating greater improvement in teaching. This finding supports the need to fulfill in particular condition three: greater improvement occurs when teachers know how to make changes. These teachers, as well as others who improved without consultation, were apparently also intrinsically motivated to make changes (as required by condition four). Moreover, teachers who were not intrinsically motivated would probably not have submitted to consultation sessions.

One reason the so-called diagnostic items on most student rating forms may not lead to greater changes in teaching is that they are not specific enough. Murray (1983) constructed a teacher behaviors inventory that included fairly specific or low-inference items for student responses. Items such as "Puts outline of lecture on board" and "Gives preliminary overview of lecture" specifically tell teachers what they can do to give better-organized lectures, and are thus low-inference items. Using this type of item, Murray (1985) found that in the nineteen studies discussed previously, teacher groups that received feedback from students at midsemester showed larger gains than those which used more traditional high-inference items, such as "Rating of how well class sessions are planned."

Some alternatives to professional consultation, which is fairly expensive, are the approaches devised by Wilson (1987). Wilson suggested that faculty members who had retired from the University of California, Berkeley, act as consultants to junior teachers. While this may be less expensive, the consultation may not be as worthwhile as that given by a faculty development specialist, unless the mentor first receives some training. Certainly mentors from the same discipline as the junior teacher can provide specialized assistance. Wilson also developed a compendium of good teaching ideas provided by professors who had received high ratings on Berkeley's student description of teaching questionnaire. His interviews with these professors resulted in some two hundred good ideas, which he matched to items on the questionnaire. Packets with compilations of these ideas were then made available to teachers to allow them to make better use of their student evaluation results. Unfortunately, as Wilson found, only a small number of teachers read the information or adopted any of the ideas.

Students' Written Comments

Most student evaluation forms allow students to offer comments about the course and the way it was taught. Such comments can be especially useful in improving instruction. Open-ended questions such as "What are the major strengths and weaknesses of the course or the instructor?" or "How do you think the course can be improved?" elicit suggestions. Some teachers, in fact, prefer a series of open-ended questions to objectively scored questionnaire items. Yet students could understandably feel inhibited about making negative comments, fearing that their handwriting would be identified. One study of students' written comments found that nearly two-thirds were positive (Braskamp, Ory, and Pieper, 1981). This behavior parallels students' tendency to be lenient in scoring instructional rating scales; generally about 60 percent of teachers at four-year colleges and universities are judged "above average" and another 25 percent or so "about average"(Educational Testing Service, 1979). Still, about 15 percent of the students are very critical of their teachers, so not all students are lenient evaluators.

Braskamp, Ory, and Pieper (1981) analyzed 3,240 written student comments and found that the instructor's ability to communicate clearly in class was the most frequently mentioned. Many of the dimensions identified from the written comments were similar to those derived from the objective items in many rating forms, including such factors as instructor preparedness, rapport with students, course content, and course organization. Naturally, some comments were much more course-specific, but it was not always clear how widely held such comments were among the students. The written comments did, however, corroborate objective items on students' general impression of instructional quality. When the overall ratings of courses or instructors taken from objective items were compared with the written comments, the correlations were highly significant (Braskamp, Ory, and Pieper, 1981). Similarly, in another study by these three Illinois researchers, objective questionnaire items, written student comments, and student group-interview summaries were found to be highly congruent, with correlations in the .81 to .94 range (Ory, Braskamp, and Pieper, 1980). Students'

comments during the group interviews (during which the instructors were not present) were much less variable than were the written
comments, possibly because of peer pressure in the group setting.
Thus it appears that the same general good-to-bad classification of
teachers occurs whether students respond to a few global ratings (for
example, by using a five-point scale to rate the teacher or the
course), write down their views, or discuss them in a group. The
latter two methods, when used together with the more course-
specific items in rating forms, however, are more likely to lead to
instructional improvement, because they offer specific suggestions.

Written comments can be obtained at any time during the
course, and some teachers have used ingenious ways to elicit these
comments. In his study of highly rated University of California,
Berkeley, professors, Wilson (1987) found one physics teacher who
asked students to write their answers to two questions at the end of
each class session: "What is the most important thing you learned
today?" and "What question is foremost in your mind as a result
of today's session?"

The teacher discovered that student responses to these questions were very useful in determining how well they were understanding the course content. I have done the same thing in many
courses and found that the students' questions also formed an excellent bridge to opening discussions at the next class session. It is
not necessary for students to respond in each class period to these
"one-minute papers," as the Berkeley professor called them (actually, students take more than a minute to respond). Questioning
students every few class sessions may be sufficient because otherwise
some may refrain from asking questions orally in class in order to
have something to write.

Computer-Aided Communications

Continuous feedback such as the one-minute papers, can be an
excellent way for instructors to keep in constant touch with students' concerns and to make needed course adjustments. Another
way to receive continuous feedback is through electronic mail.
Teachers can set up a computer account that students can use anonymously to send messages to the teacher and receive some back

(code letters are used for identification). Computer-aided communication, as this approach might be labeled, offers several advantages:

1. Students can inform teachers about how the course is progressing or ask questions about course content. Because messages can be anonymous, students can offer comments or suggestions they might not otherwise make. The teacher can respond to each student by electronic mail or answer the question in class if several students express the same concern and the answer would benefit many.

2. Comments or questions can begin early on and continue throughout the course. There is no need to wait until the end of the course, as is typically the case with student ratings. The teacher and the student can also participate in a dialogue until a point is cleared up.

3. Although computerized communication may be especially helpful in large classes, individual study projects may benefit as well.

I studied three courses that used electronic mail for teacher-student communications and my findings suggest both promise and problems with the approach (Centra, 1987). In two of the courses, only about a fourth of the students used the system, while just over half did so in the third. Of the seventy-five or so messages sent by students, 60 percent were reactions to specific course procedures, such as assignments or quizzes, or comments on the pace of the course. Such messages were often accompanied by the students' suggestions. Another 20 percent of the messages were questions about course content or requests for further information. The last 20 percent were evaluative comments, sometimes combined with a question, such as: "I'm learning a lot in this course but would you explain. . . ."

Instructors in these three courses responded to all comments or questions by electronic mail except in a few instances when they answered in class. In all three courses, teachers also encouraged students to ask questions orally or in writing, and this may have limited the messages students sent. Also, not all students had ready access to a computer terminal, and the directions for using electronic mail, while reduced to one page, may have been too involved for some students. In the future, as more students and faculty members gain access to computer terminals, computer-aided communication should provide a useful supplement to the more traditional approaches used for obtaining student comments and questions.

Tenure and Promotion Decisions

Institutions of higher education vary not only in the weight they give teaching in their summative decisions, but also in the weight they give student evaluations (Leventhal and others, 1981). Certainly, most department chairs and faculty members believe that student evaluations should be used in the summative evaluation of teaching (Centra, 1977a). However, at one research university, teaching ability in general and numerical summaries of student evaluation in particular were found to have little effect on promotion decisions (Salthouse, McKeachie, and Lin, 1978). In this study, present and former members of promotion and tenure committees were asked to judge the eligibility of hypothetical candidates for a promotion or salary increase. Research productivity was the dominant criterion. In a later study at the same university, Lin, McKeachie, and Tucker (1984) had senior faculty members vote on simulated dossiers of individuals up for promotion. One-fourth of the judges did not promote any candidates with only a medium level of research productivity, regardless of the candidate's teaching evaluations. Including students' comments about the teacher's effectiveness with the numerical summaries of their evaluations increased the credibility of the teaching evaluations for the judges and they were shown to then give teaching a weight more in line with their stated beliefs. The students' comments, which were carefully chosen to reflect the numerical summaries, apparently had greater influence on the faculty representatives than did the numerical averages alone.

Studies that investigated the impact of student evaluations on actual personnel decisions (rather than on simulations) indicate that the evaluations made a significant, though not heavy, contribution. Hoyt (1974) reported a correlation of .20 between student ratings and annual salary increments for 222 faculty members at Kansas State University some twenty years ago. Murray (1984) compared faculty members who had been granted tenure with those who had not during a ten-year span at a Canadian university. Those who received tenure had significantly higher student ratings, although the ratings did not contribute significantly to decisions on promotion to full professor. Research productivity was important as well at this university: it received about five times as much weight as student evaluations. Nevertheless, about 12 percent of the variance in tenure decisions was attributed to student evaluations. At institutions that give teaching effectiveness considerable weight in personnel decisions, student evaluations can be expected to be more influential.

Guidelines for the Use of Student Evaluations

The following guidelines are based on my interpretation of study results and on discussions I have had with other researchers, selected faculty members, and administrators who have used student evaluations.

1. *Determine how the results will be used.* Student evaluations are most often used for instructional improvement or in tenure, promotion, or salary decisions. On occasion, when the results are made public, students can use them for course or teacher selection. Faculty members and administrators need to understand clearly how the results of student evaluations will be used, who will have access to them, and how their use relates to contractual arrangements at the institution. Depending on their use—in particular, when they are used in personnel decisions—several of the following guidelines are especially critical. Students should also be informed of how the results will be used.

2. *Use several sources of information.* No matter what purpose they are put to, student evaluations represent only one source of information about teaching performance: student opinion. Other sources of information (for example, reports from colleagues, self-reports), may be less reliable or less accessible but nevertheless must be considered because they provide additional information. Research productivity, as studies have consistently shown, does not

reflect teaching effectiveness and should not be substituted for measures of teaching performance.

3. *Use several sets of evaluation results.* For tenure and promotion decisions, a pattern of evaluation results derived from different courses taught over more than one semester should be used. It is important to consider trends in results over time and to limit the undue effects of a particular course. If the faculty member teaches different types of courses (for example, lectures and small groups), each type should be sampled. Graduate and undergraduate courses taught by the same person also often differ in ratings. Using results from five or more classes is best, as we discuss in the following guideline. For instructional improvement, evaluations of a single course can be useful, particularly in improving that course.

4. *Have a sufficient number of students evaluate each course.* The absolute number of students and the proportion of students in the class responding are both important. The reliability of the results increases as the number of students increases: with fewer than ten students, the results should be treated with caution; ten to fifteen students is an acceptable number, especially if the results of five or more classes are considered; with twenty-five students, the reliability estimates are excellent. By having a sufficient number of students, the effects of a few divergent opinions are limited. For example, one or two disgruntled students out of twenty-five respondents will have much less effect on an average score than they will if a total of only eight students responds. Proportionately, two-thirds or more of a class should respond. If more than a third are absent or choose not to respond, the results may not be representative of the class. While the reliability of the ratings is especially important for summative purposes, consistent and representative results are always important.

5. *Consider course characteristics when interpreting results.* Student evaluations are affected by some course characteristics. While this effect does not always represent bias, it may not be fair to teachers to completely disregard such characteristics, which include class size and teaching method, the course subject, and the relationship of the course to the students' program. The effect of any one of these factors may not be great, but a combination could affect a teacher's mean rating by 20 to 30 percentile points. An

instructor's personal characteristics, such as personality or gender, may bias ratings under some circumstances, but generally these characteristics do not have much influence on ratings.

6. *Use comparative data, but with caution.* Student evaluations are typically skewed, that is, a relatively small proportion of teachers are rated below average. For this reason, it is useful to have comparative data that provide a context within which teachers and others can interpret class means. Some commercially available forms (for example, SIR and IDEA) publish comparative data derived from institutions that have used their service. Individual colleges also compile comparative data derived from scores they have accumulated over time. Without comparison data, teachers can easily overestimate their effectiveness. However, when local data are used, the practice can foster competitive and unrealistic expectations because half the population must by definition fall below the fiftieth percentile. For this reason, the comparison data should not be based on a very narrow population (for example, a fifteen-member department).

7. *Do not overestimate small differences.* Because student evaluations are typically quantified, there is a tendency to give them a precision they do not possess. An instructor who is at the fiftieth percentile on an item does not differ in any practical way from one at the sixtieth percentile. When using student evaluations in personnel decisions, teachers might better be classified into four or five broad groups of teaching excellence based on a pattern of evaluations (see guideline three). Similarly, mathematical formulas that weigh student evaluation scores as part of a determination of overall teaching effectiveness are not advisable.

8. *For personnel decisions, use global evaluation items and other summary scores.* Because of the difficulty of assimilating the results of a twenty- or thirty-item rating form, one should first examine the teacher's overall rating. Overall ratings of the teacher and the course tend to correlate more closely with student achievement scores than do other items. Effective teachers may not score high on every item or dimension on a rating form because of their different styles and strengths. Nevertheless, these scores should also be considered to identify which strengths support the overall evaluations.

9. *For instructional improvement, encourage teachers to*

use diagnostic information. Good rating forms help teachers diagnose their strengths and weaknesses. Some teachers can use the results to make improvements while others can profit from discussing the results with a colleague or professional consultant and getting feedback. Teachers should add their own course-related items to standardized forms and encourage written or oral communications from students. Both sources can provide the specific information that is especially useful for improvement. However, faculty members should remember that it is not possible or even desirable to satisfy all students' complaints or wishes.

10. *Use standardized procedures for administering forms in class.* When the results are used for personnel decisions, standardized procedures are needed to minimize possible biasing effects. Forms should be completed by students in class, probably during the next to last week of class (before the final exam). When students must mail back forms, the response rate is usually poor. Teachers should not be in the room when forms are completed, nor should they collect the ratings. Students should remain anonymous; they should not be expected to spend more than about fifteen minutes in responding. Written comments should either be typed by the institution or not be given to teachers until final grades are in; a quantitative summary of student responses should be given to instructors at the same time. For instructional improvement, standardized administrative procedures are less critical because the instructor has no reason to influence the ratings. Still, in fairness to students, ratings should be anonymous and should not be read by instructors until after grades are determined.

11. *Give teachers an opportunity to respond to evaluation results.* For personnel decisions, teachers should have the opportunity to describe what they were trying to accomplish in the course and how their teaching methods fit those objectives. Teachers should also be encouraged to discuss circumstances they feel affected the evaluations. What may seem to be a poor evaluation of a particular aspect of a course may, for example, be a reflection of the teacher's attempt to use a different approach. Traditional student rating forms may not reflect the effectiveness of less traditional teaching methods.

12. *Limit the use of rating forms.* The use of student rating

forms reaches a point of diminishing returns. If the same form is used in every course during every term, students may get bored or respond haphazardly. Faculty members may resent the lost class time, pay less attention to the results, and be less motivated to experiment in their instructional methods. For these reasons, ratings can be expected to change very little after a few years. Institutions and instructors need to strike a balance between attempting to obtain information for personnel decisions and not stifling faculty innovations or student interest in the process.

Summary

Student evaluations are most likely to lead to significant improvement in teaching when four conditions are met. First, the teacher must learn something from the students that was not already known. Second, the teacher must value the information. Third, the teacher must know how or be advised about how to make improvements. And fourth, the teacher must be motivated to make improvements. Studies have demonstrated the importance of some of these variables in influencing improvement, although none has yet included all four. Machine-scored objective items provide limited feedback; students' written comments can be more course specific. Collecting feedback halfway through a course rather than at the end, collecting continuous feedback through the use of computerized electronic mail, and making use of "one-minute papers" are other ways to obtain useful information from students.

Student evaluations are increasingly being used in personnel decisions. Studies have demonstrated that the evaluations are given modest weight at most schools, and even less weight at research-oriented institutions. Anecdotal evidence suggests that new studies, particularly of institutions that weigh teaching heavily, would find that student evaluations are given greater consideration.

Whether they use student evaluations for summative or formative purposes, institutions should be aware of the strengths and limitations of the evaluations. The guidelines that conclude this chapter should help institutions establish sound policies and practices for their use.

Chapter 5

Teachers' Self-Reports and Portfolios

*P*eople do not see themselves as others do. A poem that Robert Burns wrote in 1786 still rings true today:

> Oh! wad some power the giftie gie us
> To see oursels as others see us!
> It wad frae mony a blunder free us
> And foolish notion.
>
> *From "To a Louse"—Robert Burns* (1856)

This chapter reviews the research on teacher self-evaluations—or self-ratings—and distinguishes them from self-reports. The research clearly demonstrates why self-evaluations should not be emphasized in summative evaluation. Moreover, unless they are complemented by other information, self-evaluations have only limited use in instructional improvement. In contrast, self-reports, or descriptive information, together with self-reflections, are a critical part of a faculty member's annual report, dossier, or portfolio. Self-evaluations can be included in self-reports but they should not be given emphasis. This chapter examines appropriate self-report information, focusing in particular on the use of the portfolio in formative and summative evaluation. The validity and usefulness of faculty portfolios as an evaluation source is not yet certain, but they have rapidly gained acceptance as an important part of systematic evaluation procedures. I studied the teaching portfolio at one institution that used it in summative evaluation. The results of that study, which focused on how colleagues and a dean evaluated the portfolio, are presented in this chapter. The chapter concludes with a discussion of the use of classroom research as a means of improving instruction.

Research Evidence

With few exceptions, people usually overestimate their knowledge of most topics (Lichtenstein and Fischhoff, 1977). Similarly, college teachers often overestimate their performance as teachers. Feldman (1989) reviewed studies that compared self-evaluations of teaching with the evaluations given by current students, colleagues, and administrators. In nineteen studies comparing self-evaluations with those of current students, the correlation was .29. Self-ratings had a correlation of .15 with colleagues' ratings across six studies. The lowest correlation—.08—was between self- and administrator ratings across five studies. None of these indicate much agreement between teachers' view of themselves and others' view of them. The correlation between self- and student ratings was probably highest in part because teachers knew how other students had rated them in the past. This assumption is substantiated by the finding that a lower correlation existed when teachers had not been rated by students previously (Centra, 1973b). In another study, for which self-ratings and student ratings were collected in successive semesters, it was found that the two converged in the second semester because the teachers lowered their self-ratings (Braskamp and Caulley, 1978).

Although colleagues, administrators, and students do not agree with teachers' self-ratings, the three groups agree in high measure with one another (Feldman, 1989; see also discussion in Chapter Four). Clearly, the self-perceptions are out of line, although not always. When the mean ratings that teachers in a five-college sample had given themselves were compared with their students' ratings, about 27 percent were considerably higher, while about 6 percent were considerably lower (Centra, 1973b). Again, this was a sample of teachers collecting student ratings for the first time. In other studies reviewed by Feldman (1989), in which student ratings had probably been collected previously, teacher and student ratings were more similar in absolute value (that is, mean rating scores were similar).

Teachers tend to give themselves higher ratings than students do particularly on the quality and frequency of their feedback to students and on their rapport with students. Perhaps the high divergence occurs because students have higher expectations for teacher performance in these areas. Mediocre or poor teachers tend to be less accurate in their self-assessments than are excellent teachers (Centra, 1973a, 1973b; Barber, 1990). Most teacher characteristics, however, do not affect how accurately teachers view their teaching. Differences in self- and student evaluations have not been seen to correlate with a variety of teacher and course characteristics, including gender, years of teaching experience, age, tenure status, teaching load, class size, and preference for the subject (Centra, 1973b; Doyle and Webber, 1978). Although none of these characteristics may account for the skewed results, an examination by subject field does turn up interesting differences. According to studies, teachers in the natural sciences did not think the pace of their courses were as fast as students thought they were, nor did they agree with the students' contention that they put a great amount of effort into the course. Apparently, these teachers had higher expectations than most for students, or perhaps they were reacting to the large amount of material they believed should be covered and learned in their courses.

In addition to misjudging their teaching performance, college teachers also apparently misjudge how much students learn in their courses. When fifteen teachers of lecture courses were asked to estimate the percentage of items students would know on an end-of-course test, they overestimated by a considerable amount (Fox and LeCount, 1991). The teachers thought students would know 75 percent of the items, when in fact they knew only 58 percent. In contrast, when asked about the course pre-test, the teachers' estimates of student knowledge had been very accurate: only 2 percent under the students' actual performance level (teachers had estimated knowledge of 46 percent of the items, while students actually knew 48 percent). Therefore, it appears that teachers' evaluations of their own teaching as well as their estimates of student learning in their courses are not accurate and should not be taken into consideration in summative decisions.

For instructional improvement, however, self-ratings can be very useful. Studies that compared self- and student ratings indicated that teachers identified the same relative strengths and weaknesses as students did, even though the teachers gave themselves higher absolute scores (Centra, 1973b; Feldman, 1989). Therefore, some teachers are aware of the aspects of their performance that they need to improve, although corroborating evidence from other sources may be necessary to persuade them to make changes. Students and colleagues, as discussed in other chapters of this book, can often provide the catalyst for change. So, too, can video playback of segments of a teacher's class (see chap. 3, Centra, 1979, for a discussion of the use of video- and audiotapes for instructional improvement).

Not only does the literature argue against the use of self-evaluation information for summative purposes, but teachers themselves are critical of its use in this way. In a study at a research university, the faculty thought that student ratings were more useful and valid than were self-evaluations (Marsh, 1982). Most faculty members probably recognize what the research has shown, summarized as follows:

- Self-evaluations are not a meaningful measure of teaching performance.
- Self-evaluations lack validity and objectivity.
- Self-evaluations can become a justification for not improving one's own performance.

Self-Reports

While self-evaluations are judgments about one's own performance, self-reports are descriptive and, at least potentially, nonjudgmental. While self-evaluations are usually made on quantifiable rating forms, self-reports are responses to open-ended questions or activity sheets that faculty members complete for their institutions, sometimes accompanied by examples of products such as course syllabi and published articles. Both self-evaluations and self-reports can be used for formative and summative evaluation, but as the research evidence has indicated, self-evaluations do not have enough validity to warrant their use in tenure, promotion, or salary decisions. Self-reports on teaching, and their latest incarnation, the teaching portfolio, will be discussed in this section.

Annual reports, sometimes referred to as "brag sheets," are the most common type of self-report. Most institutions require faculty members to describe their teaching, scholarship, and service activities each year, and those that have merit-pay systems use this information to help allot salary increases. The reports usually include information about the following activities:

> *Teaching:* teaching load, advising load, honors received, summary of evaluations by students or others (optional), new course or curriculum development
>
> *Scholarship, creative endeavors:* publications completed or in press, works in progress, grants, awards, presentations at conferences, performances, exhibitions
>
> *Service:* service to the institution (generally committee work); service to the government or the local community; service to the profession

Annual reports are usually completed in the spring. They may include the faculty member's plans for the future. This combination self-report and development plan is especially useful for nontenured faculty members.

Some institutions or departments require the two reports to be done separately by nontenured individuals for use as what might be described as a "nontenured faculty member's survival plan." At the beginning of each academic year, nontenured faculty members submit a report describing their current activities and plans for the year. The plans are accompanied by requests for assistance (such as travel or research funds and teaching materials). Department chairs, other administrators, or a mentor may use the information to advise and assist the faculty member. It may also be compared with the second report, the individual's annual report turned in at the end of the school year, to determine whether plans and goals were met, and whether the faculty member appears to be meeting the department's and the institution's expectations for tenure or promotion.

Another type of self-report is made up of the material assembled by the faculty member when a promotion or tenure decision will be made. In addition to the annual reviews accumulated up to that point, the faculty member includes as many tangible products as possible—course syllabi, articles published or in press, letters of support, student evaluations (if not collected by the institution or department), and so forth. It is not uncommon to present a packing box filled with materials of this nature to the tenure and promotion committee.

Teaching Portfolio

The teaching portfolio has been heralded as a great new contribution to effective teaching evaluation. Borrowed from such fields as art and architecture, where the practice is for professionals to display samples of their work to prospective clients or employers, the teaching portfolio is not actually new. Not long ago, the same product was called a teaching dossier and was defined as a "summary of a professor's major teaching accomplishments and strengths" (Shore and others, 1986). The teaching dossier was developed in the mid 1980s, when the Canadian Association of University Teachers sponsored a project to identify the kinds of information a faculty member might use as evidence of teaching effectiveness. Three major areas containing forty-nine specific items were suggested (Shore and others, 1986):

1. Products of good teaching (for example, student workbooks or logs, student pre- and postexamination results)
2. Materials developed by the individual (course materials, syllabi, descriptions of how various materials were used in teaching and of innovations attempted and an evaluation of their success, curriculum development materials)
3. Material or assessments from others (evaluations from students, colleagues, or alumni)

A portfolio may include information from the professor alone or from others as well (Bird, 1990). Entries by a teacher can represent both good and bad practices, or the entries may be more selective and display only the best work, especially when they are being used in personnel decisions (Wolf, 1991). Most writers believe that a portfolio should include not only items that present the teachers' views about their teaching but also examples and artifacts (Wolf, 1991; Edgerton, Hutchings, and Quinlan, 1991). Thus, they are arguing that the portfolio should be reflective and explain the teachers' thoughts and hopes as they made instructional decisions. As Schön discussed in *The Reflective Practitioner: How Professionals Think in Action* (1983), professionals should not simply depend on established theory or technique but should react to particular situations. Thinking and doing should not be separate; people who reflect-in-action, Schön argues, become researchers in the context of their jobs. The ideal portfolio would therefore highlight "a professor's reflections about a sample of actual work" (Edgerton, Hutchings, and Quinlan, 1991) and include documentation of any classroom research that the teacher carried out (see discussion later in this chapter).

Lessons learned in portfolio design during the Stanford Teacher Assessment Project for K–12 teachers have been useful for college faculties as well (Bird, 1990; Wolf, 1991). Building on the Stanford project, Edgerton, Hutchings and Quinlan (1991) identified four domains in which the information that college professors present in a portfolio should fall. The first is course planning and preparation, represented by such samples as course syllabi and lecture notes. The second is the actual teaching presentation of the course, represented, for example, by videotapes and comments from colleagues or students based on class observations. The third is evaluating students and giving feedback; a teacher's comments on a graded essay assignment would be a sample of this kind of work. The fourth domain is keeping current in one's field—attending a professional conference, for example, and describing how the knowledge gained was used to alter the content or method of teaching a course. All samples are expected to be accompanied by the teachers' comments or reflections on their actions.

In recent years, many colleges have used teaching portfolios for both formative and summative purposes. When they are used formatively, the information can facilitate self-analysis and improvement by continuously capturing the teachers' descriptions of their activities in various courses and their reflections on them. Any judgments by others are offered as suggestions. Thus, including reflections on how a teacher might have done better is not threatening and can be useful to the individual. When the portfolio is used summatively, judgments by others about what teachers have said and presented not only are necessary but also determine the contents of the portfolio. That is, teachers are likely to use only positive illustrations of their performance in these portfolios because they are making their "best case" to the reviewers. When a portfolio is being used for summative decisions, it is reasonable to ask teachers to provide only positive examples of their work. Expecting teachers to reveal their faults in this case is not only unrealistic but also unfair to those who are willing to expose their weaknesses. In one study of three departments that experimented with portfolio construction and review, faculty members interviewed were very negative about the use of the portfolio for either formative or summative purposes (Robinson, 1993). In the study described next, one college's use of the portfolio for summative evaluation was investigated.

A Study of the Portfolio

I studied the use of the portfolio at a community college in contract renewal decisions. A portfolio for each full-time faculty member was evaluated by a dean and two peers. How well these evaluations compared with one another and with independently collected student evaluations were the primary questions addressed in the study. Because of the rich documentation usually found in portfolios, we would hope that the groups judging them would be in general agreement about the performance levels of individual teachers. We would also hope that portfolio evaluations would correlate positively with an accepted measure of teaching effectiveness such as student evaluations.

The faculty portfolio in this study included descriptive, evaluative, and reflective information. Because the results were to be used for summative decisions, most faculty members took great care in preparing the portfolios. They provided specific examples and descriptions of how they were committed to teaching, how they involved students in the subject matter, how they maintained flexibility in response to student needs, and other activities that reflected teaching skills. Faculty members were asked to document their accomplishments, and write personal statements, within four categories of activity: teaching effectiveness, service to the college and community, personal (academic) credentials, and professional activities. Although teaching effectiveness was considered the most important, receiving two-thirds of the weight in the compilation of total score, service and the other categories were also judged. Research and publications were excluded from formal rating because the policy of the college was to de-emphasize their importance.

Teaching effectiveness was described in thirteen categories that were grouped into three areas: motivational skills, interpersonal skills, and intellectual skills. These skill areas and categories were adapted from descriptions of teaching performance provided by Roueche and Baker (1987). Following is a list of the categories with some examples of the kinds of activity teachers could describe and provide products to illustrate:

Motivational Skills

1. *Commitment to teaching:* is available to students and willing to spend time with them out of class if necessary
2. *Goals orientation:* outlines goals and expectations for students
3. *Integrated perception:* helps students link classroom experiences to the broader context of their lives
4. *Positive action:* helps students achieve, motivating them and instilling in them a desire to succeed
5. *Reward orientation:* feels rewarded by teaching, shows signs of enthusiasm and satisfaction with teaching, rewards successful student performance

Interpersonal Skills

6. *Objectivity:* handles difficult situations calmly and objectively, concentrating on solving the problem rather than plac-

ing blame; communicates effectively to involve students in the subject matter

7. *Active listening:* paraphrases for clarification, attends to non-verbal clues, and shows that what the students have to say is valued

8. *Rapport:* achieves and maintains a favorable relationship with students

9. *Empathy:* reaches out to students in need and recognizes students' feelings; expresses care, yet asserts high expectations

Intellectual Skills

10. *Individualized perception:* sees students as individuals with different learning styles, interests, and motivations; adjusts courses to individual needs

11. *Teaching strategies:* employs a variety of well-organized teaching strategies; is flexible and responsive to students

12. *Knowledge:* stays current in professional field and shares new knowledge with students; teaches from a wide range of sources, including books, journals, materials derived from conferences

13. *Innovation:* Integrates new ideas in a planned, deliberate way; willingly takes risks for a successful innovation

An example of the comments given in two of the categories follows. The comments were provided by a teacher at a college that was used to pre-test the categories.

Commitment to Teaching (Motivational Skill):

My commitment to teaching is demonstrated by a variety of behaviors in and outside of the classroom. I teach five sections of a course that requires a term paper. It is a freshmen course, and many students taking it have not had a previous opportunity to write a term paper. I observed that a large number of students were either immobilized by the assignment or had an extremely high level of anxiety about it. Indeed, many of them lacked adequate skills in preparing and writing term papers. Therefore, I scheduled term paper workshop sessions on a different weekday for any students who desired extra time with me to help them prepare an "excellent" or A-type term paper. This appeals to most students, especially those who feel unsure and unconfident. For the past two semesters, more than half of the students enrolled in those sections have attended more than three sessions of the workshop. I conduct only five workshop sessions each semester. The outcome of my efforts and the students' labor has been a productive one. The total caliber of term papers has improved, and I am greatly pleased that the extra time on my part has been beneficial to all—student and teacher alike.

Individualized Perception (Intellectual Skill):

Being able to individualize teaching for my students is paramount to my understanding of how to communicate in order to reach each one of them. The classroom structure is a group system within which individuality exists and must be recognized. I believe "true" learning occurs when each individual student is ready to internalize and act upon new information, and this process does not occur for all students at the same time or in the same manner.

I constantly aim to meet the group's needs, yet I think that if I did not understand their different individual learning styles, levels of motivation, and cognitive abilities, much of what I do in and outside the classroom might be only pedestrian. Therefore, I plan learning activities related to course content on differing competency levels. I arrange small-group assignments that take student abilities into consideration. In some instances, students of diverse skill levels are assigned to the same group so that they can learn from each other. There are other group assignments where the students are more similar in academic prepared-

ness. I am endeavoring to become more knowledgeable about different student learning styles and to adjust my teaching style to accommodate all students
more often during a semester.

This person had a reputation as an excellent teacher, and it
seems to be supported by her responses. Even she, however, became
somewhat repetitive in her comments. Clearly, the thirteen categories could be collapsed into six or seven and still be representative
of the three skills. For example, the categories of active listening,
rapport, and empathy could easily be combined.

The thirteen teaching categories were rated on a six-point
scale, which ranged from "contradiction of the criterion" (0) and
"criterion is not evident" (1) to "quality is strongly evident" (5). A
total of sixty-five points could be awarded by each rater.

The service activities rated included those in the college and
community carried out within the past year only, and omitted com-
pensated activities. "No participation" was given zero point value
for either service area, while a continuous leadership role in two or
more service activities was given the highest point value: fifteen for
college service and five for community service. Personal credentials
were rated on a ten-point scale, with a doctorate or terminal degree
in the teacher's primary discipline given the highest value. Master's,
bachelor's, associate degrees, and certificates in related fields received fewer points. Finally, up to five points could be awarded for
participation in professional organizations (inactive membership
was given no points, active participation in two or more organizations four points, leadership positions five points). Altogether, raters could award up to one hundred points for four categories of
activity documented in the portfolio.

Two peers and one of four deans rated each portfolio. One
peer, designated Peer A, was selected by the individual being evaluated as an appropriate judge; the second peer, Peer B, was selected
by the area dean. Deans rated only faculty members in their individual schools. In making their judgments, the raters relied heavily
on the portfolios but did not have to limit themselves to what was
included in them; the college faculty and staff had decided that it

would be difficult to exclude other perceptions of or experiences with the person being evaluated.

The second source of information on teaching effectiveness used was student evaluations collected at the end of a course. The college selected the Educational Testing Service (ETS) Student Instructional Report (SIR) for this purpose. Of the thirty-nine items and six factors included in the SIR, two global items and three factors were emphasized by the college in summative evaluations and also seemed appropriate for this study. The two items—the overall value of the course and the overall quality of instruction—would be expected to correlate with the total teaching score and the performance in the three teaching skill areas of the portfolio. The three SIR factors corresponded to the three skill areas (motivational, interpersonal, and intellectual). The three SIR factors were as follows:

1. *Organization and planning:* the extent to which teachers are perceived by students as well organized (they prepare for each class, summarize major points in lectures or discussions, and make their instructional objectives clear)
2. *Faculty/student interaction:* the extent to which instructors are perceived to be concerned with student progress and aware of students' needs and to which students feel free to ask questions or consult with the teacher
3. *Communications:* the extent to which instructors raise challenging questions, use examples or illustrations, and give high-quality lectures

Virtually all full-time faculty at the college were evaluated during the 1990–91 academic year and included in this study. They totaled ninety-seven from four schools or divisions. Because of a change in the governance of the college, including a name change, the evaluation information was to be used for contract renewal decisions for each faculty member. Thus, a unique situation was presented in which all faculty members were summatively evaluated at the same time. In addition to the portfolio evaluations and the SIR results, each dean also made at least one unannounced visit to each teacher's classroom. The classroom visits most likely affected the deans' evaluations of portfolio information.

What We Learned

What I learned from my study has implications for the construction and use of faculty portfolios, particularly the descriptions of and reflections on teaching that are key aspects of it. For summative purposes, the validity of the peers' and deans' evaluations is critical. Taking into consideration which person makes the evaluations is also critical, as my study demonstrated; peers selected by individual faculty members were the most lenient, most likely because each faculty member was to be evaluated as well as to evaluate others. When peers are on a tenure and promotion committee (or an ad hoc committee to evaluate teaching—see Chapter Six), they may be more objective in their evaluations, although other studies have shown that peers generally give high evaluations (Centra, 1975; Root, 1987). Furthermore, the peers selected by individual faculty members did not agree with the other peers or the deans in their evaluations of teaching effectiveness, though the evaluations of service, credentials, and professional activities by all three groups were highly correlated. These results are evident in Tables 5.1 and 5.2. Correlations for Peer A, the peer named by the faculty member, with Peer B and the deans were not significant for the evaluation of total teaching and most of the three teaching skills. Nor did Peer A evaluations correlate with the student evaluations on the appropriate SIR factors or items. The SIR evaluations correlated reasonably well, however, with the teaching evaluations made by the deans and Peer B. These correlations were not quite as high as in previous studies that compared student, peer, and administrator evaluations (see the discussion in Chapter Six). Those studies compared ratings based on hearsay, reputation, or other unspecified sources of evidence, and the evaluations were generally not used to make personnel decisions. Using a portfolio in summative decisions can help provide a more complete representation of performance, although the portfolios used by the college in this study emphasized teachers' comments rather than work samples. Only positive examples were asked for, so it is not surprising that the peers and deans rated

Table 5.1. Correlations Among Raters for Motivational Skills, Interpersonal Skills, Intellectual Skills, and Total Teaching.

	Deans				Peer A			
	Motivation	Interpersonal	Intellectual	Total Teaching	Motivation	Interpersonal	Intellectual	Total Teaching
Peer A								
Motivation	.00							
Interpersonal		.04						
Intellectual			.22[a]					
Total Teaching				.04				
Peer B								
Motivation	.40[b]				.14			
Interpersonal		.39[b]				.16		
Intellectual			.24[a]				.19	
Total Teaching				.43[b]				.17

Note: N = 97

[a] $p < .05$ [b] $p < .01$

Source: Centra, 1992. Reprinted by permission of Educational Testing Service, the copyright owner.

Table 5.2. Correlations Among Raters for Scores in College Service, Community Service, Credentials, and Professional Activities.

	Deans				Peer A			
	(I) College	*(II)* Community	*(III)* Credentials	*(IV)* Professional	*(I)* College	*(II)* Community	*(III)* Credentials	*(IV)* Professional
Peer A								
I	.32[a]							
II		.47[a]						
III			.65[a]					
IV				.44[a]				
Peer B								
I	.29[a]				.27[a]			
II		.52[a]				.66[a]		
III			.68[a]				.55[a]	
IV				.40[a]				.35[a]

Note: N = 97

[a] $p < .05$

Source: Centra, 1992. Reprinted by permission of Educational Testing Service, the copyright owner.

performance highly overall: on a six-point scale most ratings were at four or above.

Better reliability (greater agreement among deans, students, and peers) would likely have been evidenced if work samples had been included. The monographs by Edgerton, Hutchins and Quinlan (1991), and Seldin (1991) included sample portfolios that contained several of the following work samples:

- A personal statement by the teacher describing instructional goals for the next several years
- Representative course syllabi
- Examples of graded student essays
- Hard evidence of student learning (examination scores pre- and postcourse)
- A videotape of the professor teaching a class

Some Further Implications of the Study

Evaluations of portfolios can undoubtedly benefit from discussion among evaluators about criteria and standards. In a study in which six elected fellow staff members rated faculty dossiers after first discussing the ratings criteria and examples of high and low ratings, agreement among peers was very high (Root, 1987; see further discussion in Chapter Six). The dossiers included various teaching materials, student evaluations of instruction, publications, grant proposals, and documentation of service activities. The brief training session produced substantial agreement within the group in its assessment of teaching, research, and service.

The ideal portfolio is put together by a faculty member over a period of several years. Because the college needed to make immediate use of portfolios as part of a complete evaluation process, the faculty in this study did not have the opportunity to do so. Thus, the portfolio was a snapshot of one moment in teaching performance, albeit with much descriptive detail, rather than a documented set of data on changes or effects over time. Nevertheless, even this less-than-ideal portfolio was helpful to evaluators in their personnel decisions.

In addition to the work samples listed previously, the portfolio should include the teacher's reflections on some key areas of teaching. The thirteen used in this study were too many. Fewer and more sharply distinguished categories would be easier for both teachers and evaluators to use. The following six seem especially appropriate: motivational skills, goals orientation, rapport, teaching strategies, knowledge, and innovation. By explaining what they were thinking, what problems they had encountered, what they did, and what their expectations were as they relate to these areas (as well as to others individual teachers may see as applicable), they are reflecting-in-action, as Schön (1983) advocates. In a similar vein, Shulman (1989) refers to contextualized episodes of teaching, in which teachers describe how they transform their knowledge of the subject matter as they interact with students in a particular teaching situation.

Teaching Portfolio for Graduate Students

The teaching portfolio is useful not only for current faculty members but for prospective members as well. As graduate students, most faculty members complete a research or teaching assistantship. Seldom do they have to demonstrate their teaching skills to prospective employers. The teaching assistantship gives many graduate students an opportunity to start a teaching portfolio early in their careers and to have it available as they enter the job market. With this in mind, the Syracuse University Teaching Assistant Program of the Graduate School made the teaching portfolio a key element of its newly created Certificate in University Teaching. With support from the Fund for the Improvement of Postsecondary Education and the Pew Charitable Trust, the certificate is awarded to teaching associates who elect to pursue a "program of professional development that results in the documentation of their preparation to assume a teaching position at a college or university" (Teaching Assistant Program of the Graduate School, 1991). In addition to the portfolio, teaching associates work closely with a teaching mentor, a faculty member from their department. The mentor provides a final assessment of the graduate student's teaching potential that becomes a part of the portfolio. In addition, the student's portfolio can include the following elements:

1. Videotapes of various teaching performances (such as lectures, labs, and studios)
2. Copies of syllabi, examinations, and papers graded by the candidate
3. Summaries of student evaluations of instruction
4. Evidence of special teaching-related projects designed or authored by the candidate
5. Descriptions of courses previously taught or which the candidate is qualified to teach
6. Notations of teaching awards (including outstanding TA awards, and service as a teaching fellow)
7. A summary statement describing the candidate's teaching experience, philosophy, and goals [Teaching Assistant Program of the Graduate School, p. 9]

Self-Improvement Through Classroom Research

Teachers can improve by systematically studying their classroom technique and how it affects student learning. Some teachers have been doing this for years. Novice teachers become experts in part by the lessons they learn through their own inquiries and insights. Cross (1990) refers to this as "classroom research" and has promoted its use as a practical alternative to traditional educational research, which seeks to advance knowledge about teaching and learning through more statistical procedures. Teachers who carry out classroom research are less concerned with statistical significance or detailed analyses than with reaching a better understanding of how students learn in their courses.

Classroom assessment is a form of classroom research. In fact, it is probably the most common form used by teachers. Cross (1989, p. 4) defines classroom assessment as "small-scale assessments conducted continuously in college classrooms by discipline-based teachers to determine what students are learning in that class." Other chapters in this book offer examples of classroom assessment techniques as approaches to formative evaluation. See Chapter Four, for example, where one-minute papers and the use of anonymous electronic mail messages are described. Cross and Angelo (1988) put together a compendium of thirty assessment techniques that have been devised and used by teachers (one-minute papers probably being the most popular).

Angelo (1991) edited an issue of the New Directions for Teaching and Learning series that featured eight assessment examples taken from different disciplines and campuses. Teachers of English composition, accounting, introductory science, psychology, and physics described classroom projects they undertook to improve student learning. The physics teacher, for example, wanted to understand how his students used visualization to solve physics problems. He videotaped students as they described or illustrated their visualization of the problems. From his research, he learned how to use visualization in his teaching.

Classroom research is an excellent example of what Schön (1983) refers to as a practitioner's reflection-in-action. Professional practitioners, according to Schön, should have an interest in transforming their current situation into a better one. Teachers, therefore, should be constantly experimenting in their classrooms to see what happens and, most importantly, to see if they like what they get. This differs from a more scientific experiment where action is taken to see if a particular hypothesis is upheld. When a practitioner-teacher reflects-in-action, he or she is part of the experiment and has a stake in understanding the situation in order to effect change. Rather than being an unbiased observer, the practitioner-teacher shapes the classroom procedure so that the hypothesis is upheld.

The success of a classroom research project or assessment depends on the extent to which it fulfills the same conditions for improvement that I introduced in Chapter One:

1. *Do teachers obtain new information, something they did not know previously?* Are teachers trying something in their classroom research?
2. *Do teachers value the information?* Because they collect it themselves, it is likely that teachers value the information. But its value also depends on the particular research or experiment they use and how well it furthers their understanding.

3. *Do the teachers understand how to change?* Can the teacher shape the classroom situation to bring about change?
4. *Are teachers motivated to change?* Because they chose to carry out classroom research, they will probably also be motivated to make any changes that are called for or that enhance student learning.

The second and fourth conditions are most likely to be fulfilled through classroom research and reflection-in-action. Fulfillment of the first and the third depend very much on how well teachers design their classroom research project or assessment procedure.

Summary

While quantifiable self-evaluations may be included in a teacher's annual self-report or portfolio, the research evidence does not support their use in summative evaluations. They can, however, be useful in instructional improvement, particularly when considered in conjunction with student or colleague evaluations. Most institutions require faculty to describe their teaching, scholarship, and service activities each year, and in greater detail when promotion or tenure decisions are made. The teaching portfolio or dossier is being used increasingly to provide continuous documentation of a teacher's performance. The portfolio should include not only what the individuals and others say about their teaching, but examples of what they actually do. A teacher's reflections about key areas of teaching should also be included. Portfolios may be used for formative and summative purposes, but when used for the latter, evaluations by administrators, colleagues, and the tenure and promotion committee are a critical component. A study I conducted indicated that the reliability of the evaluations varies according to such factors as how colleagues are chosen, whether work samples are included, and whether evaluators receive counseling and training in the procedures. Graduate students should also use teaching portfolios to document their experiences and demonstrate their potential.

Classroom research and classroom assessment are excellent

examples of ways teachers can experiment in their own classrooms. Such reflection-in-action allows teachers to understand better what they are currently doing and how they can shape situations to bring about change.

We turn our attention next to the critical role that colleagues and department chairs play in evaluations.

Chapter 6

Critical Roles of Colleagues and Department Chairs

Colleagues and department chairs can provide evaluative information that is not available from any other source. Neither students, who lack the background and perspective, nor deans, who lack the time, can contribute the kind of information that colleagues and chairs can. In this sense, they truly form the critical link in a complete and comprehensive faculty evaluation, and they are valuable for both formative and summative evaluations. This chapter examines research findings about colleague evaluations, a literature that is certainly much less extensive than that on student evaluations. Even less is known about department chair evaluations, although many of the findings on colleagues are applicable. The chapter also examines ways in which colleague evaluations can be used in both formative and summative evaluations of teaching; models of methods used at selected institutions are described. Guidelines for the use of colleague and chair evaluations are given at the end of the chapter.

The term *colleague* rather than *peer* is used throughout this chapter, although the terms are frequently used interchangeably. *Colleague* may be the more appropriate term because *peer* implies equal status, while *colleague* does not: a colleague, or fellow worker, may be of another rank, as is often the case. A department chair may be looked on as a colleague; the perception depends on institutional expectations for the position. Most chairs are at times colleagues and at other times department administrators. Rotating chairs, because of their temporary status, are more likely to see themselves and to be seen as colleagues.

Colleagues can contribute to the evaluation of teaching as well as the evaluation of research. Faculty members have little hesitancy about asking a colleague to review a draft research article or proposal, but much more hesitancy about asking for a review of a course syllabus or a visit to their class to offer suggestions about teaching. There are at least four reasons for this discrepancy. First, many faculty members believe teaching to be personal and subjective, whereas standards of good research or scholarship are widely known and objective. Second, class visits and reviews of instructional materials not only are time consuming but also can be damaging to collegial relationships. Colleagues seem especially sensitive about classroom observations; any criticisms of classroom techniques should be carefully worded. Third, in those postsecondary settings where research is the more important activity, seeking advice about teaching does not have high priority. And finally, one's scholarship, or any creative endeavor, when published or displayed, is there for all to see and evaluate; one's teaching is typically seen only by one's students. It is likely that much less research has been conducted on colleague and chair evaluations of teaching than on scholarship for the same reasons.

Research Evidence on Colleague and Chair Evaluations

Colleague or chair evaluations can be made by assigning numerical ratings to or ranking all members of a group (such as department or school). Because ratings are subject to such errors as central tendency and leniency, they are usually less reliable than ranking methods, although the results of both were found to be at acceptable levels in the military and other nonacademic settings (Love, 1981; Kane and Lawler, 1978). Ranking may be accomplished by each member conducting evaluations and in turn being evaluated by the others; this system has been used on occasion in military settings.

Another ranking method is for members to nominate others who are best (or worst) at an activity, such as teaching or research. Institutions that give teaching awards often rely on nominations, and if we can generalize from research in other settings, such nominations can produce sufficient consensus (Kane and Lawler, 1978). Whether teaching awards reflect anything more than reputation as a teacher, and whether they actually encourage good teaching at a college are another matter. Most institutions use rating methods which include scales that either quantify performance in various areas or describe and assess activities through written statements. Such information can be used for either formative or summative purposes, as will be illustrated later in this chapter.

Some people think that colleague or chair evaluations of teaching are synonymous with, or at least highly dependent on, classroom observations. This assumption is untrue; furthermore, it would be a mistake to design colleague evaluation procedures to rely heavily on classroom observation. Research has shown that when colleague ratings of teaching are based solely on classroom observation, only slight interrater agreement can be expected (Centra, 1975). In a study at an institution in its first year of operation, I analyzed three colleagues' ratings of each faculty member. The rating scale included many of the items typically found on student rating forms, questions that could be answered on the basis of observations during a class visit (for example, "Did the teacher use class time well?" and "To what extent were examples or illustrations used for clarification?"). Because teaching reputations had not yet become established at this new college, and because colleagues did not know much more about one another's teaching than what they learned from observation, their ratings were probably based primarily on the classroom visits; each colleague made two. While each colleague was consistent in the ratings he or she made both times, agreement among colleagues was poor. Apparently, each person had a notion of "excellent" or "average" performance that was not shared by the others. Training colleagues in how to rate classroom teaching behaviors would undoubtedly result in better agreement but would be time consuming, and faculty members might not see any direct benefit for themselves. However, if the training focused on criteria that faculty members could use to reflect on and improve their own teaching, learning to apply the criteria and developing the observational skills and standards needed for colleague evaluation would be side benefits.

Colleagues should also concentrate on accepted teaching effectiveness criteria, such as those identified by Cohen and McKeachie (1980). Their review of the literature identified ten criteria of effective teaching that colleagues are best able to judge:

1. Mastery of course content
2. Selection of course content
3. Course organization
4. Appropriateness of course objectives
5. Appropriateness of instructional materials (such as readings, media)
6. Appropriateness of evaluative devices (such as exams, written assignments, reports)
7. Appropriateness of methodology used to teach specific content areas
8. Commitment to teaching and concern for student learning
9. Student achievement, based on performance on exams and projects
10. Support of departmental instructional efforts (p. 148)

Colleagues could make their judgments by examining course syllabi, assignments, examinations, and other documentary evidence. Several of the ten criteria are best evaluated by colleagues in the same field as the person being evaluated. But at small institutions or in small departments it is virtually impossible to limit evaluators to those in the same departments. In fact, given possible friendships or rivalries within departments, a more balanced evaluation may be achieved by including other colleagues. Evaluations of course organization and teaching methods, and assessment of student achievement, can be done by colleagues outside a department who have some sensitivity to good instructional design.

Little or no research has been published on the reliability and validity of colleague or chair evaluations of course syllabi, student assignments, or other documentary evidence of effective teaching. Most studies have investigated colleagues' evaluations of teachers' overall effectiveness, which were based on reputation, hearsay, or other unspecified sources of information. Feldman (1989) compared colleague evaluation studies with studies in which teaching effectiveness was evaluated by two or more different groups. On the basis of fourteen studies, the correlation between colleagues' and current students' global evaluations of teachers was .55. Colleague and administrator (mainly department chairs) evaluations of teachers had a correlation of .48 (based on five studies). Administrator and student evaluations had a correlation of .39 (based on eleven studies). The lowest correlations were between self-ratings and colleague ratings (.15) and self-ratings and administrator ratings (.08).

The size of the correlations between colleague and student evaluations, while far from ideal, indicates a fairly similar ranking by both groups. Exactly why this was true could not be determined from the studies. One possibility is that faculty members learn about one another's teaching abilities from students. Feldman (1989) also noted that the studies reviewed found no difference in the rating averages given by colleagues and students. In other words, both groups rated similar percentages of teachers as "excellent," "good," and so forth. Other studies have shown that colleagues are more lenient than students in their ratings (Centra, 1975); the differences depend on such circumstances as the purpose of the evaluation. By contrast, in the Feldman study, colleagues generally gave their fellow teachers lower ratings than did administrators, although the .48 correlation indicates that they ranked teachers fairly similarly. This was not true in a study that I recently completed on portfolio evaluations, which was discussed in Chapter Five.

Colleagues are apparently better able to judge the research productivity than the teaching effectiveness of fellow faculty members. Kremer (1990) found that colleagues' evaluations of research were more reliable (that is, there was greater agreement among colleagues) than were their evaluations of teaching or service. Not surprisingly, evaluations of teaching had lower reliabilities when colleagues said they were less confident about the basis for the evaluations. While Kremer studied colleague evaluations based on general knowledge and the reputations of fellow faculty members, Root (1987) studied evaluations when six elected members of the faculty independently rated dossiers of individual faculty members. The dossiers included course outlines, syllabi, teaching materials, student evaluations, and curriculum development documentation, all of which were used to judge teaching. Faculty members submitted materials published during the year, grant proposals, works in progress, and any meritorious awards received for judgment of their research. Documentation of service was the most varied of the three areas and included committee reports or proposals, and recognition from outside groups. The committee reviewed and discussed the criteria before making ratings, using cases that illustrated high and low ratings. The committee's ratings were used each year to determine salary increases at this school within a research university, with research and teaching given twice the weight of service.

The reliabilities of the evaluations (based on average intercorrelations) of the six-member committee were very high (above .90) for each of the three performance areas. In fact, Root concluded that a three-member committee could provide sufficiently reliable evaluations. The strongest agreement was in the evaluation of research. Little agreement was found between ratings of research, teaching, and service; not a reflection on the reliability of the evaluation, this indicated that individuals who were productive in one area were not necessarily productive in the other two. Root concluded that evaluations by a committee of colleagues provide a fair basis to implement a merit pay system. (Whether annual merit pay increases should be given at all is another matter: McKeachie [1979a] maintains that they are not particularly effective incentives for faculty, and as I discuss in Chapter One, they have disadvantages.) The Root study supports the use of colleague evaluations of dossier or portfolio materials for tenure and promotion decisions, especially when the committee has previously discussed criteria and standards of performance. Because chair evaluations represent a single view, agreement among raters cannot be determined. The stability of chair ratings over time could be investigated; published studies of this type of reliability do not yet exist. A single rating, whether by chair, colleague, or student, will more likely be subject to biasing effects and fluctuations. Still, chairs have access to a wide range of information about a faculty member's performance and may therefore be able to provide a uniquely valid view.

Formative Colleague Evaluations

Informal discussions among faculty members about their work take place daily. Some departments have formalized these discussions by holding brown-bag lunches or including the discussions during monthly departmental meetings. Such discussions often focus on individual research projects; occasionally, teaching may be discussed. Some examples of efforts made to increase collaboration among faculty members on teaching include the following, which were used at some institutions.

Faculty Mentoring Faculty

Mentoring, or sponsorship, is widely practiced—by executives, academicians, hourly workers, and others (Levinson and others, 1978). In a survey of faculty at a public university, Sands, Parson, and Duane (1991) found that a third of their respondents had been mentored by a colleague at the university; many more also had been mentored at an earlier time in their careers. When asked to describe the ideal faculty mentor, the respondents in the Sands, Parson, and Duane study identified the four major roles the mentor should play:

1. Friend (offering emotional support, help with personal problems)
2. Career guide (promoting professional visibility, advising about research opportunities)
3. Information source (discussing expectations for promotion and tenure, offering information about university policies and procedures)
4. Intellectual guide (reviewing drafts of papers, offering constructive criticism and intellectual guidance)

At this public university, which primarily rewards research, help with teaching was not deemed an important service by an ideal mentor. At institutions with a different reward structure, advice about teaching could be considered more important.

Mentoring, when it exists, is generally done informally. But, increasingly, departments are assigning senior faculty members as mentors to young, untenured colleagues. A formal arrangement makes better sense than the sink-or-swim method that seems to be the alternative. Mentors may play any or all of the four roles described by Sands, Parson, and Duane (1991), thereby giving new arrivals the greatest opportunity to prove their worth and fulfill institutional expectations. If some teaching practices are discipline based, as some argue (Shulman, 1986), then a mentor from one's discipline would seem to provide unique teaching advice. Yet the contention that teaching practices can be improved only by a mentor from the same discipline is just one of several disproven by Boice (1992). In a series of studies on faculty mentoring conducted at a variety of colleges, Boice found that:

1.   Only a handful of new hires found useful mentoring on their own. They also tended to teach cautiously by emphasizing facts and principles over active student involvement.
2.   It was not necessary to pair new faculty members only with senior members from the same department. The pairing of junior faculty members and mentors from other departments was equally effective.
3.   Useful mentoring did not depend on pairs picking each other. Assigning mentors was equally effective. It was often necessary, however, to prompt pairs to meet regularly until meetings became habitual.
4.   Although mentoring was generally beneficial, many mentors were reluctant to give advice to new faculty on teaching, scholarly productivity, and time management. Thus, mentoring was not without its deficiencies.

The Master Faculty Program

Shortly before his death in 1988, Joseph Katz promoted a strategy for faculty development based on faculty members working together in pairs to understand how students learn (Katz and Henry, 1988).

Referred to as the Master Faculty Program, or the "buddy system," it is a fairly straightforward process. Each faculty pair collaborates on a set of activities designed to help them increase their knowledge about teaching and how their students learn in the classroom. The activities include classroom observations, student interviews, and discussions between colleagues. Testing students on personality and learning style dimensions was also prescribed by Katz, but it is neither necessary nor preferred by faculty participants. Each faculty member takes turns, by semester, observing a class taught by the other member of the pair. Observations should be frequent enough for the observing colleague to become familiar with the course content, the students, the assignments and testing, and the teacher's methods of instruction. The two colleagues do not have to be from the same discipline; in fact, if they are not, discussions are more likely to focus on teaching and learning than on course content. Each faculty member also interviews two to four students from the observed class. The students may be volunteers; better yet, they may be chosen to represent different genders, age groups, performance levels, or other student characteristics. Students should be interviewed several times during the semester, with questions emphasizing student learning in the course (for example, reactions to specific class sessions, topics that may be difficult, their personal motivations).

With information gathered from observations and interviews in hand, the two faculty colleagues meet once a week or so to discuss how student learning has been fostered or hindered in class. At campuses with many pairs of faculty members participating in the process, the entire group meets once a month with a campus coordinator to share insights or stories and to discuss a particular teaching or learning issue that may have emerged. The campus coordinator also recruits new participants, matches pairs, and provides any assistance needed. At the end of each semester, the members of each pair write brief essays reflecting on what they learned from the experiences.

During the late 1980s, the Master Faculty Program, under the sponsorship of the New Jersey Department of Higher Education and the New Jersey Institute on Collegiate Teaching and Learning, engaged some three hundred faculty members at twenty-one colleges in New Jersey. One assessment of the program was very favorable: "The program enabled students to not only find their voice, but also let that voice be heard. The pairing of colleagues bridged the isolation faculty often experience as members of the academy. Most important, though, we found the program encouraged faculty to become more reflective about their teaching. It is an extraordinarily effective way of introducing junior faculty to teaching. It is also an excellent source of renewal in midcareer" (Chandelar, 1991).

     While deemed successful for most faculty members who choose to participate, many teachers who most need such a source of renewal are not likely to volunteer for the Master Faculty Program or a similar activity (Centra, 1978a). Another collaborative approach was used by Anthony Grasha at the University of Cincinnati; it required three-member faculty teams (Centra, 1979). These "peer development triads" relied on shared course materials and classroom observations. Because two colleagues instead of one provide reactions, Grasha argued that the recipient is more likely to pay attention to suggestions, especially when the two reactions are similar. Since it is more difficult to get three faculty members to collaborate, and since it is more time consuming, Katz's buddy system may be easier to promote. Still, even this more moderate time investment will deter some faculty from participating. For these individuals, an abbreviated collaboration may be of interest. Another possible collaboration is with a graduate student, as described in the next section.

Graduate Students as Colleagues

A variation of the buddy system has been used at the University of Chicago's Graduate School of Business. A one-credit course for M.B.A. students is designed to provide feedback that teachers can use for course improvements. The students audit a professor's classes, videotape selected presentations, and gather suggestions from enrolled students through focus-group interviews and written questionnaires. They report their findings to the professor on a weekly basis, thereby allowing changes in midcourse. By providing the professor with timely feedback and discussing changes suggested by the students, the graduate students are acting as colleagues. At the same time, they are not only earning a credit toward their degree but learning something about teaching.

Small Group Instructional Diagnosis

Small Group Instructional Diagnosis (SGID) is another method used to improve instruction with the aid of a colleague. Designed by D. Joseph Clark at the University of Washington, SGID has been widely used among both tenured and nontenured faculty members at colleges in the state of Washington. At Seattle Community College, for example, three-fourths of the tenured faculty and more than half of the adjuncts assessed their teaching through SGID during the 1980s (Bennett, 1987). The process, which can be easily learned by colleagues, is described by Bennett as follows:

> 1. With a half hour or so left in a class period, the instructor introduces a facilitator (colleague) as a friend who will gather ideas about the students' learning experiences. The word evaluation is not used because of its pejorative connotation to students. Before leaving the room, the instructor informs the class that he or she has voluntarily requested this SGID and hopes to learn about how the course is going.
> 2. The facilitator-colleague assures students that the results are confidential and will be shared only with the teacher. Groups of four or so students are formed to discuss their learning experiences and a notetaker for each group is designated by the facilitator. The facilitator also lists three questions on the board for each group to discuss: Which aspects of instruction help you learn? Which do not help? What do you suggest to improve your learning?
> 3. After ten minutes of discussion, the facilitator records the students' responses using appropriate quantifiers ("most said," "a few said"). The facilitator summarizes the major ideas and shares the summary with the students for additions or corrections.

4. The facilitators share student responses with the teacher as soon as possible, using the students' own words whenever possible. If serious problems have emerged, the facilitator highlights solutions offered by students.

5. During the next class period, if possible, the instructor replies to the students' analysis. Instructors should try to implement at least one of the suggestions made by students; suggestions that are inconsistent with course goals or a teacher's style do not need to be given serious consideration.

Evaluations of the effects of the SGIDs have been positive (Bennett, 1987). A campus coordinator (for example, a teacher with one-third released time) who encourages participation and who arranges the visits is helpful. Some instructors exchange classroom visits and SGIDs, which can lead to fruitful discussions of teaching based on the two reports. In the rare instances when students' comments are almost entirely negative, however, facilitator-colleagues may not have the necessary skills to remain nonjudgmental in their interpretations of the students' views and in discussions of possible remedies.

Cross-Disciplinary Perspectives on Teaching

Faculty members from different disciplines may provide a teacher with a fresh perspective on teaching. For example, what if teachers in the humanities and social sciences attended classes in math and science and gave their reactions about the course to the instructor? Intrigued by this question, Tobias (1986) convinced the chair of the department of physics at the University of Chicago to try an experiment. Two teachers taught physics classes to thirty nonscientist scholars and administrators over two days. The two sets of lectures included both demonstrations and theoretical presentations, thereby offering a sample of the undergraduate learning experience in physics courses. The thirty peers dealt with two questions: What is making this subject difficult for me? and What could I or the instructor do to make it come clear? They discussed these questions

with the instructor immediately after the sessions, offering suggestions to improve the clarity of lectures and demonstrations and
discussed the nature of "truth and understanding" in physics. At a
later time, they composed letters that suggested what science
teachers might do to better reach students.

Some of the findings of this experiment were to be expected.
The nonscientist colleagues did not understand much of the material, and the lecturers had little sense of the level of understanding.
Students who have trouble learning science drop out early in their
careers; hence, teachers have little experience with such problems.
Nonscientist colleagues offered them that perspective. Tobias concluded that the outcomes of this approach were well worth the time,
and that both the teachers and colleagues enjoyed participating. While
perhaps particularly appropriate for science teachers, there is no reason why humanities teachers might not profit from the reactions of
scientist colleagues, as in fact later pairings demonstrated.

The Appraisal Interview

For the chair who wants to discuss an instructional problem with
a teacher, interview techniques developed in personnel management should be kept in mind. Consider, as an example, the case of
a chair who has received some negative comments about a new
teacher from students. How can this situation be handled in order
to avoid defensiveness and hard feelings and to find solutions to the
problem? Maier, Solem, and Maier (1975), in the chapter, "The
Appraisal Interview," made some excellent suggestions for indus-
trial supervisors that, with some modifications, provide a constructive model for department chairs dealing with a situation of this
kind.

First, the chair needs to create a supportive environment during the interview so that the teacher will feel comfortable about
expressing ideas and feelings. The chair might begin with questions
about how things are going, and discussing and praising the positive things happening in the class. Perhaps the chair has already
visited the teacher's class and can offer some encouraging comments
about the teacher's practices. It is important in this first stage of the
interview to comprehend the teacher's perception of his or her per-

formance as well as to create a nonthreatening climate. The chair then asks whether the teacher is having any difficulties. When teachers perceive that a chair wants to be helpful, they talk freely about their problems. If the teacher is not forthcoming, the chair should mention the problems raised by students (which the chair may also have observed in the classroom or ascertained from course materials). Finally, chairs ask how they or the department can help solve the problems discussed. If handled properly, teachers will be motivated to work on a solution and will see the interview as an opportunity to receive advice about a problem they may not have known about. Rather than hurting feelings, the interview can lead to a significant modification or innovation. Of course, not all problems can be dealt with in a single interview. In fact, major problems may take several interviews or require assistance from a faculty development specialist.

Summative Colleague Evaluations

Department faculty members and chairs should, and usually do, prepare formal written recommendations when a colleague is being considered for tenure or promotion. They might make a single departmental recommendation or the chair might make a separate recommendation. Separate recommendations are preferable because they allow for different perspectives. The faculty members who make the assessments and the information they use vary widely. A few departments select an anonymous group of colleagues to make evaluations (French-Lazovik, 1981; see Centra, 1979, for a description of these procedures). The anonymity of these groups can no longer be guaranteed following the Supreme Court's 1990 ruling prohibiting the University of Pennsylvania from withholding confidential peer evaluations from a faculty member who had filed a discrimination claim against the university (*University of Pennsylvania* v. *EEOC,* 110 S. Ct. 577, 1990). (See Chapter Eight for a discussion of legal considerations.)

Tenure and promotion committees always include faculty representatives, but these committee members usually do not have the time or expertise needed to obtain their own information on teaching, scholarship and creativity, or service performance. Instead, they must rely on other sources. For scholarship and creative endeavors, written or oral testimonials from colleagues in the candidate's discipline, both internal and external to the candidate's institution, are solicited. Enough lead time should be allowed for thoughtful reviews, and criteria to be used should be specified. Colleagues should be selected from a list provided by the faculty member and by others who have published on similar topics. (An example of a letter inviting an external colleague's evaluation of one's professional products and reputation is included in Centra, 1979, chap. 6.) Similar comments can be invited on the candidate's local or national service. For teaching, the sources consulted are frequently students or department members. In general, this procedure provides an incomplete picture. Following are a few examples of more systematic ways in which to carry out colleague evaluations of teaching in tenure and promotion decisions.

Ad Hoc Committees on Teaching

One college within a research university has for many years used a useful model of colleague evaluations in which an ad hoc committee on teaching is appointed for each faculty member up for tenure or promotion. Teaching performance only is assessed, and the committee's report is submitted directly to the tenure and promotions committee. Each committee on teaching consists of a senior faculty member, two junior faculty members, and a graduate or upper-level student, all from outside the candidate's department. A meeting between the committee and the candidate takes place during the semester prior to that when the decision will be made. The candidate then presents the committee with a variety of teaching-related materials: copies of syllabi, exams, teaching aids, and student evaluations of past courses. The candidate also lists names and addresses of student advisees, dissertation advisees, and enrollees in past and current courses. Through phone calls, letters, and brief survey questionnaires to a random sample of the students, the committee is able to piece together a picture of the students' views of the teacher to supplement their evaluation reports of past courses. Committee members also observe classes taught by the teacher and then write a description of their observations.

Candidates typically cooperate fully with their committees, for to do otherwise would imply lack of interest in teaching. Once all the information is collected, the committee members meet several times to discuss their individual assessments. A final eight-page report, written by the committee chair, is typically supplemented by comments from the committee members and information gathered from students. The report has six sections:

1. *Classroom performance:* evaluation of performance based on instructor work load, class observations, and current and past student reactions
2. *Instructional materials:* description and evaluation of instructional materials by committee members
3. *Advising:* amount and quality of advising as indicated by student phone calls, surveys, or letters
4. *Participation in doctoral studies:* comments from students whose committee the faculty member has chaired or served on; evaluation of quality of dissertations
5. *Special recognition for teaching:* review of awards, external use of material, teaching-related publications
6. *Summary:* ratings of the teacher by each committee member are made in each previous category, on a five-point scale, and an overall evaluation

Candidates who have accumulated a teaching dossier or portfolio (see Chapter Five) are generally in a stronger position because they can provide a more complete view of their teaching performance and growth; without such information the committee must rely on evidence from the two most recent semesters only. Although research productivity is given primary importance at this research university, committee on teaching reports have influenced close personnel decisions. At institutions in which teaching is of primary importance, this approach provides a way for colleagues to have greater influence in tenure and promotion decisions. The method is not suitable for salary decisions because of the length of time required. Faculty members usually serve on a committee once every three years or so, depending on the number of decisions to be made. While currently used for summative purposes, information from the committee could also be useful for instructional improvement. Given the positive findings about colleague evaluations of teaching effectiveness that were based on dossiers, in the Root (1987) study cited earlier, the use of ad hoc committees on teaching would seem to provide reliable assessments of teaching.

Colleagues' Evaluation Questionnaires

A wide variety of questionnaires and rating forms exist for use by colleagues or chairs. Few if any studies of the psychometric properties—reliability and validity—of these forms have been published. Most of these instruments, however, appear to have validity: they ask questions dealing with aspects of faculty behavior and performance that colleagues are likely to be able to judge. Some forms include very specific questions that are rated numerically; others ask open-ended questions. One questionnaire, reprinted in Centra (1979, pp. 78–79), asks colleagues to give numerical ratings for twenty-eight items in five categories: (1) research activity and recognition, (2) intellectual breadth, (3) participation in the academic community, (4) associated professional activities, and (5) public service and consulting.

Items on classroom teaching performance are excluded (except for a question about general concern about teaching), because of the expectation that students can better provide that information.

Another form examined in Centra, Froh, Gray, and Lambert (1987, pp. 37–39) includes open-ended questions that colleagues and chairs can use to guide their analysis of instructional materials. The questions are listed under six characteristics of good teaching. A list of the six and examples of the questions follow:

1. Good organization of subject matter and course. (Does the content appear to be appropriate and relevant?)
2. Effective communication. (Are student assignments well defined?)
3. Knowledge of and enthusiasm for subject matter and teaching. (Are tests and other sources appropriate for the course?)
4. Fairness in examinations and grading. (Do examinations test course objectives?)
5. Flexibility in approaches to teaching. (Do the course materials

include a variety of instructional approaches suggesting creativity and flexibility?)
6. Appropriate student learning outcomes. (Are student-produced
    documents consistent with the course goals and objectives?)

Many of the questions in the form are best answered by colleagues in the same department as the faculty member. Another
form, examined in Centra, Froh, Gray, and Lambert (1987), uses the
same six categories of effective teaching with a different set of questions to guide classroom observations. (See the form "Classroom
Observation by Colleagues" in the resources.) Colleagues do not
have to be in the same department to respond to these more generic
questions.

Other colleague and chair evaluation questionnaires have
been assembled by Braskamp, Brandenburg, and Ory (1984). Their
examples, based in large part on their experiences at the University
of Illinois, focus on teaching. A form designed by French-Lazovik
(1981) also deals with evaluation of teaching. Shown in the resources, the "Suggested Form for Peer Review of Undergraduate
Teaching Based on Dossier Materials" provides five broad questions, suggests which dossier materials should be reviewed in connection with each question, and suggests a focus in examining the
dossier materials. A seven-point rating scale and written comments
are added for each of the five areas of evaluation. The brevity and
sharp focus of this form make it especially appealing, although like
the others, it has not been examined for reliability or validity.

A community college undergoing a complete reorganization
made unique use of colleague and administrator evaluations. As
discussed more completely in Chapter Five, every faculty member
was evaluated by colleagues, a chair or dean, and students. The
criteria for judging teaching effectiveness were adapted from
Roueche and Baker (1987), with faculty members describing their
teaching skills within three broad areas: motivational skills, interpersonal skills, and intellectual skills.

As is often the case, particularly when all faculty members
are being evaluated at the same time, the colleague evaluations were
somewhat lenient (see Centra, 1975, for another example.) Administrator evaluations were less lenient. Student evaluations of teach-

ing for each faculty member were derived from a standard form. Special contributions to the college (for example, committee work) and to the community were also described by each faculty member and evaluated by both colleagues and administrators. Although the procedures used at this community college allowed for colleague assessments and employed a specific set of criteria for teaching effectiveness, there was unfortunately no opportunity to apply the criteria in a formative way before their adaptation for summative purposes.

The various evaluation forms for colleagues and chairs that were described in this section were designed for summative evaluation but could also be used for formative evaluation. In fact, faculty members should have the opportunity to receive formative evaluations so that they can adjust their teaching and instructional materials before being evaluated summatively.

Summary

The major points in this chapter can be best summarized in the form of guidelines for colleague and chair evaluations. The guidelines are based on the research and the examples of successful practices that this chapter presents.

1. *Use committees of colleagues to evaluate teaching for tenure and promotion decisions.* Evaluations by committees of colleagues should be based on a dossier or portfolio of instructional materials, student evaluations of a range of courses and, if possible, classroom observations. As few as three colleagues can provide sufficient reliability in an overall evaluation of teaching performance once they have integrated information from the several sources. Brief training sessions for the colleagues ensure the reliability of their judgments.

2. *Do not give classroom observations undue weight in summative evaluations.* Because of the limited amount of time that colleagues can spend observing classes, and because of the different views faculty members may have about teaching, colleague ratings based on observations alone should not be given undue weight. However, they should be used to supplement other kinds of information about teaching performance.

3. *Encourage faculty members to work together to improve instruction.* Several models for collaboration are described in this chapter. Incentives could include a reduced teaching load, monetary rewards, or acknowledgment of such efforts when tenure and promotion decisions are made. Although faculty members vary in their ability to offer useful suggestions, all teachers can provide a perspective that students or others cannot.

4. *Have colleagues from appropriate fields, both internal and external to the institution, evaluate research and creative endeavors.* Colleagues, and probably chairs as well, are able to provide more reliable judgments of research and creative endeavors than of teaching. It is often necessary to go outside an institution to obtain judgments about research, scholarship, and creative work.

5. *Use reflective judgment.* Colleagues and chairs should keep in mind the individual teacher's goals and reflections on his or her practice. Judging, like teaching, is in part an art. The best formative and summative judgments will be made by individuals who draw on rich experience and their knowledge of teaching, research, or service. Evaluations by colleagues are not unlike a Greek chorus; the collective voice of the group is what must be heard.

Chapter 7

Determining Effectiveness
in Research and Service

*N*early all the work that college faculty members perform falls into four overlapping areas: teaching, research, public service, and institutional service. This chapter discusses the areas of research and public service, focusing on how best to evaluate performance in those areas. Among the issues addressed are quantity versus quality as measures of research effectiveness, the relationship between teaching and research, differences by discipline in research productivity, ethics in research, and efforts to broaden the definition of research. The different kinds of public service, its relationship to research, and ways to evaluate it are also investigated. In their landmark study of American professors, Bowen and Schuster (1986) used the term *research* to mean activities by the faculty that advance knowledge and the arts. "Humanistic scholarship, scientific research in natural and social sciences, philosophical and religious inquiry, social criticism, public-policy analysis, and cultivation of literature and the fine arts" (p. 16) were included. In addition to the discovery of new knowledge or the creation of art, dissemination is a necessary part of research. Bowen and Schuster pointed out that only through the production of a durable publication or a piece of art do research results become widely known. But word of mouth is another form of dissemination, and both teaching and public service provide such avenues.

At research universities, faculty members in 1989 spent an equal amount of time on research and on teaching: twenty hours per week (Rees and Smith, 1991, reporting analysis of data from the 1989 Carnegie Foundation for the Advancement of Teaching faculty survey). Nevertheless, they believed their research was considered to be much more important: 83 percent said publishing was necessary for tenure, up from 44 percent in the 1969 Carnegie faculty survey. Even at comprehensive institutions and liberal arts colleges, faculty members said they spent between nine and eleven hours per week on research (Rees and Smith, 1991). The result of all the time spent on research is a barrage of publications that at least one critic claims to be often "routine and pedestrian" and "a moral and spiritual drag on the institutions in which it takes place" (Smith, 1990).

The amount of material published is indeed extensive. A U.S. Department of Education survey indicated that 70 percent of full-time faculty members at research and doctorate-granting universities published a refereed journal article during 1986 and 1987 (Mooney, 1991). At these same institutions, the average number of refereed articles for each person who published during that period was 4.9. At comprehensive institutions and liberal arts colleges, half as many faculty members published in refereed journals—35 percent—and the average number of publications was 2.6. If we look at the wide range of publications, however, 91 percent of university faculties and 78 percent of those at all other institutions published during the years 1986 and 1987. Other publications are defined to include books, chapters in books, reviews, nonrefereed articles, monographs, presentations in the popular media, technical reports distributed to clients, conference presentations, exhibitions or performances in the arts, and computer software. With such an extensive amount being published and the variety of ways in which it is disseminated, institutions must attempt to assess quality. The 1989 Carnegie survey reports faculty perceptions of the importance of some quality measures for granting tenure, as shown in Table 7.1.

Earlier surveys revealed the importance that institutions give to (in rank order) articles in quality journals, books written by the individual as sole or senior author, publications in professional

Table 7.1. Types of Publications Considered Important
for Gaining Tenure, by Type of Institution.[a]

	Research and Doctorate Granting	Compre-hensive	Liberal Arts	Two-Year
Reputations of the journal presses	38	18	7	2
Published reviews of books	8	5	3	1
Lectures or papers at professional meetings or other institutions	8	12	7	3
Research grants received	38	19	9	3
Recommendations from outside scholars	41	9	16	3
Recommendations from faculty within the institutions	14	19	38	15

[a] Percent of faculty indicating.
Source: Carnegie Foundation for the Advancement of Teaching, 1989. Reprinted by permission.

journals, and monographs or chapters in books (see Centra, 1979, p. 15). Journal and book quality, indicated by the concern with the reputation of the publisher, is still of prime importance, as Table 7.1 indicates. The table also reflects the relatively low importance that book reviews and presentations at professional meetings were given in 1989; I found them to receive equally little weight in my survey, conducted in 1979. A major difference in the findings of the more recent survey was the emphasis on research grants received, particularly in the universities. Also new was the importance university faculty placed on recommendations from outside scholars. At the three other types of institutions, recommendations from faculty within the institution are still more important, possibly because faculty members can also evaluate teaching effectiveness.

The trend toward deeper examination of quality of publications at research and doctorate-granting universities is evident elsewhere. A few research universities have discussed limiting the

number of publications a candidate can submit to tenure and promotion committees (Mooney, 1991). By doing so, they hope to stifle
trivial research, which wastes resources and can take time away from
teaching.

Comparing Quantity and Quality

If institutions were to use only the number of articles published as
a measure of research, what would the consequences be? In addition
to encouraging trivial research, some faculty members who deserved
to be rewarded for the quality of their work would not be, while some
who produced large numbers of papers of little consequence would
be unduly rewarded. How many trivial works would be produced? In
a study by Cole and Cole (1967) of 120 university physicists, they
found the number to be 33 percent of this sample. Using the number
of citations of published work as an indication of quality, they found
a correlation of .72 with total publications. Other studies have cor-
roborated this finding: there was a correlation of .71 for science department faculties (Hagstrom, 1971) and .67 (Clark, 1957), and .60
(Schrader, 1978) for psychologists.

Citation counts appear to be used increasingly as a measure of
quality of publications. Three indexes are now available: the Science
Citation Index, first published annually in 1961; the Social Science
Citation Index, first published in 1969; and the Arts and Humanities
Citation Index, first published in 1978. Thus, most fields are now
covered, although certain kinds of publications—books and art exhibits, for example—are not included in all the appropriate indexes.
If a bibliography of the person being evaluated is used, the indexes
can provide citation counts for all of that person's articles, not only
first-authored articles, and can distinguish between authors with the
same last name and first initials (Garfield, 1979).

The use of citation counts is not without its problems, however. Some of the limitations are the following: (1) authors may be
tempted to cite their own or their close friends' work frequently, (2)
works may be cited for negative rather than positive reasons, (3)
because the scientific fields differ in size, comparison of citation
counts between different fields may be unfair, (4) the significance
of some work may not be recognized in the field for many years, (5)
for younger faculty, the time lapse between publication of an arti-

cle, citations by others, and appearance in an index may be too long to give a complete evaluation of quality for tenure decisions.

In spite of these limitations, citation counts are one of the better indicators of the visibility and value of research. They are an indirect method of ascertaining peer judgments, compared with the more direct method of requesting written peer reviews. Certainly direct peer reviews will continue to be the dominant method of judging research quality, but citation counts can be useful, especially for higher-level promotions and awards.

The art world parallels the world of science in one way: scientists put forth challenging new hypotheses, while artists put forth challenging new creations. In the performing arts, traditional ways of measuring quality may not capture the uniqueness or personal creativity of an accomplishment. The arts are generally governed by poorly defined criteria and standards that vary among artists, critics, and the public (Blau, 1988). In studio art, drama, music, film, creative writing, and other creative fields, peer review may penalize an unconventional but creative accomplishment. Critics' reviews and the public's response should certainly be considered, but like peer judgments, they may have a narrow perspective. The criteria and standards of performance also vary somewhat by area, and this too must be taken into account. Generally speaking, the criteria for evaluation include originality, scope, significance, and contribution to the field. Collaborative products and events are common in such areas as drama and film, so it is necessary to ensure that the most credit is given to the individuals who had responsibility. In spite of their possible limitations, outside critiques of the work by other artists and academicians should be solicited (Wood, 1984). Whether evaluating scholarship in the performing arts or another subject field, the basic rule is the same: convergence of the various measures and sources is needed. If the results conflict, additional measures should be sought to reconcile the differences.

Relationship Between Research and Teaching

Most faculty members firmly believe that research benefits teaching, especially at the graduate level. The results of a survey of natural science faculty members at one university are probably typical: 95

percent thought that "research increases teaching effectiveness by increasing awareness and currency" (Jauch, 1976). In addition to keeping teachers current in their subjects, a number of other reasons have been proposed to support the expectation of a beneficial research-teaching connection:

1.   Some individuals' higher general ability and energy levels make them good at research and teaching (as well as in other professional roles).
2.   Research influences teaching when the instructor's excitement and involvement is communicated to students and they are able to see knowledge as constantly growing. "For a chemist to be able to share the excitement of discovery with students, it is necessary to work in a laboratory, mix compounds together, and follow the resulting reactions. For a historian to teach students how to interpret the past, it is essential to work with old documents and artifacts, to feel the materials of history . . ." (Winkler, 1992).
3.   Research helps maintain the teacher's interest in the subject matter.
4.   Stimulating discussions with students in the classroom can lead to productive research.

Compelling arguments have also been made that a negative relationship exists between research and teaching:

1.   The rewards given to research at many institutions cause faculty members to put less effort into teaching.
2.   The time faculty members spend on research takes away from time they might spend preparing class sessions, grading papers, and meeting with students. Even those who are good teachers and researchers would be even better teachers if they devoted all their time to teaching.
3.   The abilities and personality traits needed to be a good researcher are different from those needed to be a good teacher.

A variety of studies, including two by Rushton, Murray, and Paunonem (1983) support the last contention. They used a compos-

ite measure based on publication and citation counts to assess research. They based their ratings of teaching effectiveness on five
years of formal student evaluations. Peer-, student-, and self-ratings
were also collected for the faculty on twenty-nine personality traits.
Creative researchers from several different fields were described as
follows: ambitious, enduring, seeking answers, dominant, showing
leadership, aggressive, independent, bold, and nonsupportive. Effective teachers were described as liberal, sociable, showing leadership,
extraverted, calm, objective, supporting, nonauthoritarian, not defensive, intelligent, and aesthetically sensitive. The research cluster
is marked by qualities of independence, achievement, dominance,
and desire for cognitive order. The teaching cluster suggests an individual who is easygoing, intelligent, and liberal. "Showing leadership" was the only quality used to describe effective people in both
groups. They were most dissimilar in supportiveness. Of course, as
the study authors point out, not all effective teachers and researchers
are perfectly described by these profiles, and certainly cause and effect
cannot be determined from such studies. Still, the different profiles
may help explain why the relationship between effective teaching
and research performance is not very strong.

Feldman's (1987) meta-analysis of twenty-nine studies that
related teaching effectiveness with research productivity found an
average correlation of .12. While the correlation is positive, it is
fairly small, indicating that the two functions are not highly related. Being a productive researcher does not contribute to effective
teaching, but neither does it detract from teaching. The twenty-nine
studies used student evaluations as a measure of teaching effectiveness because they are most readily available for a large number of
teachers. Research productivity was assessed in a variety of ways,
including publication counts, citations, value or number of research grants, and ratings by chairs or peers.

Many other factors in the teaching-research relationship have
been analyzed. I studied some 4,600 faculty members at different
career stages and in different academic fields; I expected that research and teaching might be significantly related for faculty
members in their middle or later years and in only some disciplines
(Centra, 1983). The number of publications during the preceding
five years was used as the measure of research productivity in order

to better ascertain possible spillover effects on teaching. Some evidence for a possible spillover effect—where the research enhanced the teaching—was found in the social sciences but not in the other areas. For the teachers of humanities or professional courses (for example, business or education courses), the correlations were for the most part positive but insignificant; for natural science teachers, the correlations were either insignificant or negative. The expectation that the relationship between teaching quality and research productivity would be stronger for teachers in their middle or later years, when they no longer needed to focus on research to increase their chances of gaining tenure, was not consistently supported by my study. The subject field differences corresponded to findings in another study. Baird (1980) found that the quality of teaching, as judged by graduate students in the departments, was more highly correlated with recent journal publications for psychology department faculty members than for those in history or chemistry departments.

Why spillover effects may be somewhat more likely to occur in social science subjects is not definitely known. Perhaps it is easier to use research results in those courses, or perhaps stimulating classroom discussions are more likely to lead to productive avenues of research.

Feldman (1987) considered other factors that might mediate the association between research productivity and teaching effectiveness. These included rank and age of faculty members, their general abilities, and the amount of time or effort spent on research. None affected the relationship consistently. What may be important, however, is the type of college. Robert McCaughey (1992), dean of the faculty at Barnard College, concluded that faculty members at many of the twenty-four selective liberal arts colleges he studied were actively publishing and were also effective teachers. "Senior scholars who were identified by external reviewers as being among a college's most active scholars also were more likely to be ranked among the most effective teachers than were senior professors with little or no scholarly record" (p. 36). The sample used—senior professors at selective liberal arts colleges—and McCaughey's methodology may have produced the more positive correlations. Rather than being student evaluations, the ratings of teaching were made by deans who had not seen the rankings of scholarly productivity. But they were likely to be aware of who the productive researchers were on their faculties. Further validation of these results is needed, particularly at other types of institutions.

No one questions the need for teachers to keep current in their fields; the question is whether they must carry on research in order to do so. The studies do not provide strong support for the need. This is not to say, however, that faculty members must become generalists in their disciplines and focus only on teaching. Scholar-teachers must keep up with huge amounts of research in their fields. Not all may make original contributions, but other forms of scholarship, such as the integrative research we will discuss later in this chapter, are important for effective teaching. Finally, we emphasize that the lack of consistent negative correlations between research productivity and teacher ratings indicates that such performance does not significantly detract from performance as a teacher, as some have argued.

Disciplinary Differences

We have seen, in other chapters of this book, how teaching differs by discipline. So too does research. Knowledge of these differences is especially important if individuals' research productivity is compared. The U.S. Department of Education's 1988 survey of 11,013 full-time faculty members revealed differences in average research production, by discipline, as shown in Table 7.2 (Mooney, 1991).

Wide variations can be noted in production amount and type over the two-year period studied. Refereed articles ranged from an average of 4.3 in the health sciences to 0.8 in fine arts. Faculty in natural science and agriculture and home economics fields averaged just over 3.0. Health science and social science faculty members published the greatest number of books, chapters, and monographs, averaging slightly more than 1.0. Humanities teachers wrote the most book reviews—an average of 1.4—and engineering and agriculture and home economics faculties published the most "other reports" (for example, project reports). Fine arts faculty members had the lowest scores in every category except the last, presentations and exhibitions. There they averaged 15.6, more than twice as many

Table 7.2. Average Number of Publications by Full-Time Faculty
Members, 1986 and 1987, by Discipline, at Four-Year Institutions.

Discipline	Refereed Articles	Books, Textbooks, Chapters, Monographs	Book Reviews	Other Reports	Presentations, Exhibitions
Agriculture, Home Economics	3.3	0.6	0.2	3.1	5.4
Business	1.4	0.5	0.2	1.5	2.6
Education	1.5	0.7	0.4	2.0	5.1
Engineering	2.5	0.5	0.2	3.1	3.0
Fine Arts	0.8	0.3	0.4	0.8	15.6
Health Science	4.3	1.2	0.6	1.7	6.0
Humanities	1.4	0.8	1.4	0.9	3.3
Natural Science	3.2	0.5	0.5	2.4	2.9
Social Science	2.1	1.1	0.9	1.4	3.4

Source: Mooney, 1991. Reprinted by permission.

as in any other field. Clearly, fine arts faculty members are greatly disadvantaged if the written word is emphasized in personnel decisions. And the large difference in refereed articles by discipline probably would be reflected in citation counts, with the health and natural sciences receiving the greatest number.

Besides disciplinary differences in research productivity, career stage during which people publish also varies by discipline. I analyzed the publication rates of some 3,000 faculty members in relation to their years of teaching experience (Centra, 1979, pp. 123–124). Faculty in the natural sciences published more journal articles early in their careers than did those in the humanities or social sciences. The median number of articles for natural science teachers during their first six years of experience was well over two, while the median for humanities and social science teachers during the same period was about one and a half. During the first twelve years of experience, natural science teachers produced more articles than either humanities or social science teachers, but the picture changes later on: those in the humanities and social science publish slightly more than those in natural sciences, although all three groups publish less after twenty years of experience than at any previous time. Cole's (1979) study of faculty members in six fields found a similar curvilinear relationship between age and productivity.

An explanation for the higher publications rates by natural science researchers early in their careers is provided by Zuckerman and Merton (1973; cited by Cole, 1979). They characterized scientific fields by the extent to which knowledge is codified. In highly codified fields, such as physics and chemistry, knowledge is compacted into a relatively small number of theories, and graduate students can quickly learn the state of the field and begin productive research. In the less codified fields, such as the social sciences, descriptive facts and low-level theories that are ill understood make it more difficult to do significant research until one gains competence through experience.

If an institution compares faculty members' research productivity and does not take discipline into account (as some university-wide tenure and promotion committees might do), natural scientists (health scientists included) would have a decided edge during the early years. For faculty in the humanities and social science departments, appropriate added weight should continue to be given to the publication of books, as my survey of department heads indicated was generally done (Centra, 1977a). And for faculty in the fine arts, the documentation and evaluation of presentations and exhibitions, rather than journal publications alone, are necessary.

Ethics in Research

The pressure to publish and obtain grants in order to gain tenure has resulted in unprecedented numbers of scientific misconduct cases. A survey of 259 graduate school deans by Judith Swazey of the Acadia Institute (Maine) found that 40 percent reported cases of confirmed misconduct during the five years studied, 1983–88 (Hilts, 1992). In spite of this, only 10 percent of the graduate schools surveyed required students to take a class in ethics. The few that did emphasized case studies of misconduct and discussions of standards of behavior in conducting research. Neophyte researchers usually

learn about proper research conduct from their mentors and other
senior researchers during the doctoral socialization process (Braxton, 1991; Zuckerman, 1988). These people must take the lead, setting a proper example and offering seminars on ethics.

Robert Merton's (1973) four norms for scientific behavior
might well provide a framework for such a seminar. Descriptions
of his four norms follow:

1. *Communality.* Research findings must be made public
because they belong to the scientific community. Scientists must be
recognized for their contributions. Examples of violations include
failing to cite the pertinent work or ideas of other scholars, keeping
research findings secret, and failing to give credit to a collaborator.

2. *Disinterestedness.* Research must be conducted for the advancement of knowledge rather than for personal gain. Examples
of violations include engaging in a project solely for financial gain,
seeking publicity from the mass media, and knowingly publishing
findings based on incorrect or fraudulent data.

3. *Organized skepticism.* Scholars must critically assess the
procedures and findings of their own and others' work. Examples
of violations include failing to present data that contradict the original hypotheses, personally attacking a colleague whose findings
conflict with the researcher's, and ignoring new evidence from others that challenge the researcher's own findings.

4. *Universalism.* Scholarship must be judged on scientific
merit; favoritism or personal qualities of the scientist must not influence judgments. Examples of violations include relying on a scholar's
past work to assess current research and rejecting a scholarly finding
because of the author's rank or institutional affiliation.

Merton's four norms encompass behavior that ranges from
serious misconduct to what some people might consider minor impropriety. Publishing findings based on fraudulent data is much
more serious than seeking publicity for one's findings (universities
have public information offices to publicize the accomplishments
of the university faculty). Failing to present data that conflicts with
the researcher's expectations is a more serious breach of conduct
than failing to cite previous research because of its author's institutional affiliation. Using case studies to discuss behavioral norms
with beginning researchers should help clarify the seriousness of the

impropriety. Evaluation procedures for tenure and promotion decisions should include consideration of an individual's behavior in carrying out research. Faculty members should be forewarned that serious acts of misconduct or even a pattern of minor improprieties could affect the decision. In summary, incidents of scientific misconduct can best be decreased by educating researchers, offering proper examples, and taking into account the process as well as the products of research.

Broadening the Definition of Research

Ernest Boyer (1990) argued that it is time "to break out of the tired old teaching versus research debate and define, in more creative ways, what it means to be a scholar. It is time to recognize the full range of faculty talent and the great diversity of functions higher education must perform" (p. xii).

The definition of a scholar, in the view of many faculty members, has been too narrow. For example, more than two-thirds of the faculty in the 1989 Carnegie Foundation for the Advancement of Teaching survey said that measures other than number of publications are needed to evaluate scholarly performance (Boyer, 1990, appendix). In an attempt to clarify what scholarly work is, Pellino, Blackburn, and Boberg (1984) asked faculty members at twenty-four colleges and universities to indicate how central they believed each of thirty-two activities was to both their performance and conception of scholarship. A factor analysis of the results produced six dimensions of academic scholarship: professional activity, research and publication, creative (artistic) endeavor, engagement in the novel, community service, and pedagogy. These dimensions include a wide range of activities—teaching, service, and the several kinds of research—in their definition of scholarly work. Lynton and Elman (1987) as well as Boyer (1990) have also argued that teaching and public service should be included in a broadened definition of scholarship. They reject as too limiting the traditional view that scholarship merely means research leading to refereed publications. Boyer and Rice reject the trilogy of research, teaching, and service in favor of four interrelated components of scholarship: discovery, integration, application, and teaching. According to this more inclusive view of what it means to be a scholar, knowledge is acquired through research, synthesis, practice, and teaching. The four categories are described in Boyer's *Scholarship Reconsidered: Priorities of the Professoriate* (1990). Selected excerpts follow:

The Scholarship of Discovery

The first and the most familiar element in our model, the scholarship of discovery, comes closest to what is meant when academics speak of "research." No tenets in the academy are held in higher regard than the commitment to knowledge for its own sake, to freedom of inquiry and to following, in a disciplined fashion, an investigation wherever it may lead. Research is central to the work of higher learning, but our study here, which inquires into the meaning of scholarship, is rooted in the conviction that disciplined, investigative efforts within the academy should be strengthened, not diminished.

Thus, the probing mind of the researcher is an incalculably vital asset to the academy and the world. Scholarly investigation, in all the disciplines, is at the very heart of academic life, and the pursuit of knowledge must be assiduously cultivated and defended. The intellectual excitement fueled by this quest enlivens faculty and invigorates higher learning institutions, and in our complicated, vulnerable world, the discovery of new knowledge is absolutely crucial.

The Scholarship of Integration

In proposing the scholarship of integration, we underscore the need for scholars who give meaning to isolated facts, putting them in perspective. By integration, we mean making connections across the disciplines, placing the specialties in larger context, illuminating data in a revealing way, often educating nonspecialists, too. In calling for a scholarship of integration, we do not suggest returning to the "gentleman scholar" of an earlier time, nor do we have in mind the dilettante. Rather, what we mean is serious, disciplined work that seeks to interpret, draw together, and bring new insight to bear on original research. . . .

The scholarship of integration also means interpretation, fitting one's own research—or the research of others—into larger intellectual patterns. Such efforts are increasingly essential since specialization, without broader perspective, risks pedantry. The distinction we are drawing here between "discovery" and "integration" can be best understood, perhaps, by the questions posed. Those engaged in discovery ask, "What is to be known, what is yet to be found?" Those engaged in integration ask, "What do the findings mean? Is it possible to interpret what's been discovered in ways that provide a larger, more comprehensive understanding?" Questions such as these call for the power of critical analysis and interpretation. They have a legitimacy of their own and if carefully pursued can lead the scholar from information to knowledge and even, perhaps, to wisdom. . . . Today, interdisciplinary and integrative studies, long on the edges of academic life, are moving toward the center, responding both to new intellectual questions and to pressing human problems. As the boundaries of human knowledge are being dramatically reshaped, the academy surely must give increased attention to the scholarship of integration.

The Scholarship of Application

The first two kinds of scholarship—discovery and integration—reflect the investigative and synthesizing traditions of academic life. The third element, the application of knowledge, moves toward engagement as the scholar asks, "How can knowledge be responsibly applied to consequential problems? How can it be helpful to individuals as well as institutions?" And further, "Can social problems themselves define an agenda for scholarly investigation?" . . . To be considered scholarship, service activities must be tied directly to one's special field of knowledge and relate to, and flow directly out of, this professional activity. Such service is serious, demanding work, requiring the rigor—and the accountability—traditionally associated with research activities.

The scholarship of application, as we define it here, is not a one-way street. Indeed, the term itself may be misleading if it suggests that knowledge is first "discovered" and then "applied." The process we have in mind is far more dynamic. New intellectual understandings can arise out of the very act of application—whether in medical diagnosis, serving clients in psychotherapy, shaping public policy, creating an architectural design, or working with the public schools. In activities such as these, theory and practice vitally interact, and one renews the other.

Such a view of scholarly service—one that both applies and contributes to human knowledge—is particularly needed in a world in which huge, almost intractable problems call for the skills and insights only the academy can provide.

The Scholarship of Teaching

Finally, we come to the scholarship of teaching. The work of the professor becomes consequential only as it is understood by others. Yet, today, teaching is often viewed as a routine function, tacked on, something almost anyone can do. When defined as scholarship, however, teaching both educates and entices future scholars. Indeed, as Aristotle said, "Teaching is the highest form of understanding."

As a scholarly enterprise, teaching begins with what the teacher knows. Teaching can be well regarded only as professors are widely read and intellectually engaged. . . .

Teaching is also a dynamic endeavor involving all the analogies, metaphors, and images that build bridges between the teacher's understanding and the student's learning. Pedagogical procedures must be carefully planned, continuously examined, and relate directly to the subject taught . . . great teachers create a common ground of intellectual commitment. They stimulate active, not passive, learning and encourage students to be critical, creative thinkers, with the capacity to go on learning after their college days are over.

Further, good teaching means that faculty, as scholars, are also learners. All too often, teachers transmit information that students are expected to memorize and then, perhaps, recall. While well-prepared lectures surely have a place, teaching, at its best, means not only transmitting knowledge, but transforming and extending it as well. Through reading, through classroom discussion, and surely through comments and questions posed by students, professors themselves will be pushed in creative new directions.

In the end, inspired teaching keeps the flame of scholarship alive. . . . Without the teaching function, the continuity of knowledge will be broken and the store of human knowledge dangerously diminished [Boyer, 1990, © 1990, The Carnegie Foundation for the Advancement of Teaching. Reprinted with permission.].

More than twenty learned societies and professional groups have been examining ways to apply these four components of scholarship to their disciplines. The project, begun in mid 1992 and sponsored by both the Fund for the Improvement of Postsecondary Education and the Lilly Endowment, has been coordinated by Syracuse University's Center for Instructional Development, with Robert Diamond as project director. The goal is to enlist representatives of each professional association to develop applications to their own disciplines. Because the disciplines largely determine what kind of scholarship is valued, they may influence a redefinition of scholarship and bring about changes in the reward system. The American Historical Association is among the first groups to develop a draft document. A panel of their members proposed lists of activities under each component as follows:

1. Under the scholarship of discovery, the panel listed the typical outlets for original research in the field, such as publishing refereed articles or conference papers, or participating in museum exhibitions or other projects. Documentary or critical editions and translations were also included.
2. For the scholarship of integration, the panel included many examples of the synthesis of knowledge, such as publishing in review essays, textbooks, newsletters, magazines, conference papers, films, museum exhibitions or other public programs. Edited anthologies or a series of volumes comprising the work of other scholars were also included.
3. For the scholarship of the application, the panel included public history, for example, participating in public programs in museums or other cultural institutions; providing expert testimony on public policy, participating in film or archival administration; professional service, such as editing journals and organizing scholarly meetings; community service drawing directly on scholarship, such as working through state humanities councils, or history day competitions.
4. For the scholarship of teaching, the panel included student mentoring or advising; developing courses, curricula, and teaching materials; participating in programs with the schools; and participating in disciplinary assessment programs and in programs that educate the public (such as film, radio, and museum programs).

Clarification of the components and reduction in the overlap of activities between the categories would probably occur with further use and discussion. And while many specific activities will differ by discipline, some will likely be applicable to many, with only slight modifications.

In his monograph Boyer (1990) offered a few suggestions about how to evaluate scholarly performance when its definition is more inclusive. For the scholarship of integration, he recommended evaluating well-done textbooks. They "can reveal a professor's knowledge of the field, illuminate essential integrative themes, and powerfully contribute to excellence in teaching, too" (p. 35). Writing for nonspecialists should also be recognized: "To make complex ideas understandable to a large audience can be a difficult, demanding task, one that requires not only a deep and thorough knowledge of one's field but keen literary skills as well" (p. 35). Boyer suggested that other scholars who have written for the general public might be appropriate peer reviewers. Other integrative forms of scholarship that should be recognized are preparing quality computer software, videocassettes, and television productions. Finally, Boyer proposed that evaluation of integrative scholarship should include such curriculum-related work as developing a new core program or preparing a cross-disciplinary course. Even though Boyer states that the evaluation of these curricular innovations should focus on the integration of the relevant literature into the course, this example of integrative scholarship is different from the previous examples. In fact, it seems more appropriately considered part of the scholarship of teaching.

Boyer equated scholarship of application with public service. Like others, he argued that only those public service activities "that relate directly to the intellectual work of the professor and [are] carried out through consultation, technical assistance, policy analysis, program evaluation and the like" should be considered (p. 36; see also Lynton and Elman, 1987). The evaluation of public service will be discussed in the next section of this chapter.

To evaluate teaching—the scholarship of teaching, as he termed it—Boyer recommended gathering at least three types of information: self-assessment, peer assessments, and student assessments. Much research has already contributed to our understanding of the strengths and limitations of each of those sources, as discussed in this book. Methods of incorporating research into the teaching and learning environment should be encouraged. In graduate education, a symbiotic relationship between research and teaching already exists; at the undergraduate level, a little more effort and creative thinking is needed to encourage the relationship. A few possible methods are described in the following list. Some are already used by individual teachers or institutions. Research, as defined in these examples, includes exhibits or other kinds of presentations in the fine and performing arts.

1. Undergraduate programs could include requirements for majors to conduct research projects as part of a senior-level capstone seminar. Selected papers could be delivered to the faculty and students in the program as if it were a professional conference (that is, there would be time limits, critiques, and discussion).
2. Teachers could be encouraged to include their own research, published or not, in their courses. Even occasional digressions from the prescribed course content would be warranted to emphasize the need for students to witness the connection between active scholarship and learning.
3. While it is often difficult to involve many undergraduate students in research, faculty members could be encouraged to do so. If necessary, institutional funding could be made available, or efforts by faculty could be counted in personnel decisions.
4. Creative efforts to integrate research into teaching could be otherwise encouraged and rewarded.

In summary, broadening the definition of scholarship is no more than recognizing the wide-ranging missions and responsibilities of various institutions. The available funding and the prestige associated with basic research—the scholarship of discovery—has caused many colleges and universities to honor too narrow a range of activities. Integrative research, teaching, and public service, probably in that order, have been slighted. Including all of these other functions under the umbrella of scholarship may give them and the individual faculty members who excel in them the credit they deserve.

Evaluating Public Service

The state universities that were born following the Civil War, and the community colleges that sprang up in the decades following

World War II, placed great importance on their public service roles. Now almost every college or university talks about its service to the public, but faculty report spending only 4 percent of their time in public service (Bowen and Schuster, 1986, p. 15). This may be in part because of the lack of recognition and rewards given to those who are committed to public service. Lynton and Elman (1987) argue that recognition will come only when public service is considered a valid component of scholarship. As we have discussed, Boyer (1990) agreed with their argument.

Dressel (1976) identified three types of public service. The first type, which he referred to as "national missions," employs the model of the land-grant universities, in which agricultural extension agents consulted with farmers. Federal legislation has extended this model to business, industry, urban affairs, and the schools, with colleges and universities using their expertise to help solve problems in all the areas. Dressel's second type of public service is providing assistance to community groups, with faculty from appropriate disciplines addressing whatever needs the groups may have. The third type, continuing education, includes teaching non-degree courses, workshops, and other classes for professionals and other adults. The last category more closely resembles instruction than public service.

According to Elman and Smock (1985), public service includes those activities that draw on faculty members' professional expertise. Faculty members either apply their knowledge and skills to a problem or issue, or to public dissemination of information (Lynton and Elman, 1987). Dressel's first two categories coincide with this definition. Lynton and Elman use the term *professional activity* instead of public service to underscore the application of faculty expertise. They see a continuum of activities, ranging from applied research (which would also qualify as basic research), to teaching or providing information to general audiences (for example, giving continuing education classes.) Between the two ends of the spectrum are contracted research, consultation, technical assistance, policy analysis, program evaluation, targeted briefings, and other didactic activities, such as teaching sessions for newly elected government officials (p. 152).

For public service to be rewarded, proper documentation and

evaluation based on known criteria are needed. Documentation should be included in a faculty member's annual report or portfolio. A written description of the public service activity along with contracts, proposals, final reports, articles, and so forth could be made available. The individual's description of the objectives, intended audience, perceived outcomes, and time involved could also be provided. Criteria for the evaluation would depend on the particular activity and its context. Lynton and Elman (1987, pp. 152–158) offered some evaluation questions derived from basic criteria. Many of the same questions can be asked about other kinds of research, as Lynton and Elman point out. They can be summarized as follows:

1. What was the complexity of the problem or situation and the level of skill needed to deal with it?
2. Were state-of-the art knowledge and methodologies used?
3. Were innovative approaches used? Are they applicable to other contexts? Has the work influenced the faculty member's teaching or research pursuits?
4. Did the final product take into account all factors in reaching conclusions and recommendations? Was the work objective in its presentation of alternative approaches and the advantages and disadvantages of each?

Tenure and promotion committees would need to seek answers to such questions, just as they would in evaluating traditional research. They may need to seek internal and external reviews of public-service activities, as they do when evaluating research. In some cases, they could consider comments by agencies, firms, the public, or others involved in the activity.

Summary

Although research, teaching, and service are often seen as separate and distinct functions, they are related in crucial ways. Some people see them all as different aspects of scholarship and thus want to broaden the definition of that term. Because basic research currently receives the most recognition at many types of institutions, broadening the definition of scholarship may lead to recognition of exemplary performance in teaching and service and strengthen the connections among all three. As the studies reviewed in this chapter reveal, teaching performance has not been found to be strongly related to traditional measures of scholarly productivity.

Quantity and quality have both been used to evaluate research performance; the trend is toward a deeper examination of quality. There are disciplinary differences in research production, including the numbers and types of publications and the stage at which faculty members become most productive; these differences should be considered in summative evaluations. Because of the pressure to publish and the resulting high incidence of scientific misconduct, it is also important to apply ethical norms in summative decisions and to discuss them in graduate training.

Public service has a long tradition as a function of higher education. Yet faculty performance in public service does not receive appropriate recognition. A wide range of faculty activities that draw on professional expertise qualify as public service. Evaluation of faculty performance in public service, like evaluation of research, often requires internal and external reviews of finished products.

Chapter 8

Legal Considerations in Faculty Evaluation

Consider the following four scenarios:

A faculty member at a state college claims that he was
denied tenure without being given reasons for the decision. Moreover, he was not given the option of a
hearing, which he requested, to challenge the decision. He and his lawyer claim that his Fourteenth
Amendment rights were denied. This amendment requires public institutions in particular to defend their
employees' rights to due process and equal protection.
The procedures used to evaluate this faculty member
may indeed have been unfair and a violation of his
due-process rights.

A faculty member at a private college claims that the
institution's faculty handbook specified that written
evaluations by peers, students, and the department
chair be used in assessing teaching, research, and service. Yet these sources were not used in the evaluation
that led to his denial of tenure, he alleges. The faculty

member claims that, under common law, he can sue the college for breach of contract. The institution's lawyers believe that such a suit will be unsuccessful: the institution can produce evidence of formal written evaluations that supports its evaluation of the faculty member.

A faculty member at another college was also denied tenure, and claims that a false negative evaluation had hurt her chances at another position unlawfully, because it was defamation of her character. The college's lawyer is not concerned about this tort claim: she believes that the peers and administrators involved in the decision acted within the scope of their jobs, did not act maliciously, did not invent falsehoods, and took into consideration the faculty member's on-the-job performance.

A female faculty member denied tenure is challenging the decision on the basis of sexual discrimination. Moreover, she believes that she was held to higher standards of performance than are her male peers. Her suit will be based on Title VII of the Civil Rights Act of 1964. She expects to be granted access to peer evaluations because of recent court decisions on the confidentiality of peer reviews.

These are examples of four major legal challenges that institutions face in evaluating faculty members for summative purposes (Lee and Olswang, 1985). Although only the first faculty member described is claiming a violation of his constitutional rights, the First or Fourteenth amendments to the Constitution and various federal statutes are involved in all four cases. Should faculty members and administrators be intimately familiar with these laws and the many interpretations that the various state and national courts have rendered? Probably not, at least not unless they want to make a career of doing so. There are, after all, more than one hundred separate federal jurisdictions and state court systems, any of which may have judged a relevant case. A decision in one of the twelve U.S. circuit courts of appeals or the ninety-four federal district courts represents the law only in the states within their jurisdiction. Even United States Supreme Court decisions, the only decisions binding throughout the country, are subject to varying interpretations. Nevertheless, because of their national significance, this chapter highlights Supreme Court decisions whenever applicable.

Faculty members and administrators should have a general awareness of their legal rights and responsibilities, as stated in federal or state laws and interpreted in court cases; faculty members are both employees, about whom decisions are made, and peers who sit in judgment. In the past few years the confidentiality of peer reviews has been questioned in several court cases. Given the significance of peer judgments in tenure and promotion decisions, the impact of these cases is discussed in this chapter. The chapter also examines the role of legal counsel, faculty contract rights, due-process rights under the Constitution, and potential employment discrimination. The chapter closes with a set of legal guidelines and recommendations for faculty evaluation.

Role of Legal Counsel

Administrators need to work with legal counsel and equal opportunity officers to formulate personnel policies and to reduce the chances of legal challenges. Kaplin (1985) refers to this process as an aspect of preventive law, which he contrasts with the more typical practice of treatment law. In addition to formulating policies and legal parameters, legal counsel can both identify the legal consequences of decisions made by the institutions and determine the impact of new laws or court decisions on institutional policy. Kaplin also suggests that a lawyer and administrator team periodically perform a legal audit to determine whether every office and function on campus is in compliance with "the full range of legal constraints to which it is subject" (Kaplin, 1985, p. 33).

Treatment law is typically put into practice when an institution is sued or wishes to sue. Every institution has or should have legal counsel for this purpose. Some larger institutions employ their own counsel on staff, some arrange with one or more private law firms for legal services, while some use a combination of in-house and private counsel. The practice of preventive law as a proactive measure has not been a priority for colleges and universities but should be as indispensable as treatment law (Kaplin, 1985).

Contract Rights

The first two situations described at the beginning of this chapter are examples of possible breaches of contract rights. One of the faculty members was not given a hearing or told why he was denied tenure; the second claimed that the institution's requirement for use of written evaluations was not fulfilled. While every institution has a contract system, there is considerable variation in what a contract may be. Some contracts are standard notices of appointments which may also refer to other documents, such as the faculty handbook or the American Association of University Professors (AAUP) guidelines. Others may be collective bargaining agreements.

Disputes over the agreement are handled differently and may be subject to National Labor Relations Board (NLRB) jurisdiction, depending on whether an institution is private or public, and, if private, on what type of private institution it is. The Supreme Court's well-known *Yeshiva* decision of 1980 (*NLRB* v. *Yeshiva University*, 100 S. Ct., 856) held that the faculty were "managerial employees" and therefore not covered by the Taft-Hartley Act, which guarantees union membership and collective bargaining. In debating the case, the Supreme Court justices discussed at length the role of faculty and in particular the role of the faculty at Yeshiva University. As the Court's majority opinion stated: "The faculty at each school [within Yeshiva] make the recommendations to the dean or the director in every case of faculty hiring, tenure, sabbaticals, termination, and promotion. Although the final decision is reached by the central administration on the advice of the dean or the director, the overwhelming majority of faculty recommendations are implemented" (100 S. Ct., 860). Yeshiva and institutions like it are thus not subject to the NLRB.

For institutions that are not like Yeshiva, that is, where the faculty has limited decision-making authority, the faculty were not deemed to be managerial employees (*Loretto Heights College* v. *NLRB,* 742 F.2d 245, 10 Cir. 1984). Such institutions are not subject to NLRB jurisdiction and, at this time, neither are public institutions. About half the states allow some form of collective bargaining in public higher education. Several books and monographs have included discussions of the *Yeshiva* decision and other issues related to faculty collective bargaining (for example, Clarke, 1981; Baldridge, Kemerer, and Associates, 1982).

The contract between an institution and its faculty members generally includes established criteria to be used in faculty appointments, promotions, and tenure decisions; the institution may also include the grounds for firing staff and faculty members. Such written criteria and standards are legally binding, and both public and private institutions must comply with the procedures. Criteria usually define what aspects of a performance will be evaluated in decisions, and standards define the desired level of performance. The courts allow institutions to be fairly broad in their statements of criteria and standards. For example, the contract may state that teaching excellence is the primary criterion, and that research or creative activities, together with service, are the others.

Ideally, the weight given to each of the criteria should be specified in the contract. Some institutions, in fact, give the percentage weight for each criterion. If they want to, institutions can vary the criteria or the weight of each criterion by department. Professors in the performing arts, for example, can and probably should be evaluated on different criteria than biology professors. More importantly, it is not the substance of standards or criteria but the procedures for enforcement that concern the courts; these should be uniform for all faculty members. The courts, however, can still subject standards or criteria to legal scrutiny, especially when they are part of the faculty contract. Federal statutes prohibit discriminatory standards or criteria. In the case of public institutions, standards and criteria can be further scrutinized for adherence to the First and Fourteenth amendments (Kaplin, 1985). According to the First Amendment, which guarantees free speech, a standard or criterion cannot be so broadly worded that it restricts a faculty member's right of free expression. And according to the Fourteenth

Amendment, which guarantees procedural due process, standards or criteria must be clear enough that faculty members understand the reasons for their dismissal, their rights to a hearing, and so forth. The courts have not yet entirely determined when standards and criteria in postsecondary education are "overbroad" or "vague," as reflected when a Michigan court did not support a faculty member's suit against Oakland University for negligence in conducting an evaluation of the faculty member (*Dohlman* v. *Oakland University*, 432 N.W.2d 304, Mich. App. 1988).

The specific content of the faculty contract is especially crucial in termination decisions caused by financial exigency or program discontinuance. According to the Statement of Principles on Academic Freedom and Tenure, issued by the AAUP and the Association of American Colleges (AAC) in 1940, "termination of a continuous appointment because of financial exigency should be demonstrably bona fide." But what does bona fide mean here? The *Krotkoff* v. *Goucher College* case (585 F.2d 675, 4th Cir. 1978) probably provides the most far-reaching analysis of this issue (Kaplin, 1985). Krotkoff was a tenured professor of German at Goucher College whose appointment was terminated during a retrenchment caused by a financial shortfall. The court ruled that (1) the contract did not exempt Krotkoff from a bona fide dismissal of exigency, (2) the college did not breach this contract, and (3) the college had made a reasonable effort to find Krotkoff alternative employment at Goucher. These findings were in stark contrast with an earlier case involving Bloomfield College, in which the New Jersey Supreme Court ruled that financial exigency was a pretext for undercutting tenure to replace older faculty members with younger, less costly ones (*AAUP* v. *Bloomfield College*, 129 N.J. Super. 249 322 A.2d 846, 1974).

The written criteria attached to the contract, or those that are implied by the contract, can be used to forestall a potential legal challenge. In one instance, a court ruled that a faculty member could interpret affirmative-action language in the college handbook to mean she had a right to have gender considered in her tenure deliberation (*Sola* v. *Lafayette College*, 804 F.2d 40, 3d Cir. 1986).

To reiterate, criteria and standards not only should be specified in contracts, but should be assigned relative weights, for teaching, research, and any other activity or characteristic indicated.

Constitutional Rights

The constitutional rights that are important in faculty evaluation are the rights to due process under the Fourteenth Amendment and freedom of speech under the First Amendment. Although contracts should spell out due-process procedures at both private and public institutions, employees of public colleges and universities also have constitutional rights to due process. The two landmark cases on constitutional due process are *Board of Regents* v. *Roth*, 408 U.S. 564 (1972), and *Perry* v. *Sindermann*, 408 U.S. 593 (1972). Using the due-process clause, the Supreme Court ruled that faculty members have a right to a fair hearing whenever a personnel decision deprives them of a "property" or "liberty" interest. As stated by the Fourteenth Amendment, states shall not "deprive any person of life, liberty, or property without due process of law."

In the *Roth* case, the Court ruled that there was no legitimate claim to loss of property interest; in the *Perry* case, however, the Court ruled that there was a legitimate claim to loss of property interest. Roth had completed a one-year contract at Wisconsin State University, Oshkosh, and was not rehired. Wisconsin law provided that teachers in any state university be hired for one-year terms and become eligible for tenure after four years of continuous service. Roth was given no reason for nonrenewal nor any opportunity to challenge the decision in a hearing. He alleged that he was dismissed because he had criticized the university administration, and he claimed a violation of his freedom of speech; he also alleged that he was neither given reasons for nonrenewal nor allowed a hearing, a violation of the due-process clause. The Supreme Court reversed lower courts in ruling that the teacher's Fourteenth Amendment rights had not been violated because he had no protected liberty or property interest; the institution was therefore not obligated to provide reasons for nonrenewal or allow a hearing. Concerning liberty interests, the Court stated that no charge had been made against Roth "that might seriously damage his standing and associations in his community." Nor did the Court find that there had been a suggestion that the state "imposed on him a stigma or other disability that foreclosed his freedom to take advantage of other employment activities." Concerning property interests, the Court stated: "To have a property interest in a benefit, a person clearly must have more than an abstract need or desire for it. He must have more than a unilateral expectation of it. He must, instead, have a legitimate claim of entitlement to it" (408 U.S., 578).

Sindermann had been employed in the Texas public college system on a series of one-year contracts for ten consecutive years when the board elected not to rehire him. During his employment he had been openly critical of the board of regents. No reasons were given for the nonrenewal of his contract nor was he given an opportunity for a hearing. Unlike in the Roth case, the Supreme Court ruled that the professor's claim to de facto tenure was genuine. The Court found that an implied contract may have existed, because the tenure guidelines for the particular college and the state system made note that there was no formal tenure system but that "the college wishes the faculty member to feel that he has permanent tenure as long as his teaching services are satisfactory and as long as he displays a cooperative attitude toward his co-workers and his superiors." In light of the politics and practices of the institution, the Court ruled that Sindermann had a legitimate claim to loss of property interest. Although this did not entitle him to reinstatement, it did entitle him to an impartial hearing in which he could be informed of the grounds of his dismissal and challenge their sufficiency.

When an institution has a formal published policy on tenure, a faculty member cannot expect a claim of de facto tenure to be supported as it was in *Perry* v. *Sindermann*. For this reason, every institution should have a formal policy on tenure. In one case, a faculty member who had been at an institution for six years claimed de facto tenure because other faculty members in a position to influence his tenure vote had assured him that he would receive it. The circuit court ruled in the university's favor because it had a formal tenure system (*Haimowitz* v. *U. of Nevada*), 579 F.2d 526, 9th Cir. 1978). Several other cases, including a 1989 decision, affirmed that "a nontenured faculty member of a university has no entitlement to tenure on a de facto basis, where the university has a formal system which provides that tenure may be obtained only by formal grant of such privilege" (*Omlor* v. *Cleveland State University*, 45 Ohio St. 3d 187, 543 N.E. 2d 1238, quote 3d at 189).

Liberty interests under the Fourteenth Amendment can be created when an institution, in the course of nonrenewal, seriously damages the faculty member's reputation or standing in the community. Charges of dishonesty or immorality are examples of actions that could infringe on a faculty member's liberty interests. A nonrenewal that results in a "stigma or other disability," for example because of charges of professional incompetence that may bar the faculty member from other employment, also infringes on liberty interests. Thus, public institutions should be careful about the reasons they give and the evidence they use for nonrenewal and should provide a hearing of charges; taking the case to court, as in most circumstances, should be the last option. If a hearing is held, an impartial person should preside. The confidentiality of the reasons given for nonrenewal or termination, at least in relation to peer reviews, has undergone recent legal challenges that will be discussed later in this chapter.

The *Roth* and *Perry* decisions were applied in a late 1980s case in which tenured faculty members were involuntarily transferred from one engineering department to another within Auburn University (*Maples* v. *Martin*, 858 F.2d 1546, 11th Cir. 1988). The court ruled that the transfer did not infringe on their property or liberty interests. Neither the faculty handbook nor state law protected the professors from the transfers; moreover, because they had not suffered loss of rank or salary and could not show that their professional reputations were damaged, their liberty interests were not infringed on. Finally, the faculty members had been given notice of the transfers and could have used the grievance procedures outlined in the faculty contract, so they had not been denied procedural due process. Thus the court asserted that "transfers and reassignments have generally not been held to implicate a property interest" (858 F.2d, 1550). Under conditions of financial exigency, institutions that apply transfer procedures like those at Auburn would seem to satisfy the Fourteenth Amendment's due-process clause.

In cases involving the First Amendment, state institutions

that have used a faculty member's course content or teaching methods as the basis for nonrenewal have not been found to have infringed on the faculty member's right to free speech. In one case, a faculty member believed that her students should be free to organize assignments according to their individual interests, while the institution expected her to use a more traditional approach. The court refused to accept the faculty member's assertion that her First Amendment rights had been abridged, stating that the right to academic freedom does not exempt a nontenured teacher's teaching style from tenure review. That her methods and philosophy are considered acceptable somewhere in the teaching profession does not make them acceptable at her institution (*Hetrich* v. *Martin*, 480 F.2d 705, 6th Cir. 1973). There were other reasons the college administrators disapproved of her "pedagogical attitude"; still, knowledge of decisions like this one could seriously curtail less traditional approaches to teaching, at least among nontenured individuals at public institutions.

In contrast, accusations of violations of First Amendment rights including academic freedom have been supported by two circuit courts. In a more general instance, for example, the right of a nontenured faculty member to make public statements critical of the administration was upheld (*Smith* v. *Losee* 485 F.2d 334, 10th Cir. 1973). Personal grooming is an example of a private matter that was protected under the First Amendment in *Hander* v. *San Jacinto Junior College*, 519 F.2d 273, 5th Cir. 1975.

Charges of Discrimination

The courts expect the evidence obtained for personnel decisions to be job related and nondiscriminatory. The Constitution and some eight federal statutes, especially Title VII of the Civil Rights Act of 1964, cover employment discrimination. The Constitution is important in discrimination cases for persons not covered by federal statutes, such as people under age forty. Many states also have fair employment practice laws (Kaplin, 1985). Sexual discrimination is covered by Title IV of the Education Amendments Act of 1972, as well as Title VII and other statutes. Age discrimination is covered largely, although not exclusively, by the Age Discrimination in

Employment Act (ADEA). People with disabilities are protected against discrimination by the Rehabilitation Act of 1973 and the Americans with Disabilities Act of 1992.

The most cases by far have arisen under Title VII, which states:

> It shall be an unlawful employment practice for an employer (1) to fail or refuse to hire or to discharge any individual, or otherwise to discriminate against any individual with respect to his compensation, terms, conditions, or privilege of employment, because of such individual's race, color, religion, sex or national origin; or (2) to limit, segregate, or classify his employees or applicants for employment in any way which would deprive or tend to deprive any individual of employment opportunities or otherwise adversely affect his status as an employee, because of such individual's race, color, religion, sex or national origin [p. 254].

Various court cases have established that colleges and universities are subject to the same standards of discrimination as are other types of employers. Title VII does not prevent institutions from distinguishing among faculty members in determining salary, promotion, and tenure decisions as long as the distinctions are not based on race, color, religion, sex, or national origin.

Title VII claims by faculty members are termed either disparate treatment claims or adverse impact claims. Individuals who allege that they have lost a job or been denied a promotion because of discriminatory treatment may file a disparate treatment claim. When an institution's policy has a demonstrated discriminatory impact on a class of people, an adverse impact or disparate impact suit may be filed. The Supreme Court ruled in one case that Title VII protection against discrimination includes white persons (*McDonald* v. *Santa Fe Trail Transportation Co.*, 421 U.S. 273, 1976). Several suits brought by white professors against predominantly black institutions were decided in favor of the plaintiffs by circuit courts. For example, in *Whiting* v. *Jackson State University*,

616 F.2d 116 (5th Cir. 1980), a white professor's claim that his discharge was due to racial discrimination was supported by the U.S. Court of Appeals for the Fifth Circuit.

In the *Board of Trustees of Keene State College* v. *Sweeney,* 439 U.S. 25 (1978) on remand, 604 F.2d 106 (1st Cir. 1980), a female faculty member claimed that she had been denied promotion because of sexism. Although the case also involved critical burden-of-proof issues, the courts ruled in favor of the faculty member because of both the subjectivity of the peer reviews and findings of sexism. Some of the reasons cited by the plaintiff for the denial of her promotion were that "she was perceived as being narrow-minded, rigid, old-fashioned, and . . . she tended to personalize professional matters" (Flygare, 1980, p. 102). Thus, in this instance, both the peer process and sexism were investigated in the court's decisions.

An illuminating study of litigation under Title VII indicated that only one in five faculty members prevailed in suits over denied hiring, promotion, or tenure decisions. LaNoue and Lee (1987) analyzed all published opinions between 1972 and 1984 dealing with Title VII litigation; they also surveyed all participants, and interviewed the plaintiffs, administrators, and others involved in six of the cases. According to LaNoue and Lee, the 20 percent who prevailed encountered further difficulties in their careers; moreover, the authors noted the negative effects of the litigation on campus morale and governance, and in other areas. The goal of Title VII remedies is "to make persons whole for injuries suffered on account of unlawful employment discrimination" (*Albermarle Paper Co.* v. *Moody,* 422, U.S. 405 1975). Based on the results of the LaNoue and Lee study, court decisions are frequently not able to achieve this goal.

Other areas that Title VII and other statutes have dealt with are sexual harassment, other forms of sexual discrimination, and discrimination based on religion and national origin (see Kaplin, 1985, and Kaplin and Lee, 1990, for further discussion).

Confidentiality of Peer Evaluations

Questions about the confidentiality of faculty peer reviews have obvious implications for faculty evaluation. A 1990 Supreme Court decision helped clarify an issue over which four federal appellate courts had been split: whether these reviews can be subpoenaed in contested decisions. In the *University of Pennsylvania* v. *EEOC*, 110 S. Ct. 577 (1990), the court denied that the university had "academic freedom privilege" to withhold the confidential peer evaluations for a plaintiff and five male faculty members. Rosalie Tung, an Asian Wharton School faculty member alleged discrimination based on race and sex in her tenure denial. The Equal Employment Opportunity Commission (EEOC) subpoenaed the confidential peer evaluations and the university denied the request, arguing that releasing the files would destroy collegiality. As in previous suits, the argument presented was that postsecondary institutions are organized on a collegial basis and must maintain the confidential nature of the peer-review process. Legally, the university argued for a First Amendment or a common-law academic freedom privilege (examples of other such privileges are the attorney-client privilege and the priest-penitent privilege). The Court ruled that Title VII does not exclude peer evaluation from discovery, and regarded the possible injury to academic freedom as speculative (Kaplin and Lee, 1990). Postsecondary institutions did not need special treatment, according to the Court.

> We are not so ready as petitioner seems to be to assume the worst about those in the academic community. Although it is possible that some evaluations may become less candid as the possibility of disclosure increases, others may simply ground their evaluations in specific examples and illustrations in order to deflect potential claims of bias or unfairness. Not all academics will hesitate to stand up and be counted when they evaluate their peers [110 S. Ct., 588].

The Supreme Court opinion echoed an earlier Fifth Circuit decision in the highly publicized case of a University of Georgia professor who refused to disclose his vote in a tenure committee decision (in re: *Dinnan*, 661 F.2d 426, 5 Cir. 1981). That court stated that people "must have the courage to stand up and publicly account for [their] decisions" (9, p. 432). Furthermore, the court implied that faculty members should not accept positions on tenure and promotion committees if they cannot handle such responsibility.

The outcome of the *Pennsylvania* case does not mean that any faculty member has access to information used to make a contested employment decision; the faculty member or the EEOC must first file a claim of discrimination to subpoena such information.

Concluding Remarks

Which legal principles should institutions consider in establishing faculty personnel procedures? At the least, public institutions must comply with constitutional due process. Under the Fourteenth Amendment, faculty members at all public institutions are guaranteed due-process rights; faculty members at private institutions are also guaranteed this right if it is specified in their contract, as is often the case. These so-called procedural due-process rights include the right to notice of dismissal and a hearing. Substantive due-process rights include freedom of speech, religion, and privacy under the First and Fourteenth amendments. The particular methods of evaluation or the criteria that institutions apply are of little concern to the courts, but they do expect the information used in personnel decisions to be job related and nondiscriminatory. The courts also prefer that college administrators deal directly with faculty members in disputes over course content, teaching behavior, or classroom behavior, rather than expect that such disputes be handled legally.

Readers who want to learn more about legal issues in faculty evaluation should consult the periodic reviews by Kaplin, and by Kaplin (1985) and Lee (1990) titled *The Law of Higher Education*.

Summary

The following section summarizes guidelines and recommendations for institutions in today's legal climate, based on the discussion in this chapter.

- With the help of legal counsel, institutions should formulate policies that will prevent most legal challenges before they occur. Also, "legal audits" of every office on campus should be conducted periodically. Periodic performance evaluations should also be conducted, to let employees know how they are doing.

- The faculty should be involved in the design of an evaluation system as well as in making evaluations.
- Institutions must comply with procedures specified in the contract or handbook.
- Appraisals should be as accurate and as forthright as possible, providing employees with adequate knowledge of peer performance when appropriate.
- Evidence used for personnel decisions must be job related and nondiscriminatory.
- All decisions should be documented by specific examples of the faculty's performance.
- The faculty member should be allowed to respond to individual evaluation reports or to clarify information.
- Procedures used in internal review of decisions should be available to the staff.
- Standards may vary by subject discipline; this should be taken into account in contracts.
- Teaching styles also vary; allowance should be made for less traditional approaches that can be shown to be effective.
- Judicial review should be avoided if possible. Both the employees involved and the institutions often suffer in consequence, regardless of the decision.

Chapter 9

Closing Reflections
on Determining Faculty Effectiveness

*N*ot yet discussed as a direct source for evaluation of teaching effectiveness are measures of student learning. Can teaching effectiveness be determined by the amount students learn in a course? Should the quality of the assessment measures used by a teacher be considered? Test scores, test score gains, and the criteria that might be used to judge the quality of assessment measures used by teachers are briefly discussed in this chapter. The chapter ends with some final thoughts on evaluating and improving teaching.

Measures of Student Learning

There are no simple explanations for learning. A cartoon I have pictures an indignant boy confronting his teacher with his results on an exam and exclaiming: "I think you'll find that these test results are a good indication of your ability as a teacher."

If only it were so simple! Fortunately, we know that many factors other than teacher competence affect students' examination results. One of these is the student's effort. Even effective teachers can do only so much to motivate students; in fact, some college teachers believe it is not their job to motivate students at all. They argue that college students should be self-motivated and responsible learners or should not be in college. The professors' responsibility, they say, is simply to present the course material. Fortunately, most college teachers do not seem to subscribe to this extreme view, and try to provide students with at least some motivation for learning. However, in the end, students must make an effort to learn. As one of my colleagues says, "I don't teach, I simply cause learning to occur."

Probably of greater importance to examination results than student motivation are the students' prior knowledge of the subject matter and their ability and skills. The results of an end-of-course examination are often heavily influenced by what students knew at the outset. Testing students at the beginning of a course as well as at the conclusion and computing "gain scores" is one way to assess learning. Certainly, teachers who want to measure student learning in this way for their own reflections or to design their instruction would have good reason to employ such a test. But gain scores are both easily misinterpreted and finagled and therefore should not be used for summative purposes.

For teachers to achieve high gain scores they could give a difficult pretest and an easy end-of-course examination. The temptation to "teach to the test" (that is, confine instruction to the material that will be on the final exam) is also great. Moreover, if gain scores were emphasized in decisions, how would an evaluator know when a sizable gain had occurred? What would the basis for comparison be? Other courses would not be likely to provide appropriate comparison; other sections of the same course would not be equivalent either, because both the students and the examinations would likely be very different. In brief, using precise and systematic measures of student learning such as gain scores in teacher evaluations is fraught with pitfalls. But this does not mean that measures of student learning should be ignored. Evidence of student learning and student products in a course (for example, papers, artistic pieces) could be included in a teacher's portfolio, as discussed earlier, although evaluating teacher effectiveness based on them may still be problematic. Writing samples collected at different times in a semester have been used to assess student progress in some writing courses and do not present as many problems in interpretation as do score gains. Learning (or the lack of it) should be considered when a teacher's students perform consistently low in subsequent courses or on the portions of a certification or comprehensive exam that are related to the teacher's courses. Such red-flag occurrences signify a problem, and, barring contrary evidence or explanations, should be investigated during summative deliberations.

Analysis of examination results is critical in improving instruction, especially for self-paced approaches to instruction or for adjusting instruction to suit student needs and ability better (Centra, 1979). If significant numbers of students do not understand an important concept, instructional changes are needed. Consider the following quote by a respected Princeton professor, Marvin Bressler:

> Good teachers evaluate themselves with a pitiless gaze and measure their successes not by their virtuosity as performers but by their contribution to the transformation of students. A lecture, for example, should not be conceived as a self-contained art form but as a vehicle for expanding and deepening students' comprehension of the universe, intellectual and moral. The proper questions are: What was I trying to teach? What, if anything, did they actually learn? What modifications of my teaching repertoire would bring aims and outcomes into closer alignment? Not: Did I perform brilliantly? [McLeery, 1991, p. 14].

Bressler is advocating that teachers look critically not only at how they teach but also, in particular, at what they contribute to the students' growth. Their performance in the classroom and the techniques they use are only effective if they enable their aims and course objectives to be realized.

Judging a Teacher's Assessment Practices

A teacher's course-level assessment practices are an important part of teaching. There are a number of discernible criteria for good assessment practices. The match between the course objectives and the assessment activities used is the first. By looking at examination questions and assignments, it is possible to determine the extent to which the course objectives match the level of understanding that is assessed. It may be the case that while objectives emphasize the higher-order learning skills (such as analysis and critical thinking), examination questions reflect only the lower-level skills (such as knowledge recall) described in the Bloom (1956) taxonomy. It may also be true that examinations focus on a narrow segment of the course. Milton and Edgerly (1976) found that in many instances, teachers' examinations did not represent the entire content of a course and contained ambiguous or poorly worded questions.

Finally, the grading standards used and the feedback given to students reflect the quality of assessment practices. Grading standards should be clearly explained to students and based on the level of understanding stated in the course objectives. The basis for grades should also be stated in the syllabus, and the teacher may further explain it to the class. In addition to providing students with a grade or other assessment of achievement level, teachers should comment on the strengths and weaknesses exhibited in the exams, essays, or projects, and let students know how they can improve future performance. High-quality feedback, while time-consuming, is a great help in furthering learning and development. In sum, all the ways of measuring student learning discussed could be used to evaluate teaching for both formative and summative purposes.

Some Final Thoughts

For some psychometricians, it seems that an object or an effect does not exist unless it can be measured. Yet an old adage seems more applicable to many of life's phenomena: Not everything that counts can be counted and not everything that can be counted counts. Reported to have been posted in Albert Einstein's office, these words epitomize what is most important to remember in the evaluation of teaching, research, and service. Teaching, in particular, is too complex to reduce to quantifiable indicators. Whether based on rating scales or test results, such indicators tend to minimize the kind of thought and reflection that is critical to good evaluation. Some qualification systems prescribed for summative evaluations assign

weights to ratings from different sources and total them for an overall performance score. For example, student evaluation might average 3.90 for an instructor and be assigned a weight of .70 (in other
words, 70 percent of the teaching score). The resulting total of 2.73
(.70 × 3.90) is then added to ratings by colleagues and department
chairs, perhaps weighted at 15 percent each, to arrive at a final score.
The final score implies a level of preciseness and objectivity that
does not exist and, more importantly, may overlook aspects of a
performance that cannot be quantified. An alternative approach,
which does not preclude the use of quantitative measures, is to
encourage narrative reports from chairs, colleagues, students, and
the teachers themselves. In the latter, teachers should address such
major questions as How do I teach? Why do I teach in this way?
What evidence do I have that my technique is effective? The narratives allow evaluators and faculty developers to review the evidence of effectiveness presented and also offer additional information. Such narratives allow evaluators and teachers to clarify their
own values and reasoning as they make judgments; in so doing,
they become aware of the degree of subjectivity inherent in evaluations, and what I have referred to as reflective evaluation is
encouraged.

Reflective evaluation makes use of reflective thinking. John
Dewey (1933) described reflective thinking as a special kind of intellectual activity different from other kinds of thinking; it begins
with a question, hypothesis, or "perplexity" and leads a person to
an inquiry to resolve it. Experience, relevant knowledge, and reasoning ability are all important in this activity. In contrast to routine or impulsive thinking, reflective thinking, according to Dewey,
is disciplined and orderly.

Building on Dewey's theories of inquiry and thinking, Schön
(1983, 1987) applies reflective thinking to professional practice. He
argued that professionals often depend less on established theories
or strict decision-making models than on their own abilities to reflect on what they have done before taking action. Furthermore,
reflection-in-action allows practitioners to modify their actions
while they are doing them. On-the-spot experimentation is used to
test ideas for intended results, but contrary to Dewey's theory, it does
not have to be predicated on a perplexity or hypothesis. What dis-

tinguishes reflection-in-action from other kinds of reflection, according to Schön, is its immediate significance for action, which in turn leads to further thinking about one's activity.

In this book, I have pointed out how teachers might use reflective thinking in describing their teaching. Also discussed were reasons why college teachers should become researchers in the context of their job, and how such informal classroom experiments could then be discussed in their portfolios or annual reports. The portfolio should also include the teacher's reflections about instructional strategies, efforts to set goals and motivate students, and other aspects of their teaching.

Reflection is also important in evaluations because there are no established theories; just as there is no broadly accepted theory of teaching, there is no generally applicable theory of evaluation of teaching. There is, however, a model or framework that can help guide summative and formative evaluations, although it is not a strict decision-making model either. I have earlier referred to it as a comprehensive model of instructional assessment (Centra, 1979, pp. 149–159). The comprehensive model simply advocates the use of multiple sources of information to triangulate or confirm results. Each source—student reports, self-reports, reports by colleagues and chairs, measures of student learning—has particular strengths and limitations. The weight of the accumulated evidence will lead to the most valid summative decisions. Using a variety of evaluation materials can also lead to greater improvement in teaching, because different sources are helpful to different teachers and can help identify weaknesses in different areas of instruction.

College teaching has not changed dramatically over the years. The recent resurgence of interest in involving students as active participants in learning should not be stifled by traditional thinking about teaching evaluation. Teachers, colleagues, administrators, and faculty development specialists all need to reflect first on what is best for student learning and development; they then can determine which evaluation procedures will best contribute.

Available Student
Rating Instruments

A number of student rating forms or systems are available for use by institutions or researchers. Brief descriptions of eight of the most widely used follow. A contact person for each is listed, and, for several, a copy of the instrument is included.

The costs of the forms and scoring are provided for those instruments that are commercially available. Costs are, of course, subject to change. At least two of the instruments are available at no cost; permission to use them should be obtained from the contact person. Finally, most of the instruments listed have been used in research studies. The contact person can also provide a list of these studies.

Name:	Instructional Assessment System (IAS)
Description:	The IAS presently consists of nine distinct forms, each tailored to provide diagnostic information for a broad course type (large lecture, small lecture-discussion, seminar, problem-solving course, skill acquisition course, quiz sec-

tion, homework section, lab section, and clinical section). The forms have three sections. Section 1 contains four global evaluative items whose major purpose is normative. Section 2 contains eleven items designed to provide diagnostic information. Section 3 contains seven items designed to provide information to students as well as to be diagnostic. Sections 1 and 3 contain items common to all forms.

Contact: Gerald M. Gillmore
                    Educational Assessment Center
                    PB-30, University of Washington
                    Seattle, Washington 98195

Specimen Set: A booklet describing the system and containing sample forms and computer-generated results is available at no cost. Various statistical information is available at no cost.

Availability: IAS forms may be purchased alone or together with processing services as well. Forms cost 8 cents each, processing costs 6 cents per sheet scanned, and an additional $1.20 per course or class. Additional reports of results cost 20 cents per class. All postage is also due. The participating institution is responsible for distribution. The rates are the same regardless of the number of classes surveyed.

Name: Instructor and Course Evaluation (ICE)

Description: ICE is an OPSCAN form for student evaluations that is processed through FORTRAN programs on an IBM computer to provide instructor summaries on fifty-six standard items and eighteen optional items. A computerized item bank is available for selection of optional items. Analyses provide mean, standard deviation, and distribution percentage for each of the fifty-six items.

Contact:	Douglas Bedient, Director Instructional Evaluation Southern Illinois University Carbondale, Illinois 62901
Specimen Set:	The instrument and sample output were first made available in June 1978.
Availability:	Contact director
Name:	Instructor and Course Evaluation System (ICES)
Description:	ICES is a computer-based system through which faculty can select items from a catalogue of more than 400 items classified by content (that is, by course management, student outcomes, instructor characteristics and style, instructional environment, student preferences, and settings) and by specificity (global, general concept, and specific). Global and general concept items are normed by rank of instructor and required or elective status whereas specific, or diagnostic, items, recommended for course improvement purposes, are not normed.
Contact:	Richard C. Williams Instructor and Course Evaluation System 307 Engineering Hall 1308 West Green Street University of Illinois Urbana, Illinois 61801
Specimen Set:	The catalogue, instrument, newsletters describing the rationale and suggested uses of ICES, and faculty user's guide are available at no cost.
Availability:	The student questionnaires must be ordered from the University of Illinois and returned to the university for processing. Purchasers will re-

ceive back two copies of a faculty report for
each class section evaluated. Local institutional
norms will be available for the three global
items and items selected as part of an institutional core. The distribution and confidentiality
of the faculty reports is at the discretion of the
local institution. The cost is 27 cents per student questionnaire (on orders of five thousand
or more). Catalogues cost $1.00, and the remain-
ing newsletters are 25 cents.

Name: Instructional Development and Effectiveness
                   Assessment (IDEA) System

Description: Most student rating forms use the teacher's be-
                   havior to define effective teaching. IDEA uses
                   students' ratings of progress on ten course goals
                   selected as "important" or "essential" by the in-
                   structor. Thus, no single model of effective
                   teaching is implied. The diagnostic form (con-
                   taining thirty-eight items with space for fifteen
                   additional items) offers comparisons with all
                   courses in the comparative database. The 1992–
                   93 database includes 104,237 classes from 135
                   colleges and universities selected from a pool of
                   more than 140,000 classes from 257 institutions.
                   Comparisons are also made with similar
                   courses; these courses are similar only in level of
                   motivation—the students' desire to take the
                   course—and class size. "Similar" does not mean
                   the same academic field, although table look-up
                   data are available for forty-four different aca-
                   demic fields (using data from more than 80,000
                   classes). The computer-generated diagnostic
                   summary identifies relevant teaching strengths
                   and weaknesses when three conditions are met:
                   students report unsatisfactory progress on one
                   or more of the teacher's goals; they report that

the instructor did not frequently use specific
teaching methods; the research shows that the
two are related. In the fall of 1991, a fourth page
was added to the report which contains a narrative summary. The narrative summary explains
in words the major findings of the diagnostic
summary. There is also a short (fourteen-item)
evaluation form available for use in personnel
decisions only.

Contact: William Cashin Center for Faculty Evaluation
and Development
Kansas State University
1615 Anderson Avenue
Manhattan, Kansas 66502–1604
Telephone (800) 255-2757

Specimen Set: An information packet includes all the forms, a
sample IDEA report, and a list of the center's
publications. Single packets are available at no
charge. IDEA technical reports and other of the
center's publications are available for purchase.

Availability: There are separate charges for the materials and
the processing; charges vary according to vol-
ume. Materials must be ordered from the center
and returned for computer processing. Purchas-
ers will receive back three copies of an IDEA report for each class. Institutional summary
reports, which combine data from many classes,
can be ordered specially.

Extent of Use: During 1990–91, 106 institutions used IDEA.
They ranged from two-year community colleges
and technical institutes to four-year liberal arts
colleges and research universities. The center
processed the diagnostic form for almost 25,000
classes and the evaluation form for almost 7,000
classes.

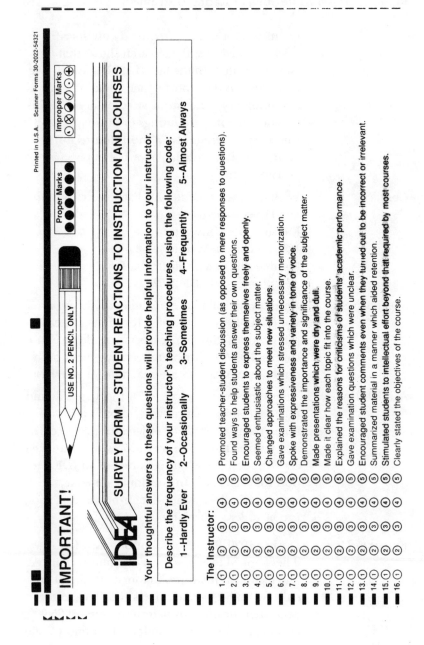

IMPORTANT!

USE NO. 2 PENCIL ONLY

Proper Marks

Improper Marks

Printed in U.S.A. Scanner Forms 30-2022-54321

iDEA SURVEY FORM -- STUDENT REACTIONS TO INSTRUCTION AND COURSES

Your thoughtful answers to these questions will provide helpful information to your instructor.

Describe the frequency of your instructor's teaching procedures, using the following code:

1--Hardly Ever   2--Occasionally   3--Sometimes   4--Frequently   5--Almost Always

The Instructor:

1. Promoted teacher-student discussion (as opposed to mere responses to questions).
2. Found ways to help students answer their own questions.
3. Encouraged students to express themselves freely and openly.
4. Seemed enthusiastic about the subject matter.
5. Changed approaches to meet new situations.
6. Gave examinations which stressed unnecessary memorization.
7. Spoke with expressiveness and variety in tone of voice.
8. Demonstrated the importance and significance of the subject matter.
9. Made presentations which were dry and dull.
10. Made it clear how each topic fit into the course.
11. Explained the reasons for criticisms of students' academic performance.
12. Gave examination questions which were unclear.
13. Encouraged student comments even when they turned out to be incorrect or irrelevant.
14. Summarized material in a manner which aided retention.
15. Stimulated students to intellectual effort beyond that required by most courses.
16. Clearly stated the objectives of the course.

17. ① ② ③ ④ ⑤ Explained course material clearly, and explanations were to the point.
18. ① ② ③ ④ ⑤ Related course material to real life situations.
19. ① ② ③ ④ ⑤ Gave examination questions which were unreasonably detailed (picky).
20. ① ② ③ ④ ⑤ Introduced stimulating ideas about the subject.

On each of the objectives listed below, rate the progress you have made in this course compared with that made in other courses you have taken at this college or university.

In this course my progress was:

1 - Low (lowest 10 percent of courses I have taken here)
2 - Low Average (next 20 percent of courses)
3 - Average (middle 40 percent of courses)
4 - High Average (next 20 percent of courses)
5 - High (highest 10 percent of courses)

Progress on:

21. ① ② ③ ④ ⑤ Gaining factual knowledge (terminology, classifications, methods, trends).
22. ① ② ③ ④ ⑤ Learning fundamental principles, generalizations, or theories.
23. ① ② ③ ④ ⑤ Learning to apply course material to improve rational thinking, problem-solving and decision making.
24. ① ② ③ ④ ⑤ Developing specific skills, competencies and points of view needed by professionals in the field most closely related to this course.
25. ① ② ③ ④ ⑤ Learning how professionals in this field go about the process of gaining new knowledge.
26. ① ② ③ ④ ⑤ Developing creative capacities.
27. ① ② ③ ④ ⑤ Developing a sense of personal responsibility (self-reliance. self-discipline).
28. ① ② ③ ④ ⑤ Gaining a broader understanding and appreciation of intellectual-cultural activity (music. science. literature. etc.).
29. ① ② ③ ④ ⑤ Developing skill in expressing myself orally or in writing.
30. ① ② ③ ④ ⑤ Discovering the implications of the course material for understanding myself (interests. talents. values. etc.).

On the next four questions, **compare this course with others you have taken at this institution**, using the following code:

1--Much Less than Most Courses   2--Less than Most   3--About Average   4--More than Most   5--Much More than Most

The Course:

31. ① ② ③ ④ ⑤   Amount of reading.
32. ① ② ③ ④ ⑤   Amount of work in other (non-reading) assignments.
33. ① ② ③ ④ ⑤   Difficulty of subject matter.
34. ① ② ③ ④ ⑤   Degree to which the course hung together (various topics and class activities were related to each other).

Describe your attitudes toward and behavior in this course, using the following code:

1--Definitely False   2--More False than True   3--In Between   4--More True than False
5--Definitely True

Self-rating:

35. ① ② ③ ④ ⑤   I worked harder on this course than on most courses I have taken.
36. ① ② ③ ④ ⑤   I had a strong desire to take this course.
37. ① ② ③ ④ ⑤   I would like to take another course from this instructor.
38. ① ② ③ ④ ⑤   As a result of taking this course, I have more positive feelings toward this field of study.
39. ① ② ③ ④ ⑤   Leave this space blank. Continue with question A.

For the following questions, A-G, indicate how descriptive each statement is by blackening the proper space.

1--Definitely False   2--More False than True   3--In Between   4--More True than False
5--Definitely True

A. ① ② ③ ④ ⑤   The instructor gave tests, projects, etc., that covered IMPORTANT POINTS of the course.
B. ① ② ③ ④ ⑤   The instructor gave projects, tests, or assignments that required ORIGINAL OR CREATIVE THINKING.
C. ① ② ③ ④ ⑤   I really wanted to take a course FROM THIS INSTRUCTOR.
D. ① ② ③ ④ ⑤   I really wanted to take this course REGARDLESS OF WHO TAUGHT IT.
E. ① ② ③ ④ ⑤   Overall, I rate this INSTRUCTOR an excellent teacher.
F. ① ② ③ ④ ⑤   Overall, I rate this an excellent COURSE.
G. ① ② ③ ④ ⑤   Overall, I LEARNED A GREAT DEAL in this course.

EXTRA QUESTIONS:
If your instructor has extra questions, answer them in the space designated below (questions 40-64).

Your comments are invited on how the instructor might improve this course or teaching procedures.
Use the space below for comments (unless otherwise directed.)
Note: Your written comments will be returned to the instructor.
You may want to PRINT to protect your anonymity.

Institution:

Instructor:

Course No.:

Time and Days Class Meets:

40. ① ② ③ ④ ⑤
41. ① ② ③ ④ ⑤
42. ① ② ③ ④ ⑤
43. ① ② ③ ④ ⑤
44. ① ② ③ ④ ⑤
45. ① ② ③ ④ ⑤
46. ① ② ③ ④ ⑤
47. ① ② ③ ④ ⑤
48. ① ② ③ ④ ⑤
49. ① ② ③ ④ ⑤
50. ① ② ③ ④ ⑤
51. ① ② ③ ④ ⑤
52. ① ② ③ ④ ⑤
53. ① ② ③ ④ ⑤
54. ① ② ③ ④ ⑤
55. ① ② ③ ④ ⑤
56. ① ② ③ ④ ⑤
57. ① ② ③ ④ ⑤
58. ① ② ③ ④ ⑤
59. ① ② ③ ④ ⑤
60. ① ② ③ ④ ⑤
61. ① ② ③ ④ ⑤
62. ① ② ③ ④ ⑤
63. ① ② ③ ④ ⑤
64. ① ② ③ ④ ⑤

Name: Student Instructional Report (SIR)

Description: The Student Instructional Report program in-
                     cludes a machine-scorable answer sheet with
                     thirty-nine questions, plus space for responses
                     to ten additional questions that may be inserted
                     locally. SIR covers such areas as instructor-
                     student interaction, tests and exams, course or-
                     ganization, student interest, and course chal-
                     lenge. Student responses are presented as
                     percentages responding to the alternatives for
                     each item; item means; percentile equivalents of
                     the means; and scores on six factors. Compara-
                     tive data, based on national use of SIR, are
                     available separately for two-year colleges and
                     four-year colleges and universities. Comparative
                     data for approximately thirty academic disci-
                     plines are included.

Contact: Carol Owen
                     Student Instructional Report
                     Educational Testing Service
                     Princeton, New Jersey 08541

Specimen Set: A specimen set is available and includes a sam-
                     ple of the questionnaire, a sample of the out-
                     put, instructions for administering, an order
                     form, a list of institutions that have used SIR,
                     reports on development and uses of SIR, and on
                     reliability and the factor structure ($10.00). Nu-
                     merous research reports on utility, validity, and
                     other issues are available as separate
                     publications.

Availability: SIR is available to any institution or instructor
                     wishing to use it. The questionnaire must be
                     purchased from the Educational Testing Service
                     (ETS). Answer sheets are available for ETS scor-
                     ing and reporting or for local scoring (NCS and

Scantron Scanners). ETS scoring and reporting results in three copies of a two-page report for each class or section in which SIR is administered. Reports are returned to the purchaser within three weeks of receipt by ETS of the completed answer sheets. Combined reports are available when designated by the purchaser (such as departmental reports, total institutional reports, and so forth).

	Costs	*Answer sheets sold in packages of fifty*
Answer sheets ordered		*Answer sheets scored*

First	20,000(	1–20,000)	$.25	First	5,000(	1– 5,000)	$.40
Next	20,000(20,001–40,000)		.22	Next	15,000(5,001–20,000)		.38
Next	20,000(40,001–60,000)		.18	Next	20,000(20,001–40,000)		.35
Over	60,000(60,001+	)	.15	Next	20,000(40,001–60,000)		.33
				Over	60,000(60,001+	)	.25

There are cumulative price reductions for the answer sheets and scoring from one year to the next for each institution that uses the instrument over time.

STUDENT INSTRUCTIONAL REPORT

This questionnaire gives you an opportunity to express anonymously your views of this course and the way it has been taught. Indicate the response closest to your view by filling in the appropriate circle. Use a soft lead pencil (No. 2) for all responses to the questionnaire. Do not use a pen (ink, ball-point, or felt-tip).

SIR Report Number

SECTION I. Items 1-20. Fill in one response number for each question.

NA (0) = Not Applicable or don't know. The statement does not apply to this course or instructor, or you simply are not able to give a knowledgeable response.

SA (4) = Strongly Agree. You strongly agree with the statement as it applies to this course or instructor.

A (3) = Agree. You agree more than you disagree with the statement as it applies to this course or instructor.

D (2) = Disagree. You disagree more than you agree with the statement as it applies to this course or instructor.

SD (1) = Strongly Disagree. You strongly disagree with the statement as it applies to this course or instructor.

	NA	SA	A	D	SD
1. The instructor's objectives for the course have been made clear	0	4	3	2	1
2. There was considerable agreement between the announced objectives of the course and what was actually taught	0	4	3	2	1
3. The instructor used class time well	0	4	3	2	1
4. The instructor was readily available for consultation with students	0	4	3	2	1
5. The instructor seemed to know when students didn't understand the material	0	4	3	2	1
6. Lectures were too repetitive of what was in the textbook(s)	0	4	3	2	1
7. The instructor encouraged students to think for themselves	0	4	3	2	1
8. The instructor seemed genuinely concerned with students' progress and was actively helpful	0	4	3	2	1

9. The instructor made helpful comments on papers or exams ....
10. The instructor raised challenging questions or problems for discussion ....
11. In this class I felt free to ask questions or express my opinions ....
12. The instructor was well prepared for each class ....
13. The instructor told students how they would be evaluated in the course ....
14. The instructor summarized or emphasized major points in lectures or discussions ....

15. My interest in the subject area has been stimulated by this course ....
16. The scope of the course has been too limited; not enough material has been covered ....
17. Examinations reflected the important aspects of the course ....
18. I have been putting a good deal of effort into this course ....
19. The instructor was open to other viewpoints ....
20. In my opinion, the instructor has accomplished (is accomplishing) his or her objectives for the course ....

SECTION II. Items 21-31. Fill in one response number for each question.

21. For my preparation and ability, the level of difficulty of this course was:
① Very elementary ④ Somewhat difficult
② Somewhat elementary ⑤ Very difficult
③ About right

22. The work load for this course in relation to other courses of equal credit was:
① Much lighter ④ Heavier
② Lighter ⑤ Much heavier
③ About the same

23. For me, the pace at which the instructor covered the material during the term was:
① Very slow ④ Somewhat fast
② Somewhat slow ⑤ Very fast
③ Just about right

24. The instructor used examples or illustrations to help clarify the material:
④ Frequently ② Seldom
③ Occasionally ① Never

Questionnaire continued on the other side. ➤

I.N. 401642

25. Was class size satisfactory for the method of conducting the class?
① Yes, most of the time
② No, class was too large
③ No, class was too small
④ It didn't make any difference one way or the other

26. Which one of the following best describes this course for you?
① Major requirement or elective within major field
② Minor requirement or required elective outside major field
③ College requirement but not part of my major or minor field
④ Elective not required in any way
⑤ Other

27. Which one of the following was your most important reason for selecting this course?
① Friend(s) recommended it
② Faculty advisor's recommendation
③ Teacher's excellent reputation
④ Thought I could make a good grade
⑤ Could use pass/no credit option
⑥ It was required
⑦ Subject was of interest
⑧ Other

28. What grade do you expect to receive in this course?
① A
② B
③ C
④ D
⑤ Fail
⑥ Pass
⑦ No credit
⑧ Other

29. What is your approximate cumulative grade-point average?
① 3.50-4.00
② 3.00-3.49
③ 2.50-2.99
④ 2.00-2.49
⑤ 1.50-1.99
⑥ 1.00-1.49
⑦ Less than 1.00
⑧ None yet - first year or transfer

30. What is your class level?
① Freshman
② Sophomore
③ Junior
④ Senior
⑤ Graduate
⑥ Other

31. Sex:
① Female
② Male

SECTION III. Items 32-39. Fill in one response number for each question.

	Not applicable, don't know, or there were none	Poor	Fair	Satisfactory	Good	Excellent
32. Overall, I would rate the textbook(s)	⓪	①	②	③	④	⑤
33. Overall, I would rate the supplementary readings	⓪	①	②	③	④	⑤
34. Overall, I would rate the quality of the exams	⓪	①	②	③	④	⑤

35. I would rate the general quality of the lectures .... ⑤ ④ ③ ② ①

36. I would rate the overall value of class discussions .... ⑤ ④ ③ ② ①

37. Overall, I would rate the laboratories .... ⑤ ④ ③ ② ①

38. I would rate the overall value of this course to me as .... ⑤ ④ ③ ② ①

39. How would you rate the quality of instruction in this course? (Try to set aside your feelings about the course itself.) Fill in one response number.

Excellent	Good	About Average	Fair	Poor
⑤	④	③	②	①

	NA										
40.	ⓞ	①	②	③	④	⑤	⑥	⑦	⑧	⑨	
41.	ⓞ	①	②	③	④	⑤	⑥	⑦	⑧	⑨	
42.	ⓞ	①	②	③	④	⑤	⑥	⑦	⑧	⑨	
43.	ⓞ	①	②	③	④	⑤	⑥	⑦	⑧	⑨	

SECTION IV. Items 40-49. If the instructor provided supplementary questions and response options, use this section for responding. Fill in only one response number for each question.

	NA										
44.	ⓞ	①	②	③	④	⑤	⑥	⑦	⑧	⑨	
45.	ⓞ	①	②	③	④	⑤	⑥	⑦	⑧	⑨	
46.	ⓞ	①	②	③	④	⑤	⑥	⑦	⑧	⑨	
47.	ⓞ	①	②	③	④	⑤	⑥	⑦	⑧	⑨	
48.	ⓞ	①	②	③	④	⑤	⑥	⑦	⑧	⑨	
49.	ⓞ	①	②	③	④	⑤	⑥	⑦	⑧	⑨	

If you would like to make additional comments about the course or instruction, use a separate sheet of paper. You might elaborate on the particular aspects you liked most as well as those you liked least. Also, how can the course or the way it was taught be improved? PLEASE GIVE THESE COMMENTS TO THE INSTRUCTOR.

If you have any comments, suggestions, or complaints about this questionnaire (for example, the content or responses available), please send them to: Student Instructional Report. Educational Testing Service, Princeton, New Jersey 08541.

ETS 1642

92 93 Mark Reflex` by NCS EP-45305:321   Printed in U.S.A.

Name: Student Instructional Rating System (SIRS)

Description: The Student Instructional Rating System is a
                     means of collecting, analyzing, displaying, and
                     interpreting student reactions to classroom in-
                     struction and course content. SIRS is designed
                     to assess student reactions to provide feedback
                     for use in instructional improvement and in ad-
                     ministrative decisions regarding instructors.
                         The resolution of the academic council
                     establishing the present SIRS stipulates that ev-
                     ery teaching unit shall approve one or more stu-
                     dent rating instruments; each teaching unit
                     shall make regular and systematic use of student
                     instructional ratings as part of the evaluation of
                     instructional performance; and every instructor
                     shall use unit-approved instructional rating
                     forms in all classes. In addition, results of in-
                     structional ratings shall be returned promptly
                     to the instructor for use in improving course de-
                     sign and instruction.
                         A standard SIRS form is available to
                     Michigan State University teaching units that
                     choose to adopt it. The form contains twenty
                     items on five factors: instructor involvement,
                     student interest, student-instructor interaction,
                     course demands, and course organization. In ad-
                     dition to the twenty items, there are four stu-
                     dent background items, one general affect item,
                     and space for responses to eight optional items
                     generated by the instructor. Instructors receive
                     back an SIRS report that includes the frequency
                     distribution, the mean and standard deviation
                     of the responses to individual items, and the
                     mean and standard deviation of the five SIRS
                     factors.

Contact: ·   Professor LeRoy A. Olson
Computer Laboratory
Michigan State University
East Lansing, Michigan 48824

Specimen Set: Available

Availability: While SIRS materials are copyrighted, educational institutions may request permission to adapt the SIRS form for their own use. Forms and processing are available on a contract basis.

MICHIGAN STATE UNIVERSITY
STUDENT INSTRUCTIONAL RATING SYSTEM

Your instructor hopes to use your thoughtful responses for the improvement of instruction. Please omit any of the items which do not pertain to the course that you are rating. With a number 2 pencil, respond to the items using the **KEY**. ⟶

S - SUPERIOR: exceptionally good course or instructor
AA - ABOVE AVERAGE: better than the typical course or instructor
AV - AVERAGE: typical of courses or instructors
BA - BELOW AVERAGE: not as good as the typical course or instructor
I - INFERIOR: exceptionally poor course or instructor

S AA AV BA I

1. The instructor's enthusiasm when presenting course material
2. The instructor's interest in teaching
3. The instructor's use of examples or personal experiences to help get points across in class
4. The instructor's concern with whether the students learned the material
5. Your interest in learning the course material
6. Your general attentiveness in class
7. The course as an intellectual challenge
8. Improvement in your competence in this area due to this course
9. The instructor's encouragement to students to express opinions
10. The instructor's receptiveness to new ideas and others' viewpoints
11. The student's opportunity to ask questions
12. The instructor's stimulation of class discussion
13. The appropriateness of the amount of material the instructor attempted to cover
14. The appropriateness of the pace at which the instructor attempted to cover the material
15. The contribution of homework assignments to your understanding of the course material relative to the amount of time required
16. The appropriateness of the difficulty of assigned reading topics
17. The instructor's ability to relate the course concepts in a systematic manner
18. The course organization
19. The ease of taking notes on the instructor's presentation
20. The adequacy of the outlined direction of the course
21. Your general enjoyment of the course

STUDENT BACKGROUND: Select the most appropriate alternative.

22. Was this course required in your degree program?   Yes No
23. What is your sex?   M F
24. What is your overall GPA? (a) 1.9 or less (b) 2.0-2.2 (c) 2.3-2.7 (d) 2.8-3.3 (e) 3.4-4.0   A B C D E
25. What is your class level? (a) Freshman (b) Sophomore (c) Junior (d) Senior (e) Graduate or other   A B C D E

O-14018

1 ① ② ③ ④ ⑤   3 ① ② ③ ④ ⑤   5 ① ② ③ ④ ⑤   7 ① ② ③ ④ ⑤

2 ① ② ③ ④ ⑤   4 ① ② ③ ④ ⑤   6 ① ② ③ ④ ⑤   8 ① ② ③ ④ ⑤

STUDENT INSTRUCTIONAL RATING SYSTEM FORM (Written Comments)

One way in which an instructor can improve his or her class is through thoughtful student reactions. This instructor hopes to use your responses for self-examination and self-improvement. If you have any comments to make concerning the instructor or the course, please write them in the shaded area below.

Do Not Write In This Area

The Michigan State University **Code of Teaching Responsibility** holds all instructors to certain obligations with respect to, e.g., course content consistent with approved descriptions, timely statement of course objectives and grading criteria, regular class attendance, published office hours, and timely return of examinations and term papers. This **Code** is printed in full in the **Schedule of Courses and Academic Handbook.** It includes specifics about complaint procedures available to students who believe that their instructors have violated the **Code**.

Name: Purdue's Cafeteria System

Description: Purdue's Cafeteria System consists of four FOR-
                      TRAN computer programs, a two hundred–
                      page operations manual, a computer-managed
                      catalogue containing two hundred diagnostic
                      items, and a norm library. The system can be
                      installed for local operation easily on virtually
                      any computer with FORTRAN capability, and
                      it functions equally well as a sheet- or a card-
                      based system. Cafeteria supports both adminis-
                      trative and instructional improvement
                      processes.

Contact: M. J. Cree
                      CIS, STEW 1092
                      Purdue University
                      West Lafayette, Indiana 47907–1092

Specimen Set: Available.

Availability: Cafeteria was designed for installation at local
                      institutions as a locally operated service. The
                      one-time fee for the system is $955; the system is
                      shipped, on floppy disks, within five working
                      days of receipt of a purchase order. Institutions
                      may elect to contract for evaluation services
                      from Purdue Center for Instructional Services.
                      CIS provides all materials, and the cost is ap-
                      proximately 34 cents per student evaluator.

INSTRUCTOR AND COURSE APPRAISAL

PLEASE RESPOND TO ANY ITEMS IN THIS SECTION BY MARKING THE APPROPRIATE SPACES.
USE NO 2 PENCIL ONLY   ERASE CHANGES OR CORRECTIONS COMPLETELY.

0001   SAMPLE   QUESTIO   NNAIRE

CLASS		SCHOOL		SCI		EXPECTED		COURSE	
----------	O	----------	O	TECH	O	GRADE	O	REQUIRED	O
FRESHMAN	O	AGR	O	VET SCI	O	----------	O	----------	O
SOPHOMORE	O	ENGR	O	HLS	O	A/PASS	O	YES	O
JUNIOR	O	CFS	O	SEX		B	O	NO	O
SENIOR	O	HSSE	O	----------		C	O		O
GRADUATE	O	MGMT	O	FEMALE	O	D	O		O
OTHER	O	PHARM	O	MALE	O	F/FAIL	O		O

SAMPLE RESPONSE

PLEASE READ EACH STATEMENT CAREFULLY. THEN SELECT ONE OF THESE FIVE ALTERNATIVES:
STRONGLY AGREE (SA), AGREE (A), UNDECIDED (U), DISAGREE (D), STRONGLY DISAGREE (SD).

SA ● U D SD

MY INSTRUCTOR DISPLAYS A CLEAR UNDERSTANDING OF COURSE TOPICS.
MY INSTRUCTOR HAS AN EFFECTIVE STYLE OF PRESENTATION.
MY INSTRUCTOR SPEAKS AUDIBLY AND CLEARLY.
MY INSTRUCTOR HOLDS THE ATTENTION OF THE CLASS.
MY INSTRUCTOR STIMULATES INTEREST IN THE COURSE.
MY INSTRUCTOR DISPLAYS ENTHUSIASM WHEN TEACHING.
THIS COURSE SUPPLIES ME WITH AN EFFECTIVE RANGE OF CHALLENGES.
MY INSTRUCTOR HAS STIMULATED MY THINKING.
MY INSTRUCTOR HAS PROVIDED MANY CHALLENGING NEW VIEWPOINTS.
MY INSTRUCTOR TEACHES ONE TO VALUE THE VIEWPOINT OF OTHERS.
MY INSTRUCTOR ENCOURAGES STUDENT CREATIVITY.
MY INSTRUCTOR EMPHASIZES CONCEPTUAL UNDERSTANDING OF MATERIAL.
MY INSTRUCTOR MAKES GOOD USE OF EXAMPLES AND ILLUSTRATIONS.
MY INSTRUCTOR IS ACTIVELY HELPFUL WHEN STUDENTS HAVE PROBLEMS.
MY INSTRUCTOR IS CAREFUL AND PRECISE WHEN ANSWERING QUESTIONS.
MY INSTRUCTOR IS READILY AVAILABLE FOR CONSULTATION.
MY INSTRUCTOR REGULARLY CHECKS AND REWARDS PROGRESS IN LEARNING.
MY INSTRUCTOR SUGGESTS SPECIFIC WAYS I CAN IMPROVE.
MY INSTRUCTOR TAILORS THIS COURSE TO HELP MANY KINDS OF STUDENTS.
I WAS ABLE TO KEEP UP WITH THE WORK LOAD IN THIS COURSE.
I AM FREE TO EXPRESS AND EXPLAIN MY OWN VIEWS IN CLASS.
WHEN I HAVE A QUESTION OR COMMENT I KNOW IT WILL BE RESPECTED.
MY INSTRUCTOR RELATES TO ME AS AN INDIVIDUAL.
MY INSTRUCTOR READILY MAINTAINS RAPPORT WITH THIS CLASS.
I UNDERSTAND WHAT IS EXPECTED OF ME IN THIS COURSE.
THIS COURSE MATERIAL IS PERTINENT TO MY PROFESSIONAL TRAINING.
MY TECHNICAL SKILLS WERE IMPROVED AS A RESULT OF THIS COURSE.
THERE IS SUFFICIENT TIME IN CLASS FOR QUESTIONS AND DISCUSSIONS.
THIS COURSE PROVIDES AN OPPORTUNITY TO LEARN FROM OTHER STUDENTS.
EXAMS ACCURATELY ASSESS WHAT I HAVE LEARNED IN THIS COURSE.
EXAMS STRESS IMPORTANT POINTS OF THE LECTURES/TEXT.
EXAMS ARE COORDINATED WITH MAJOR COURSE OBJECTIVES.
GRADES ARE ASSIGNED FAIRLY AND IMPARTIALLY.
THE GRADING SYSTEM WAS CLEARLY EXPLAINED.
DIRECTIONS FOR COURSE ASSIGNMENTS ARE CLEAR AND SPECIFIC.
THE NUMBER OF COURSE ASSIGNMENTS IS REASONABLE.
STUDENT PRESENTATIONS SIGNIFICANTLY CONTRIBUTE TO THIS COURSE.
I WOULD ENJOY TAKING ANOTHER COURSE FROM THIS INSTRUCTOR.
THESE ITEMS LET ME APPRAISE THIS COURSE FULLY AND FAIRLY.
MY INSTRUCTOR IDENTIFIES MAJOR OR IMPORTANT POINTS IN THE COURSE.
MY INSTRUCTOR MOTIVATES ME TO DO MY BEST WORK.
MY INSTRUCTOR EXPLAINS DIFFICULT MATERIAL CLEARLY.
COURSE ASSIGNMENTS ARE INTERESTING AND STIMULATING.
OVERALL, THIS COURSE IS AMONG THE BEST I HAVE EVER TAKEN.
OVERALL, THIS INSTRUCTOR IS AMONG THE BEST TEACHERS I HAVE KNOWN.

STUDENTS' EVALUATION OF EDUCATIONAL QUALITY (SEEQ)

Do not put your name on this survey. Please complete it as accurately and as candidly as possible. This is part of a larger project to improve teaching effectiveness at the University. The purpose of this survey is to provide your lecturer with feedback about his/her teaching effectiveness. For this reason you should base your responses on his/her teaching in this subject. If any items are not applicable simply put NA in the corresponding blank.

Instructor _____ Subject/Class _____ Date ____ / ____ /91

Please indicate the EXTENT of your agreement/disagreement with the following statements as descriptions of this subject by using the following scale.

NA	1	2	3	4	5	6	7	8	9
Not Applicable	Strongly Disagree		Disagree		Neutral		Agree		Strongly Agree

LEARNING/ACADEMIC VALUE

____ You found the class intellectually challenging and stimulating.

____ You have learned something which you considered valuable.

____ Your interest in the subject has increased as a consequence of this class.

____ You have learned and understood the subject materials in this class.

INSTRUCTOR ENTHUSIASM

____ Lecturer was enthusiastic about teaching the class.

____ Lecturer was dynamic and energetic in conducting the class.

____ Lecturer enhanced presentations with the use of humour.

____ Lecturer's style of presentation held your interest during class.

ORGANISATION/CLARITY

____ Lecturer's explanations were clear.

____ Class materials were well prepared and carefully explained.

____ Proposed objectives agreed with those actually taught so you knew where the class was going.

____ Lecturer gave presentations that facilitated taking notes.

____ Lecturer made students feel welcome in seeking help/advice in or outside of class.

____ Lecturer was adequately accessible to students during office hours or after class.

BREADTH OF COVERAGE

____ Lecturer contrasted the implications of various theories.

____ Lecturer presented the background or origin of ideas/concepts developed in class.

____ Lecturer presented points of view other than his/her own when appropriate.

____ Lecturer adequately discussed current developments in the field.

EXAMINATIONS/GRADING

____ Feedback on examinations/graded material was valuable.

____ Methods of evaluating student work were fair and appropriate.

____ Examinations/graded materials tested class content as emphasised by the lecturer.

ASSIGNMENTS/READINGS

____ Required readings/texts were valuable.

GROUP INTERACTION

___ Students were encouraged to participate in class discussions.

___ Students were invited to share their ideas and knowledge.

___ Students were encouraged to ask questions and were given meaningful answers.

___ Students were encouraged to express their own ideas and/or question the lecturer.

INDIVIDUAL RAPPORT

___ Lecturer was friendly towards individual students.

___ Lecturer had a genuine interest in individual students.

BACKGROUND SUBJECT/CLASS CHARACTERISTICS

___ Subject difficulty, relative to other subjects, was (1-Very Easy..3-Easy..5-Medium..7-Hard..9-Very Hard).

___ Subject workload, relative to other subjects, was (1-Very Light..3-Light..5-Medium..7-Heavy..9-Very Heavy).

___ Subject pace was (1-Too slow..5-About Right..9-Too Fast).

___ Average number of hours per week required outside of class (0=none, 1=1 hr., 2=2 hrs., etc.).

___ Gender(1-Male,2-Female)

___ Your expected subject mark: (1-Fail, 2-Pass, 3-Credit, 4-Dist, 5-Hi Dist, 6-Other)

___ Your marks in previous university subjects (1-Mostly Passes with a few Fails, 2-Mostly Passes, 3-Mostly Passes with a few Credits, 4-Mostly Credits, 5-Mostly Distinctions and High Distinctions, NA-no previous marks)

___ Readings, homework, etc. contributed to appreciation and understanding of the subject.

OVERALL RATING

___ Overall, how does this class compare with other classes at this institution? (1-Very Poor...3-Poor...5-Average...7-Good... 9-Very Good)

___ Overall, how does this lecturer compare with other lecturers at this institution? (1-Very Poor...3-Poor...5-Average...7-Good... 9-Very Good)

___ Based on a representative sample of 100 university lecturers at this institution, how would you rank this lecturer (1=Lowest...50=Average...100=Highest).

___ In comparison with other subjects at this institution, how easy is it to get good marks in this subject. (1-Very Easy.. 3-Easy..5-About Average.. 7-Difficult.. 9-Very Difficult).

___ Reason For Taking Subject (1-Course Requirement, 2-Course Elective, 3-General Education Elective Programme, 5-General Interest Only, 6-Other)

___ Level of interest in the subject before the start of the class (1-Very Low..3-Low..5-Medium..7-High..9-Very High).

___ Course (1-Assoc Dip, 2-Undergrad Dip, 3-Undergrad Degree, 4-Grad Dip, 5-Masters, 6-PhD, 7-Other)

___ Year in Course (1-1st, 2-2nd, 3-3rd, 4-4th)

___ Your School (1-Arts & Gen Stud, 2-Bus & Tech, 3-Educ & Lang, 4-Comm & Welf, 5-Nursing, 6-Other.)

LECTURER-SUPPLIED QUESTIONS (leave blank if no additional questions are provided)

1. ___   3. ___   5. ___   7. ___   9. ___   11. ___   13. ___   15. ___

2. ___   4. ___   6. ___   8. ___   10. ___   12. ___   14. ___   16. ___

Please Turn Over

c 1976, 1991 Professor Herbert W. Marsh

OPEN-ENDED COMMENTS

Your written comments will be returned to your lecturer. If you have concern for your anonymity, please print your comments.

Please indicate the important characteristics of this lecturer/class that have been most valuable to your overall learning experience.

1. _____

_____

_____

2. _____

_____

_____

3. _____

_____

_____

Please indicate characteristics of this lecturer/class that you feel are most important for him/her to improve (particularly aspects not covered by the rating items).

1. _____

_____

_____

_____

2. _____

_____

_____

3. _____

_____

_____

Please use the additional space to clarify any of your responses or to make other comments.

_____

_____

_____

_____

Name: Student's Evaluation of Educational Quality
                   (SEEQ) Instrument (U.S. and Australian
                   versions)

Description: Included here is a somewhat "Australianized"
                   version of the SEEQ instrument (incorporating
                   minor modifications to reflect Australian spell-
                   ing and usage). Interested faculty members are
                   invited to use the instrument freely for their
                   own individual purposes. People interested in
                   using SEEQ on a wider scale are requested to
                   obtain permission from Herbert Marsh; permis-
                   sion will be given free of charge. This proce-
                   dure allows the application and performance of
                   the SEEQ to be monitored. In addition, the first
                   author can provide preliminary software mate-
                   rial to analyze the questionnaire and produce
                   individualized summary reports.
                           Certain background items and sometimes
                   the introductory paragraph need to be modified
                   to suit individual institutions. The term *in-
                   structor,* used on the American version, may be
                   more appropriate than *lecturer,* used in some
                   Australian settings. All other aspects of the
                   questionnaire should be left intact.

Contact: Herbert Marsh
                   University of Western Sydney, Macarthur
                   P.O. Box 555
                   Campbelltown, NSW 2560
                   Australia

Resource B

Sample Forms
for Classroom Observation
and Colleague Evaluation

Many colleges have composed their own classroom observation and peer evaluation forms. Following are observation forms developed at Syracuse University (Centra, Froh, Gray, and Lambert, 1987), and a peer evaluation form developed by Grace French-Lazovik in 1979.

Technique: Classroom Observations by Colleagues

Evaluators: Faculty and Appropriate Administrators

Purpose: Along with student ratings of instruction, classroom observation is one of the more frequently used forms of instructional evaluation. Direct observations provide a counterpoint to the view offered by student rating surveys, alumni surveys, or administrator comments.

                    At some institutions, members of the promotion and tenure committee, or other faculty, visit classes and report observations in an unstructured way. They may comment on such items as discussion topics, mastery of content, and student interest level. Objectivity is ensured when they conduct a number of observations before making decisions.

Other institutions have developed both a worksheet to guide the observations and a procedure for the performance of the observations. For example, a committee may be designated to conduct all classroom observations. This more structured process helps ensure that a full picture of the evaluated professor's strengths and weaknesses is presented.

Classroom observations are typically complemented by a number of the other observation and evaluation techniques, particularly reviews of course materials and syllabi.

Including this additional information is critical because such a small number of people can actually make the observations, the selection of the classes is necessarily limited, and the specific characteristics evaluated are only a small sample of the total that could be observed. It is useful for the instructor and the observer to meet before an observation to summarize course objectives and materials and determine areas of focus for the observation. Moreover, it is critical that as many observations as possible take place over as long a period of time as possible to afford a more comprehensive basis for conclusions.

Example: Classroom Observation Factors
The following list of items can be used to guide classroom observations. Sample items, with appropriate scaled-response and open-ended questions, are listed under each effective teaching characteristic. The characteristics shown are examples of those that can be evalu-

ated during a classroom observation; others, such as fairness in examination and grading, are not possible to evaluate in this way.

Good organization of subject matter and course

Scaled-response items:
Made a clear statement of the purpose of the lesson
Presented topics in a logical sequence
Summarized the major points of the lesson

Written-response question:
How did the instructor demonstrate organization of the subject matter?

Effective communication

Scaled-response items:
Projected voice so it was easily heard
Listened to student questions and comments
Offered examples to clarify points

Written-response question:
What were the most and least helpful things the instructor did to communicate effectively?

Knowledge of and enthusiasm for both the subject matter and teaching

Scaled-response items:
Presented material appropriate to the stated purpose of the lesson
Demonstrated command of the subject matter
Encouraged student involvement

Motivated students through
own enthusiasm for the
subject

Written-response question: What content appeared to be
the most and least suitable to
the lesson?

Positive attitude toward students

Scaled-response items: Encouraged student discussion
Encouraged students to answer
difficult questions
Used questions to determine if
students were having
difficulty

Written-response question: How did the instructor show
interest in the students and
their learning?

Flexibility in approaches to teaching

Scaled-response items: Used appropriate instructional
techniques
Made appropriate choices between presentation and
discussion

Written-response question: To what extent did the instructor vary the instructional
methods for the material
presented? What other methods might have been
appropriate?

Classroom Observation Worksheet

Instructor _____ Course _____

Date _____ Observer _____

Directions: Below is a list of instructor behaviors that may occur within a given class or course. Please use it as guide to making observations, not as a list of required characteristics. When this worksheet is used for making improvements to instruction, it is recommended that the instructor highlight the areas to be focused on before the observation takes place.

Respond to each statement using the following scale:

Not observed	More emphasis recommended	Accomplished very well
1	2	3

Circle the number at the right that best represents your response. Use the comment space below each section to provide more feedback or suggestions.

Content Organization	*Not observed* 1	*More emphasis recommended* 2	*Accomplished very well* 3
1. Made clear statement of the purpose of the lesson	1	2	3
2. Defined relationship of this lesson to previous lessons	1	2	3
3. Presented overview of the lesson	1	2	3
4. Presented topics with a logical sequence	1	2	3
5. Paced lesson appropriately	1	2	3
6. Summarized major points of lesson	1	2	3
7. Responded to problems raised during lesson	1	2	3
8. Related today's lesson to future lessons	1	2	3

Comments:

Presentation	Not observed	More emphasis recommended	Accomplished very well
	1	2	3
9. Projected voice so easily heard	1	2	3
10. Used intonation to vary emphasis	1	2	3
11. Explained things with clarity	1	2	3
12. Maintained eye contact with students	1	2	3
13. Listened to student questions and comments	1	2	3
14. Projected nonverbal gestures consistent with intentions	1	2	3
15. Defined unfamiliar terms, concepts, and principles	1	2	3
16. Presented examples to clarify points	1	2	3
17. Related new ideas to familiar concepts	1	2	3
18. Restated important ideas at appropriate times	1	2	3
19. Varied explanations for complex and difficult material	1	2	3
20. Used humor appropriately to strengthen retention and interest	1	2	3
21. Limited use of repetitive phrases and hanging articles	1	2	3

Comments:

Instructor-Student Interactions	Not observed 1	More emphasis recommended 2	Accom- plished very well 3
22. Encouraged student questions	1	2	3
23. Encouraged student discussion	1	2	3
24. Maintained student attention	1	2	3
25. Asked questions to monitor students' progress	1	2	3
26. Gave satisfactory answers to student questions	1	2	3
27. Responded to nonverbal cues of confusion, boredom, and curiosity	1	2	3
28. Paced lesson to allow time for note taking	1	2	3
29. Encouraged students to answer difficult questions	1	2	3
30. Asked probing questions when student answer was incomplete	1	2	3
31. Restated questions and answers when necessary	1	2	3
32. Suggested questions of limited interest to be handled outside of class	1	2	3

Comments:

Instructional Materials and Environment	Not observed 1	More emphasis recommended 2	Accomplished very well 3
33. Maintained adequate classroom facilities	1	2	3
34. Prepared students for the lesson with appropriate assigned readings	1	2	3
35. Supported lesson with useful classroom discussions and exercises	1	2	3
36. Presented helpful audio-visual materials to support lesson organization and major points	1	2	3
37. Provided relevant written assignments	1	2	3

Comments:

Content Knowledge and Relevance	Not observed 1	More emphasis recommended 2	Accomplished very well 3
38. Presented material worth knowing	1	2	3
39. Presented material appropriate to student knowledge and background	1	2	3
40. Cited authorities to support statements	1	2	3
41. Presented material appropriate to stated purpose of course	1	2	3
42. Made distinctions between fact and opinion	1	2	3
43. Presented divergent viewpoints when appropriate	1	2	3
44. Demonstrated command of subject matter	1	2	3

Comments:

45. What overall impressions do you think students left this lesson with in terms of content or style?

46. What were the instructor's major strengths as demonstrated in this observation?

47. What suggestions do you have for improving upon this instructor's skills?

SUGGESTED FORM FOR PEER REVIEW OF UNDERGRADUATE TEACHING BASED ON DOSSIER MATERIALS

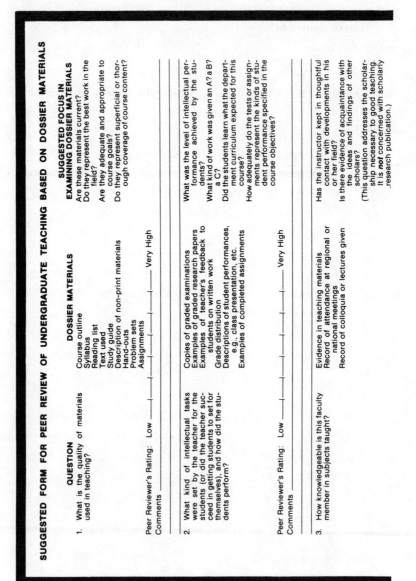

QUESTION	DOSSIER MATERIALS	SUGGESTED FOCUS IN EXAMINING DOSSIER MATERIALS
1. What is the quality of materials used in teaching?	Course outline Syllabus Reading list Text used Study guide Description of non-print materials Hand-outs Problem sets Assignments	Are these materials current? Do they represent the best work in the field? Are they adequate and appropriate to course goals? Do they represent superficial or thorough coverage of course content?

Peer Reviewer's Rating: Low ——|——|——|——|—— Very High

Comments _____

| 2. What kind of intellectual tasks were set by the teacher for the students (or did the teacher succeed in getting students to set for themselves), and how did the students perform? | Copies of graded examinations
Examples of graded research papers
Examples of teacher's feedback to students on written work
Grade distribution
Descriptions of student performances, e.g., class presentation, etc.
Examples of completed assignments | What was the level of intellectual performance achieved by the students?
What kind of work was given an A? a B? a C?
Did the students learn what the department curriculum expected for this course?
How adequately do the tests or assignments represent the kinds of student performance specified in the course objectives? |

Peer Reviewer's Rating: Low ——|——|——|——|—— Very High

Comments _____

| 3. How knowledgeable is this faculty member in subjects taught? | Evidence in teaching materials
Record of attendance at regional or national meetings
Record of colloquia or lectures given | Has the instructor kept in thoughtful contact with developments in his or her field?
Is there evidence of acquaintance with the ideas and findings of other scholars?
(This question addresses the scholarship necessary to good teaching. It is *not* concerned with scholarly research publication.) |

Peer Reviewer's Rating: Low ————|————|————|————|———— Very High

Comments —————————————————————————

4. Has this faculty member assumed responsibilities related to the department's or University's teaching mission?

Record of service on department curriculum committee, honors program, advising board of teaching support service, special committees (e.g., to examine grading policies, admission standards, etc.)

Description of activities in supervising graduate students learning to teach.

Evidence of design of new courses.

Has he or she become a departmental or college citizen in regard to teaching responsibilities?

Does this faculty member recognize problems that hinder good teaching and does he or she take a responsible part in trying to solve them?

Is the involvement of the faculty member appropriate to his or her academic level? (e.g., assistant professors may sometimes become over-involved to the detriment of their scholarly and teaching activities.)

Peer Reviewer's Rating: Low ————|————|————|————|———— Very High

Comments —————————————————————————

5. To what extent is this faculty member trying to achieve excellence in teaching?

Factual statement of what activities the faculty member has engaged in to improve his or her teaching.

Examples of questionnaires used for formative purposes.

Examples of changes made on the basis of feedback.

Has he or she sought feedback about teaching quality, explored alternative teaching methods, made changes to increase student learning?

Has he or she sought aid in trying new teaching ideas?

Has he or she developed special teaching materials or participated in cooperative efforts aimed at upgrading teaching quality?

Peer Reviewer's Rating: Low ————|————|————|————|———— Very High

Comments —————————————————————————

——————————————————————————————
Peer Reviewer's Signature

——————————————————————————————
Date

G.F. LAZOVIK 1979
UNIVERSITY OF PITTSBURGH

REFERENCES

Abbott, A. *The System of Professions*. Chicago: University of Chicago Press, 1988.

Abbott, R. D., Wulff, D. H., and Kati Szego, C. "Review of Research on Teaching Assistant Training." In J. D. Nyquist, R. D. Abbott, and D. H. Wulff (eds.), *Teaching Assistant Training in the 1990s*. New Directions for Teaching and Learning. San Francisco: Jossey-Bass, 1989.

Abrami, P. C., and d'Apolonia, S. "The Dimensionality of Ratings and Their Use in Personnel Decisions." In M. Theall, and J. Franklin (eds.), *Student Ratings of Instruction: Issues for Improving Practice*. New Directions for Teaching and Learning, no. 43. San Francisco: Jossey-Bass, 1990.

Abrami, P. C., d'Apolonia, S., and Cohen, P. A. "The Validity of Student Ratings of Instruction: What We Know and What We Don't." *Journal of Educational Psychology*, 1990, *82*, 219-231.

Abrami, P. C., Levanthal, L., and Perry, R. P. "Educational Seduction." *Review of Educational Research*, 1982, *52*, 446-464.

Aleamoni, L. M. "Student Ratings of Instruction." In J. Millman (ed.), *Handbook of Teacher Evaluation*. Newbury Park, Calif.: Sage, 1981, 110-145.

Angelo, T. A. (ed.). *Classroom Research: Early Lessons from Success.* New Directions for Teaching and Learning, no. 46. San Francisco: Jossey-Bass, 1991.

Axelrod, J. *The University Teacher as Artist: Toward an Aesthetics of Teaching with Emphasis on the Humanities.* San Francisco: Jossey-Bass, 1973.

Baird, L. L. "The Relationship Between Ratings of Graduate Departments and Faculty Publication Rates." Research Report 80–127. Princeton, N.J.: Educational Testing Service, 1980.

Baldridge, J. V., Kemerer, F., and Associates. *Assessing the Impact of Faculty Collective Bargaining.* ASHE-ERIC Higher Education Report, no. 8. Washington, D.C.: Association for the Study of Higher Education, 1982.

Baldwin, R. G. "Faculty Career Stages and Implications for Professional Development." In J. H. Schuster, D. W. Wheeler, and Associates (eds.), *Enhancing Faculty Careers: Strategies for Development and Renewal.* San Francisco: Jossey-Bass, 1990.

Barber, L. W. "Self-Assessment." In J. Millman, and L. Darling-Hammond (eds.), *The New Handbook of Teacher Evaluation.* Newbury Park, Calif.: Sage, 1990, 216–228.

Barnes, S. B., and Dolby, R.G.A. "The Scientific Ethos: A Deviant Viewpoint." *European Journal of Sociology,* 1970, *11,* 3–25.

Basow, S. A., and Silberg, N. T. "Student Evaluations of College Professors: Are Female and Male Professors Rated Differently?" *Journal of Educational Psychology,* 1987, *79,* 308–314.

Belenky, M. F., Clinchy, B. M., Goldberger, N. R., and Tarule, J. M. *Women's Ways of Knowing.* New York: Basic Books, 1986.

Bennett, S. K. "Student Perceptions of and Expectations for Male and Female Instructors: Evidence Relating to the Question of Gender Bias in Teaching Evaluation." *Journal of Educational Psychology,* 1982, *74,* 170–179.

Bennett, W. E. "Small Group Instructional Diagnosis: A Dialogic Approach to Instructional Improvement for Tenured Faculty." *The Journal of Staff, Program, and Organizational Development,* 1987, *5*(3), 100–104.

Berlant, J. L. *Profession and Monopoly.* Berkeley: University of California Press, 1975.

Bird, T. "The Schoolteacher's Portfolio: An Essay on Possibilities."

In J. Millman, and L. Darling-Hammond (eds.), *The New Handbook of Teacher Evaluation: Assessing Elementary and Secondary School Teachers*. Newbury Park, Calif.: Sage, 1990, 241–256.

Black, D. *The Behavior of Law*. San Diego: Academic Press, 1976.

Blackburn, R. T., and Clark, M. J. "An Assessment of Faculty Performance: Some Correlates Between Administrators, Colleagues, Student, and Self-Ratings." *Sociology of Education*, 1975, *48*, 242–256.

Blackburn, R. T., Pellino, G., Boberg, A., and O'Connell, C. "Are Instructional Improvement Programs Off-Target?" *Current Issues in Higher Education*, 1980, 32–48.

Blau, J. R. "Study of the Arts: A Reappraisal." *Annual Review of Sociology*, 1988, *14*, 269–292.

Bloom, B. S. (ed.). *Taxonomy of Educational Objectives*. Vol. 1: *Cognitive Domain*. New York: McKay, 1956.

Boice, R. "New Faculty as Teachers." *Journal of Higher Education*, 1991, *62*, 150–173.

Boice, R. *The New Faculty Member*. San Francisco: Jossey-Bass, 1992.

Bonwell, C. C., and Eison, J. A. *Active Learning: Creating Excitement in the Classroom*. ASHE-ERIC Higher Education Report, no. 1. Washington, D.C.: School of Education and Human Development, George Washington University, 1991.

Bowen, H. R., and Schuster, J. H. *American Professors, A National Resource Imperiled*. New York: Oxford University Press, 1986.

Boyer, E. L. *Scholarship Reconsidered: Priorities of the Professoriate*. Lawrenceville, N.J.: Princeton University Press, 1990.

Braskamp, L. A., Brandenburg, D. C., and Ory, J. C. *Evaluating Teaching Effectiveness*. Newbury Park, Calif.: Sage, 1984.

Braskamp, L. A., and Caulley, D. "Student Rating and Instructor Self-Ratings and Their Relationship to Student Achievement." Urbana-Champaign: Measurement and Research Division, University of Illinois, 1978.

Braskamp, L. A., Ory, J. C., and Pieper, D. M. "Student Written Comments: Dimensions of Instructional Quality." *Journal of Educational Psychology*, 1981, *73*, 65–70.

Braxton, J. M. "The Normative Structure of Science: Social Control in the Academic Profession." In J. C. Smart (ed.), *Higher Edu-*

cation: Handbook of Theory and Research, Vol. 2. New York: Agathon Press, 1986, 309–357.

Braxton, J. M. "The Influence of Graduate Department Quality on the Sanctioning of Scientific Misconduct." *Journal of Higher Education,* 1991, *62(1),* 87–108.

Braxton, J. M., Bayer, A. E., and Finkelstein, M. J. "Teaching Performance Norms in Academia." *Research in Higher Education,* 1992, *33(5),* 533–569.

Broad, W. J. "Fraud and the Structure of Science." *Science,* Apr. 10, 1981, *212,* 137–141.

Brubacher, J. S., and Rudy, W. *Higher Education in Transition.* New York: HarperCollins, 1976.

Bruffee, K. A. "Liberal Education and the Social Justification of Belief." *Liberal Education,* 1982, *68,* 95–114.

Bruffee, K. A. *A Short Course in Writing.* Boston: Little, Brown, 1985.

Bucher, R., and Strauss, A. "Professions in Process." *American Journal of Sociology,* 961, *66,* 325–334.

Burns, R. "To a Louse." *The Poetical Works of Robert Burns.* Edinburgh: James Nichol, 1856.

Callahan, D. "Should There Be an Academic Code of Ethics?" *Journal of Higher Education,* 1982, *53(3),* 335–344.

Camp, R. C., Gibbs, M. C., Jr., and Masters, R. J., II. "The Finite Increment Faculty Merit Pay Allocation Model." *Journal of Higher Education,* 1988, *59,* 652–667.

Carnegie Foundation for the Advancement of Teaching. National Survey of Faculty, 1989. In Boyer, E. L. *Scholarship Reconsidered: Priorities of the Professoriate.* Lawrenceville, N.J.: Princeton University Press, 1990.

Carroll, G. "Effects of Training Programs for University Teaching Assistants." *Journal of Higher Education,* 1980, *51,* 167–183.

Cashin, W. E. "Students Do Rate Different Academic Fields Differently." In M. Theall and J. Franklin (eds.), *Student Ratings of Instruction: Issues for Improving Practice.* New Directions for Teaching and Learning, no. 43. San Francisco: Jossey-Bass, 1990.

Centra, J. A. *The Student Instructional Report: Its Development and Uses.* Student Instructional Report, no. 1. Princeton, N.J.: Educational Testing Service, 1972a.

Centra, J. A. *The Utility of Student Ratings for Instructional Improvement.* Project Report 72-16. Princeton, N.J.: Educational Testing Service, 1972b.

Centra, J. A. "Effectiveness of Student Feedback in Modifying College Instruction." *Journal of Educational Psychology,* 1973a, *65(3),* 395-401.

Centra, J. A. "Self-Ratings of College Teachers: A Comparison with Student Ratings." *Journal of Educational Measurement,* 1973b, *10(4),* 287-295.

Centra, J. A. *Item Reliabilities, the Factor Structure, Comparison with Alumni Ratings.* Student Instructional Report, no. 3. Princeton, N.J.: Educational Testing Service, 1973c.

Centra, J. A. "The Relationship Between Student and Alumni Ratings of Teachers." *Educational and Psychological Measurement,* 1974, *34(2),* 321-326.

Centra, J. A. "Colleagues as Raters of Classroom Instruction." *Journal of Higher Education,* 1975, *46,* 327-337.

Centra, J. A. "The Influence of Different Directions on Student Ratings of Instruction." *Journal of Educational Measurement,* 1976, *13(4),* 277-282.

Centra, J. A. *How Universities Evaluate Faculty Performance: A Survey of Department Heads.* GREB Research Report, no. 75-56R. Princeton, N.J.: Educational Testing Service, 1977a.

Centra, J. A. "Student Ratings of Instruction and Their Relationship to Student Learning." *American Educational Research Journal,* 1977b, *14,* 17-24.

Centra, J. A. "Faculty Development in Higher Education." *Teachers College Record,* 1978a, *80,* 188-201.

Centra, J. A. "Using Student Assessments to Improve Performance and Vitality." In W. R. Kirschling (ed.), *Evaluating Faculty Performance and Vitality.* New Directions for Institutional Research, no. 20. San Francisco: Jossey-Bass, 1978b.

Centra, J. A. *Determining Faculty Effectiveness.* San Francisco: Jossey-Bass, 1979.

Centra, J. A. "Research Productivity and Teaching Effectiveness." *Research in Higher Education,* 1983, *18(2),* 379-389.

Centra, J. A. "Faculty Evaluation: Past Practices, Future Directions." Manhattan: Kansas State University, Center for Faculty Evaluation and Development, 1987.

Centra, J. A. *The Use of the Teaching Portfolio and the Student Instructional Report (SIR) for Summative Evaluation.* SIR Report no. 6. Princeton, N.J.: Educational Testing Service, 1992.

Centra, J. A., and Bonesteel, P. "College Teaching: An Art or a Science?" In M. Theall, and J. Franklin (eds.), *Student Ratings of Instruction: Issues for Improving Practice.* New Directions for Teaching and Learning, no. 43. San Francisco: Jossey-Bass, 1990.

Centra, J. A., and Creech, F. R. *The Relationship Between Student Teachers and Course Characteristics and Student Ratings of Teacher Effectiveness.* Project Report 76-1. Princeton, N.J.: Educational Testing Service, 1976.

Centra, J., Froh, R. C., Gray, P. J., and Lambert, L. M. *A Guide to Evaluating Teaching for Promotion and Tenure.* Acton, Mass.: Copley Publishing Group, 1987.

Chandelar, S. "Issues in Evaluating Multi-Institutional Models." Paper presented at the American Educational Research Association symposium, Chicago, Apr. 1991.

Chickering, A. W., and Gamson, Z. "Seven Principles for Good Practice in Undergraduate Education." *American Association for Higher Education Bulletin,* 1987, *39,* 3–7.

Chickering, A. W., and Gamson, Z. (eds.). *Applying the Seven Principles for Good Practice in Undergraduate Education.* New Directions for Teaching and Learning, no. 47. San Francisco: Jossey-Bass, 1991.

Clark, K. E. *America's Psychologists: A Survey of a Growing Profession.* Washington, D.C.: American Psychological Association, 1957.

Clarke, C. A. "The Yeshiva Case: An Analysis and an Assessment of its Potential Impact on Public Universities." *Journal of Higher Education,* 1981, *52,* 449–469.

Cleery, W. "A Teacher Reflects." *Princeton Alumni Weekly,* Nov. 25, 1992, pp. 11–14.

Cohen, P. A. "Using Student Rating Feedback for Improving College Instruction: A Meta-Analysis of Findings." *Research in Higher Education,* 1980, *13,* 321–341.

Cohen, P. A. "Student Ratings of Instruction and Student Achievement: A Meta-Analysis of Multisection Validity Studies." *Review of Educational Research*, 1981, *51*, 281–309.

Cohen, P. A., and McKeachie, W. J. "The Role of Colleagues in the Evaluation of College Teaching." *Improving College and University Teaching*, 1980, *28*, 147–154.

Cole, S. "Age and Scientific Performance." *American Journal of Sociology*, 1979, *84(4)*, 958–977.

Cole, S., and Cole, J. R. "Scientific Output and Recognition: A Study in the Operation of the Reward System in Science." *American Sociological Review*, 1967, *32(3)*, 377–399.

Cross, K. P. " 'What's in That Black Box?' or 'How Do We Know What Students Are Learning?' " Howard R. Bowen lecture presented at the Claremont Graduate School, Claremont, California, Nov. 8, 1989.

Cross, K. P. "Classroom Research: Helping Professors Learn More About Teaching and Learning." In P. Seldin and Associates (eds.), *How Administrators Can Improve Teaching: Moving from Talk to Action in Higher Education*. San Francisco: Jossey-Bass, 1990.

Cross, K. P., and Angelo, T. A. *Classroom Assessment Techniques: A Handbook for Faculty*. Ann Arbor, Mich.: National Center for Research to Improve Postsecondary Teaching and Learning, 1988.

Deci, E. L. *Intrinsic Motivation*. New York: Plenum, 1975.

Deci, E. L., and Ryan, R. M. *Intrinsic Motivation and Self-Determination in Human Behavior*. New York: Plenum, 1985.

Deming, W. E. *Out of the Crisis*. Cambridge: Center for Advanced Engineering Study, Massachusetts Institute of Technology, 1982.

Dewey, J. *How We Think*. Lexington, Mass.: Heath, 1933.

Dill, D. D. "Introduction: Ethics and the Academic Profession." *Journal of Higher Education*, 1982, *53(3)*, 243–254.

Donlon, T. F. (ed.), *The College Board Technical Handbook for The Scholastic Aptitude Test and Achievement Tests*. New York: College Entrance Examination Board, 1984.

Dowell, D. A., and Neal, J. A. "A Selective Review of the Validity of Student Ratings of Teaching." *Journal of Higher Education*, 1982, *53*, 51–62.

Doyle, K. O., Jr., and Webber, P. L. "Self-Ratings of College Instruction." Minneapolis: Measurement Services Center, University of Minnesota, 1978. Mimeograph.

Dressel, P. L. *Handbook of Academic Evaluation: Assessing Institutional Effectiveness, Student Progress, and Professional Performance for Decision Making in Higher Education.* San Francisco: Jossey-Bass, 1976.

Dressel, P. L. *College Teachers as a Profession: The Doctor of Arts Degree.* East Lansing: Michigan State University (with assistance from the Carnegie Corporation), 1982.

Drucker, A. J., and Remmers, H. H. "Do Alumni and Students Differ in Their Attitudes Toward Instructors?" *Journal of Educational Psychology,* 1951, *42(3)*, 129–143.

Eble, K. E. *The Aims of College Teaching.* San Francisco: Jossey-Bass, 1983.

Eble, K. E., and McKeachie, W. J. *Improving Undergraduate Education Through Faculty Development: An Analysis of Effective Programs and Practices.* San Francisco: Jossey-Bass, 1985.

Edgerton, R., Hutchings, P., and Quinlan, K. *The Teaching Portfolio: Capturing the Scholarship in Teaching.* Washington, D.C.: The American Association for Higher Education, 1991.

Educational Testing Service. *Comparative Data Guide, Student Instructional Report.* Princeton, N.J.: College and University Programs, Educational Testing Service, 1979.

Educational Testing Service. *Interpretative Guide and Comparative Data, Student Instructional Report.* Princeton, N.J.: Higher Education Assessment, Educational Testing Service, 1990.

Elliot, D. H. "Characteristics and Relationships of Various Criteria of College and University Teaching." *Purdue University Studies in Higher Education,* 1950, *70*, 5–61.

Elman, S. E., and Smock, S. *Professional Service and Faculty Rewards: Toward an Integrated Structure.* Washington, D.C.: National Association of State Universities and Land-Grant Colleges, 1985.

Erickson, G. "A Survey of Faculty Development Practices." *To Improve the Academy,* 1986, *5*, 182–193.

Feldman, K. A. "The Superior College Teacher from the Student's View." *Research in Higher Education,* 1976, *5*, 243–288.

Feldman, K. A. "Course Characteristics and College Students' Ratings of Their Teachers and Courses: What We Know and What We Don't." *Research in Higher Education,* 1978, *9,* 199–242.

Feldman, K. A. "The Significance of Circumstances for College Students' Ratings of Their Teachers and Courses." *Research in Higher Education,* 1979, *10,* 149–171.

Feldman, K. A. "Class Size and College Students' Evaluations of Teachers and Courses: A Closer Look." *Research in Higher Education,* 1984, *21,* 45–115.

Feldman, K. A. "The Perceived Instructional Effectiveness of College Teachers as Related to Their Personality and Attitudinal Characteristics: A Review and Synthesis." *Research in Higher Education,* 1986, *24,* 139–213.

Feldman, K. A. "Research Productivity and Scholarly Accomplishments: A Review and Exploration." *Research in Higher Education,* 1987, *26,* 227–298.

Feldman, K. A. "Effective College Teaching from the Students' and Faculty's View: Matched or Mismatched Priorities?" *Research in Higher Education,* 1988, *28,* 291–344.

Feldman, K. A. "Instructional Effectiveness of College Teachers as Judged by Teachers Themselves, Current and Former Students, Colleagues, Administrators and External (Neutral) Observers." *Research in Higher Education,* 1989, *30,* 137–189.

Feldman, K. A. "College Students' Views of Male and Female College Teachers: Part I—Evidence from the Social Laboratory and Experiments." *Research in Higher Education,* 1992, *33(3),* 317–375.

Feldman, K. A. "College Students' Views of Male and Female College Teachers: Part II—Evidence from Students' Evaluations of Their Classroom Teachers." *Research in Higher Education,* 1993, *34(2),* 151–211.

Festinger, L. A. *A Theory of Cognitive Dissonance.* Stanford, Calif.: Stanford University Press, 1957.

Flygare, T. J. "Board of Trustees of Keene State College v. Sweeney: Implications for the Future of Peer Review in Faculty Personnel Decisions." *Journal of College and University Law,* 1980, *7,* 100–110.

Fox, P. W., and LeCount, J. "When More Is Less: Faculty Misestimation of Student Learning." Paper presented at the American Educational Research Association, Chicago, Apr. 1991.

Frankhouser, W. M., Jr. "The Effects of Different Oral Directions as to Disposition of Results on Student Ratings of College Instruction." *Research in Higher Education*, 1984, *20*, 367-374.

Franklin, J., and Theall, M. "Who Reads Ratings: Knowledge, Attitudes, and Practice of Users of Student Ratings of Instruction." Paper presented at the American Educational Research Association, San Francisco, Apr. 1989.

Franklin, J., and Theall, M. "Communicating Student Ratings to Decision Makers: Design for Good Practice." In M. Theall, and J. Franklin (eds.), *Student Ratings of Instruction: Issues for Improving Practice*. New Directions for Teaching and Learning, no. 43. San Francisco: Jossey-Bass, 1990.

Frederick, P. J. "Student Involvement: Active Learning in Large Classes." In M. G. Weimer (ed.), *Teaching Large Classes Well*. New Directions for Teaching and Learning, no. 32. San Francisco: Jossey-Bass, 1987.

Freire, P. *Pedagogy of the Oppressed*. New York: Seaview, 1971.

French-Lazovik, G. "Peer Review: Documentary Evidence in the Evaluation of Teaching." In J. Millman (ed.), *Handbook of Teacher Evaluation*. Newbury Park, Calif.: Sage, 1981, 73-89.

Fuhrmann, B. S., and Grasha, A. F. *A Practical Handbook for College Teachers*. Boston: Little, Brown, 1983.

Gage, N. L. *The Scientific Basis of the Art of Teaching*. New York: Teachers College Press, 1978.

Gagne, R. M., and Dick, W. "Instructional Psychology." *Annual Review of Psychology*, 1983, *34*, 261-295.

Garfield, E. *Citation Indexing: Its Theory and Application in Science, Technology, and Humanities*. New York: Wiley, 1979.

Gilmore, G. M., Kane, M. T., and Naccarato, R. W. "The Generalizability of Student Ratings of Instruction: Estimation of Teacher and Course Components." *Journal of Educational Measurement*, 1978, *15(1)*, 1-13.

Gray, P. J., Froh, R. C., and Diamond, R. M. *A National Study of Research Universities on the Balance Between Research and Undergraduate Teaching*. Syracuse, New York: Center for Instructional Development, Syracuse University, 1992.

Guthrie, E. R. *The Evaluation of Teaching: A Progress Report.* Seattle: University of Washington Press, 1954.

Hackman, J. R., and Lawler, E. E. "Employee Reactions to Job Characteristics." *Journal of Applied Psychology,* 1970, *55,* 259–286.

Hackman, J. R., and Oldham, G. R. "Work Design in the Organizational Context." *Research in Organizational Behavior,* 1980, *2,* 247–278.

Hagstrom, W. D. "Inputs, Outputs, and the Prestige of University Science Departments." *Sociology of Education,* 1971, *44,* 375–397.

Heider, F. *The Psychology of Interpersonal Relationships.* New York: Wiley, 1958.

Hiemstra, R., and Sisco, B. *Individualizing Instruction.* San Francisco: Jossey-Bass, 1990.

Higher Education Research Institute. *The American College Teacher: National Norms for the 1989–90 H.E.R.I. Faculty Survey.* Los Angeles: University of California, 1991.

Highet, G. *The Art of Teaching.* New York: Vintage Books, 1959.

Hilts, P. J. "A Question of Ethics." *The New York Times,* Aug. 2, 1992 (*4A*), 26–28.

Holmes, D. S. "Effects of Grades and Disconfirmed Grade Expectancies on Students' Evaluations of Their Instructor." *Journal of Educational Psychology,* 1972, *63,* 130–133.

Hoyt, D. P. "Interrelations Among Instructional Effectiveness, Publication Record, and Monetary Reward." *Research in Higher Education,* 1974, *2,* 81–88.

Jauch, L. R. "Relationships of Research and Teaching: Implications for Faculty Evaluation." *Research in Higher Education,* 1976, *5,* 1–13.

Kane, J. S., and Lawler, E. E. "Methods of Peer Assessment." *Psychological Bulletin,* 1978, *85,* 555–586.

Kaplin, W. A. *The Law of Higher Education.* San Francisco: Jossey-Bass, 1985.

Kaplin, W. A., and Lee, B. A. *The Law of Higher Education, 1985–1990 Update.* Washington, D.C.: National Association of College and University Attorneys, 1990.

Kaschak, E. "Sex Bias in Student Evaluations of College Professors." *Psychology of Women Quarterly,* 1978, *3,* 235-243.

Kaschak, E. "Another Look at Sex Bias in Students' Evaluations of Professors: Do Winners Get the Recognition That They Have Been Given?" *Psychology of Women Quarterly,* 1981, *5,* 767-772.

Katz, J., and Henry, M. *Turning Professors into Teachers: A New Approach to Faculty Development and Student Learning.* New York: Macmillan, 1988.

Keith-Spiegel, P., and Koocher, G. P. *Ethics in Psychology.* New York: Random House, 1985.

Keller, F. "Goodbye Teacher. . . ." *Journal of Applied Behavior Analysis,* 1968, *1,* 79-89.

Kremer, J. "Constant Validity of Multiple Measures in Teaching, Research, and Service and Reliability of Peer Ratings." *Journal of Educational Psychology,* 1990, *82,* 213-218.

Kulik, J. A., Kulik, C.L.C., and Cohen, P. "A Meta-Analysis of Outcome Studies of Keller's Personalized System of Instruction." *American Psychologist,* 1979, *34,* 307-318.

LaNoue, G. R., and Lee, B. A. *Academics in Court: The Consequences of Faculty Discrimination Litigation.* Ann Arbor: University of Michigan Press, 1987.

Lee, B. A., and Olswang, S. G. "Legal Parameters of the Faculty Employment Relationships." In J. Smart (ed.), *Higher Education: Handbook of Theory and Research,* Vol. 1. New York: Agathon Press, 1985, 213-253.

Lepper, M. R., and Green, D. (eds.). *The Hidden Costs of Reward.* New Jersey: Erlbaum, 1978.

Levanthal, L., and others. "Experimental Investigation of Tenure/ Promotion in American and Canadian Universities." Paper presented at the American Educational Research Association, Los Angeles, Apr. 1981.

Levinson, D. J., and others. *The Seasons of a Man's Life.* New York: Ballantine, 1978.

L'Hommedieu, R., Menges, R. J., and Brinko, K. T. "The Effects of Student Ratings Feedback to College Teachers: A Meta-Analysis and Review of Research." Unpublished manuscript, Center for the Teaching Professions, Northwestern University, 1988.

Lichtenstein, S., and Fischhoff, B. "Do Those Who Know More Also Know More About How Much They Know?" *Organizational Behavior and Human Performance*, 1977, *20*, 159–183.

Lin, Y. G., McKeachie, W. J., and Tucker, D. G. "The Use of Student Ratings in Promotion Decisions." *Journal of Higher Education*, 1984, *55*, 583–589.

Linn, R. L., Centra, J. A., and Tucker, L. "Between, Within, and Total Group Factor Analyses of Student Ratings of Instruction." *Multivariate Behavioral Research*, 1975, *10*, 277–288.

Lloyd, M. E., and Lloyd, K. E. "Has Lightning Struck Twice? Use of PSI in the College Classroom." *Teaching of Psychology*, 1986, *133*, 149–151.

Lombardo, J., and Tocci, M. "Attribution of Positive and Negative Characteristics of Instructors as a Function of Attractiveness and Sex of Instructor and Sex of Subject." *Perceptual and Motor Skills*, 1979, *48*, 491–494.

Love, K. G. "Comparison of Peer Assessment Methods: Reliability, Validity, Friendship, Bias, and User Reaction." *Journal of Applied Psychology*, 1981, *66*, 451–457.

Lowman, J. *Mastering the Techniques of Teaching.* San Francisco: Jossey-Bass, 1984.

Lynton, E. A., and Elman, S. E. *New Priorities for the University.* San Francisco: Jossey-Bass, 1987.

McCaughey, R. A. "Why Research and Teaching Can Coexist." *The Chronicle of Higher Education*, Aug. 5, 1992, *48(38)*, A36.

MacGregor, J. "Collaborative Learning: Shared Inquiry as a Process of Reform" In M. Svinicki (ed.), *The Changing Face of College Teaching.* New Directions for Teaching and Learning, no. 42. San Francisco: Jossey-Bass, 1990.

McKeachie, W. J. "Financial Incentives Are Ineffective for Faculty." In D. R. Lewis and W. E. Becker (eds.), *Academic Reward in Higher Education.* Cambridge, Mass.: Ballinger, 1979a, 3–20.

McKeachie, W. J. "Student Ratings of Faculty: A Reprise." *Academe*, Oct. 1979b, 384–397.

McKeachie, W. J. "The Rewards of Teaching." In J. L. Bess (ed.), *Motivating Professors to Teach Effectively.* New Directions for Teaching and Learning, no. 10. San Francisco: Jossey-Bass, 1982.

McKeachie, W. J. *Teaching Tips: A Guidebook for the Beginning Teacher.* (8th Ed.) Lexington, Mass.: Heath, 1986.

McKeachie, W. J., Lin, Y., and Mann, W. "Student Ratings of Teacher Effectiveness: Validity Studies." *American Educational Research Journal,* 1971, *8,* 435–445.

McKeachie, W. J., Pintrich, P. R., Lin, Y., and Smith, D.A.F. *Teaching and Learning in the College Classroom: A Review of the Research Literature.* University of Michigan: National Center for Research to Improve Postsecondary Teaching and Learning, 1986.

McLeery, W. "A Teacher Reflects." *Princeton Alumni Weekly,* Nov. 25, 1992, pp. 11–14.

McLeish, J. *The Lecture Method.* Cambridge: Cambridge Institute of Education, 1968.

Maier, N.R.F., Solem, A. R., and Maier, A. A. *The Role-Play Technique: A Handbook for Management and Leadership Practice.* La Jolla, Calif.: University Associates, 1975.

Marlin, J. W. "Student Perceptions of End of Course Evaluations." *Journal of Higher Education,* 1987, *58,* 704–716.

Marques, T. E., Lane, D. M., and Dorfman, P. W. "Toward the Development of a System for Instructional Evaluation: Is There a Consensus Regarding What Constitutes Effective Teaching?" *Journal of Educational Psychology,* 1979, *71,* 840–849.

Marsh, H. W. "Validity of Students' Evaluations of College Teaching: A Multitrait-Multimethod Analysis." *Journal of Educational Psychology,* 1982, *74,* 264–279.

Marsh, H. W. "Student Evaluations of University Teaching: Research Findings, Methodological Issues, and Directions for Future Research." *International Journal of Educational Research,* 1987, *11,* 253–388.

Maslow, A. H., and Zimmerman, W. "College Teaching Ability, Scholarly Activity, and Personality." *Journal of Educational Psychology,* 1956, *47,* 185–189.

Merton, R. K. *The Sociology of Science: Theoretical and Empirical Investigations.* Chicago: University of Chicago Press, 1973.

Milton, O., and Edgerly, J. W. *The Testing and Grading of Students.* New Rochelle, N.Y.: Change Publications, 1976.

Mooney, C. J. "Efforts to Cut Amount of 'Trivial' Scholarship Win

New Backing from Many Academics." *Chronicle of Higher Education*, May 22, 1991, *37*, 1.

Murray, H. G. "Low Inference Classroom Teaching Behaviors and Student Ratings of College Teaching Effectiveness." *Journal of Educational Psychology*, 1983, *71*, 856-865.

Murray, H. G. "The Impact of Formative and Summative Evaluation of Teaching in North American Universities." *Assessment and Evaluation in Higher Education*, 1984, *9*, 117-132.

Murray, H. G. "Classroom Teaching Behaviors Related to College Teaching Effectiveness." In J. G. Donald, and A. M. Sullivan (eds.), *Using Research to Improve Teaching*. New Directions in Teaching and Learning, no. 23. San Francisco: Jossey-Bass, 1985, 21-34.

Murray, H. G., Rushton, P. J., and Paunonen, S. V. "Teacher Personality Traits and Student Instructional Ratings in Six Types of University Courses." *Journal of Educational Psychology*, 1990, *82*, 250-261.

Naftulin, D. H., Ware, J. E., and Donnelly, F. A. "The Doctor Fox Lexture: A Paradigm of Educational Seduction." *Journal of Medical Education*, 1973, *48*, 630-635.

Olson, L. A. "A Third-Generation Student Instructional Rating System (SIRS)." Paper presented at the Association for Institutional Research Conference, Montreal, Oct. 1977.

Ory, J. C., Brandenburg, D. C., and Pieper, D. M. "Selection of Course Evaluation Items by High and Low Rated Faculty." *Journal of Research in Higher Education*, 1980, *12*, 245-253.

Ory, J. C., Braskamp, L. A., and Pieper, D. M. "The Congruency of Student Evaluative Information Collected by Three Methods." *Journal of Educational Psychology*, 1980, *72*, 181-185.

Osterman, D. "Designing an Alternate Teaching Approach (Feedback Lecture) Through the Use of Guided Decision-Making." In Bass, R. K., and Dills, C. R. (eds.) *Instructional Development: The State of the Art, II*. Dubuque, Iowa: Kendall-Hunt, 1984. *27*, MF-01; PC-02. (Ed 298 903).

Outcalt, D. L. (ed.). *Report of the Task Force on Teaching Evaluation*. Berkeley: University of California Press, 1980.

Overall, J. U., and Marsh, H. W. "Students' Evaluations of Instruction: A Longitudinal Study of Their Stability." *Journal of Educational Psychology*, 1980, *72*, 321–325.

Pellino, G. R., Blackburn, R. T., and Boberg, A. L. "The Dimensions of Academic Scholarship: Faculty and Administrator Views." *Research in Higher Education*, 1984, *20(1)*, 103–115.

Peverly, S. L. "The First College Teaching Experience: The Teaching Assistantship." Unpublished doctoral dissertation, Department of Higher Education, Syracuse University, 1992.

Rashdall, H. *The Universities of Europe in the Middle Ages*, Vol. 1. Edited by F. M. Powicke and A. B. Emden. London: Oxford University Press, [1936] 1964.

Rees, A., and Smith, S. P. *Faculty Retirement in the Arts and Sciences*. Princeton, N.J.: Princeton University Press, 1991.

Remmers, H. H. "To What Extent Do Grades Influence Student Ratings of Instruction?" *Journal of Educational Research*, 1930, *21*, 314–316.

Remmers, H. H. "Reliability and Halo Effect on High School and College Students' Judgments of Their Teachers." *Journal of Applied Psychology*, 1934, *18*, 619–630.

Robinson, J. "Faculty Orientations Toward Teaching and the Use of Teaching Portfolios for Evaluating and Improving University-Level Instruction." Paper presented at the annual meeting of the American Research Association, Apr. 1993.

Roueche, J., and Baker, G. *Access and Excellence: The Open-Door College*. Washington, D.C.: The Community College Press, 1987.

Root, L. S. "Faculty Evaluation: Reliability of Peer Assessments of Research, Teaching, and Service." *Research in Higher Education*, 1987, *26*, 71–84.

Rudolph, F. *Curriculum: A History of the American Undergraduate Course of Study Since 1636*. San Francisco: Jossey-Bass, 1977.

Rushton, J. P., Murray, H. G., and Paunonen, S. V. "Personality, Research Creativity, and Teaching Effectiveness in University Professors." *Scientometrics*, 1983, *5(2)*, 93–116.

Salthouse, T., McKeachie, W. J., and Lin, Y. G. "An Experimental Investigation of Factors Affecting University Promotion Decisions: A Brief Report." *Journal of Higher Education*, 1978, *49*, 177–183.

Sands, R. G., Parson, L. A., and Duane, J. "Faculty Mentoring Faculty in a Public University." *Journal of Higher Education,* 1991, *62,* 174–193.

Schön, D. A. *The Reflective Practitioner: How Professionals Think in Action.* New York: Basic Books, 1983.

Schön, D. A. *Educating the Reflective Practitioner.* San Francisco: Jossey-Bass, 1987.

Schrader, W. B. *Admissions Test Scores as Predictors of Career Achievement in Psychology.* GREB no. 76-1R. Princeton, N.J.: Educational Testing Service, 1978.

Schurr, G. M. "Toward a Code of Ethics for Academics." *Journal of Higher Education,* 1982, *53(3),* 318–334.

Scriven, M. "Professional Ethics." *Journal of Higher Education,* 1982, *53(3),* 307–317.

Seldin, P., and Associates. *How Administrators Can Improve Teaching.* San Francisco: Jossey-Bass, 1990.

Seldin, P. *The Teaching Portfolio.* Boston: Anker Publishing, 1991.

Sherman, T. M., and others. "The Quest for Excellence in University Teaching." *Journal of Higher Education,* 1987, *58,* 66–84.

Shore, B. M., and others. *The Teaching Dossier: A Guide to Its Preparation and Use.* (Rev. ed.) Montreal: Canadian Association of University Teachers, 1986.

Shulman, L. S. "Those Who Understand: Knowledge Growth in Teaching." *Educational Researcher,* 1986, *15,* 4–14.

Shulman, L. S. "Toward a Pedagogy of Substance." *AAHE Bulletin,* 1989, *41(10),* 8–13.

Smith, P. *Killing the Spirit.* New York: Viking Press, 1990.

Stevens, E. "Tinkering with Teaching." *Review of Higher Education,* 1988, *12,* 63–78.

Stratham, A., Richardson, L., and Cook, J. A. *Gender and University Teaching.* Albany: State University of New York Press, 1991.

Stuart, J., and Rutherford, R.J.D. "Medical Student Concentration During Lectures." *Lancet,* 1978, 514–516.

Study Group on the Conditions of Excellence in American Higher Education. *Involvement in Learning: Realizing the Potential of American Higher Education.* Washington, D.C.: National Institute of Education/U.S. Dept. of Education, 1984.

Teaching Assistant Program of the Graduate School. *Preparing the*

Future Professoriate for Teaching. Syracuse, New York: Syracuse University, 1991.

Thielens, W., Jr. "The Disciplines and Undergraduate Lecturing." Paper presented at the annual meeting of the American Educational Research Association, Washington, D.C., April 1987. (ED 286436) *57,* MF-01; PC-03.

Tobias, S. "Peer Perspectives on the Teaching of Science." *Change,* March/April 1986, 36–41.

Treisman, U. "A Study of the Mathematics Performance of Black Students at the University of California, Berkeley." Ph.D. diss., University of California, Berkeley, 1985.

Verner, C., and Dickinson, G. "The Lecture: An Analysis and Review of Research." *Adult Education,* 1967, *17,* 85–100.

Weimer, M. *Teaching Large Classes Well.* New Directions for Teaching and Learning, no. 32. San Francisco: Jossey-Bass, 1987.

Weimer, M. *Improving College Teaching.* San Francisco: Jossey-Bass, 1990.

Weston, C., and Cranston, P. A. "Selecting Instructional Strategies." *Journal of Higher Education,* 1986, *57,* 259–288.

Wiener, H. S. "Collaborative Learning in the Classroom: Guide to Evaluation." *College English,* 1986, *48(1),* 52–61.

Wilson, R. C. "Toward Excellence in Teaching." In L. M. Aleamoni (ed.), *Techniques for Evaluating and Improving Instruction.* New Directions for Teaching and Learning, no. 31. San Francisco: Jossey-Bass, 1987.

Wilson, T., and Stearns, J. "Improving the Working Relationship Between Professor and TA." In J.D.W. Andrews (ed.), *Strengthening the Teaching Assistant Faculty.* New Directions for Teaching and Learning, no. 22. San Francisco: Jossey-Bass, 1985.

Winer, B. J. *Statistical Principles in Experimental Design.* New York: McGraw-Hill, 1962.

Winkler, A. M. "The Faculty Workload Question." *Change,* July/August, 1992, pp. 36–41.

Wolf, K. "The Schoolteacher's Portfolio: Practical Issues in Design, Implementation, and Evaluation." *Phi Delta Kappa,* October 1991, pp. 129–136.

Wood, R. V. "Evaluation of Artistic Work for Purposes of Faculty

Reappointment, Promotion, and Tenure." *Association for Communication Administration Bulletin,* 1984, *48,* 43–45.

Zuckerman, H. A. "The Sociology of Science." In N. J. Smelser (ed.), *Handbook of Sociology.* Newbury Park, Calif.: Sage, 1988.

Zuckerman, H. A., and Merton, R. K. "Age, Ageing, and Age Structure in Science." In R. K. Merton, *The Sociology of Science: Theoretical Empirical Investigations,* edited by N. Storer. Chicago: University of Chicago Press, 1973, 497–559.

INDEX

A

AAUP. *See* American Association of University Professors
AAUP v. *Bloomfield College,* 163
Abbott, R. D., 17
Abrami, P. C., 54, 61, 63
Active learning methods, 23, 24–28, 33
Age Discrimination in Employment Act (ADEA), 167–168
Albermarle Paper Co. v. *Moody,* 169
Aleamoni, L. M., 47
American Association of University Professors (AAUP), 161
American Historical Association, 152
Americans with Disabilities Act of 1992, 168
Angelo, T. A., 111, 112
Annual reports, 98–99
Appraisal interview, 127–128
Arts, criteria for evaluation of, 139
Auburn University, 166
Axelrod, J., 38, 42, 44

B

Baird, L. L., 142
Baldridge, J. V., 162
Baldwin, R. G., 2
Barber, L. W., 96
Bascow, S. A., 75
Bayer, A. E., 35
Bedient, D., 181
Behaviorist approach to teaching, 43
Belensky, M. F., 25
Bennett, S. K., 125, 126
Bird, T., 100
Blackburn, R. T., 23, 81
Blau, J. R., 139
Bloom, B. S., 33, 176
Bloom's cognitive levels, 27
Bloomfield College, 163
Board of Regents v. *Roth,* 164
Board of Trustees of Keene State College v. *Sweeney,* 169
Boberg, A., 23
Boice, R., 6, 122
Bonwell, C. C., 28
Bowen, H. R., 135, 155

Boyer, E., 2, 147, 148, 151, 153, 155
Braskamp, L. A., 85, 95, 132
Braxton, J. M., 35, 146
Bressler, M., 175
Brinko, K. T., 83
Brubacher, J. S., 21, 22, 23
Bruffee, K. A., 29, 32
Burns, R., 94

C

Callahan, D., 34
Camp, R. C., 8
Canadian Association of University
    Teachers, 99
Carnegie Foundation for the Ad-
    vancement of Teaching, 3, 136,
    137, 147, 151
Cashin, W. E., 68, 70, 183
Caulley, D., 95
Centra, J. A., 2, 4, 8, 11, 12, 15, 39,
    42, 43, 50, 54, 62, 63, 78, 87, 96,
    97, 129, 131, 132, 141, 175, 178,
    207
Chair evaluations: and classroom
    observations, 117–118; guide-
    lines for, 133–134; and interview
    techniques, use of, 127–128; and
    merit pay increases, 120; ranking
    methods of, 116–117; research
    evidence on, 116–121; of research
    productivity, 119–120; and stu-
    dent evaluations, similarities in,
    119; teaching effectiveness crite-
    ria in, 118–119; and tenure and
    promotion recommendations,
    128–129
Chandelar, S., 124
Chickering, A. W., 24, 25
Citation indexes, 138–139
Clark, J., 125
Clark, K. E., 138
Clark, M. J., 81
Clarke, C. A., 162
Classroom Observation by Col-
    leagues form, 205–215
Classroom research, as classroom
    assessment, 111–113
Clinchy, B. M., 25

Code of ethics, proposed, 33–34, 36,
    37
Cognitive theories of learning, in
    teaching approach, 44
Cohen, P. A., 33, 38, 51, 60, 61, 63,
    82, 118, 120
Cole, S., 138, 145
Colleague(s): buddy system of, 122–
    125; as facilitator, 125–126; grad-
    uate students as, 124–125; as
    mentor, 121–122; versus peer,
    115–116. *See also* Colleague
    evaluation(s)
Colleague evaluation(s): and ad hoc
    committees, 129–131; and class-
    room observation, 117–118; for-
    mative, 121–128; guidelines for,
    133–134; and merit pay system,
    120; questionnaire and rating
    forms for, 131–133; ranking
    methods for, 116–117; research
    evidence on, 116–121; of research
    productivity, 119–120; and stu-
    dent evaluations, similarities in,
    119; teaching effectiveness crite-
    ria in, 118–119; and tenure and
    promotion recommendations,
    128–129
College teaching preparation:
    credit courses in, 17–18; role of
    evaluation in, 15–17
Community colleges, public service
    role of, 154–155
Connected teaching, 25
Constitutional rights, in faculty
    evaluation, 164–167
Consumer, accountability to and
    evaluations for, 6
Continuing education, 155
Contract rights, in faculty evalua-
    tion, 161–164
Cree, M. J., 197
Creech, F. R., 66, 71, 72
Cross, K. P., 111, 112

D

d'Apolonia, S., 54, 61, 63
Deci, E. L., 11, 12

Deming, W. E., 7
Department chairs. *See* Chair
  evaluations
Dewey, J., 29, 33, 177
Diamond, R. M., 3, 151
Dick, W., 27
Dinnan case, 170
Discipline, research productivity
  variations by, 143-145
Doctor of Arts (D.A.) degree, 18
Dohlman v. *Oakland University*,
  163
Donlon, T. F., 51
Dorfman, P. W., 40
Dowell, D. A., 61
Doyle, K. O., Jr., 96
Dressel, P. L., 18, 155
Drucker, A. J., 49, 64

E

Eble, K. E., 12, 47
Edgerton, R., 100, 109
Educational Testing Service (ETS),
  53, 67, 69
Educational-seduction studies, 76,
  77
EEOC. *See* Equal Employment
  Opportunity Commission
Eison, J. A., 28
Eliot, C., 22
Elliot, D. H., 72
Elman, S. E., 2, 147, 153, 155, 156
Employment discrimination, 167-
  169
Equal Employment Opportunity
  Commission (EEOC), 170
ERIC system, 38-39
Erickson, G., 11
Ethics: in research, 145-147; frame-
  work for seminar on, 146
ETS. *See* Educational Testing
  Service
Extrinsic motivation: and external
  rewards, 12-13; and intrinsic
  motivation, 13

F

Factor analysis, 54-58
Faculty: and liberty interests, pro-
  tection of, 166; and peer reviews,
  confidentiality of, 169-171;
  transfer procedures, legality of,
  166
Faculty development centers, 11-12
Fair employment practice laws, 167
Feedback lecture, 28
Feldman, K. A., 39, 41, 54, 66, 67,
  71, 73, 74, 75, 77, 78, 95, 96, 97,
  119, 141, 142
Festinger, L. A., 82
Finkelstein, M. J., 35
First Amendment rights, 162, 164,
  166-167, 171
Fischhoff, B., 95
Flygare, T. J., 169
Formative evaluation, 5-6; col-
  league evaluations as, 121-128;
  and faculty development activi-
  ties, 11-12; and information
  value, 10-11; model for, 9-14;
  and motivation for change, 12-
  14; new knowledge in, 9-10
Fourteenth Amendment rights, 158,
  162, 164, 166, 171
Fox, P. W., 96
Frankhouser, W. M., Jr., 78
Franklin, J., 48, 65
Frederick, P. J., 28
Freire, P., 25, 44
French-Lazovik, G., 128, 132
Froh, R. C., 3, 42, 43, 131, 132, 207
Fuhrmann, B. S., 43, 44, 45
Fund for the Improvement of Post-
  secondary Education, 151

G

Gage, N. L., 38, 44
Gagne, R. M., 27
Gamson, Z., 24, 25
Garfield, E., 138
Gibbs, M. C., Jr., 8
Gillmore, G. M., 58, 60, 180
Goldberger, N. R., 25

Goucher College, 163
Graduate students, teaching portfolio for, 110–111
Grasha, A. F., 43, 44, 45, 124
Gray, P. J., 3, 42, 43, 131, 132, 207
Guthrie, E. R., 49

H

Hackman, J. R., 12
Hagstrom, W. D., 138
Haimowitz v. U. of Nevada, 165
Hander v. San Jacinto Junior College, 167
Heider, F., 82
Henry, M., 122
Hetrich v. Martin, 167
Hiemstra, R., 26
Higher Education Research Institute, 3
Highet, G., 37, 39, 44
Hilts, P. J., 145
Holmes, D. S., 74
Hoyt, D. P., 88
Humanistic teaching approach, 44
Hutchings, P., 100, 109

I

IAS. *See* Instructional Assessment System
ICE. *See* Instructor and Course Evaluation
ICES. *See* Instructor and Course Evaluation System
IDEA. *See* Instructional Development and Effectiveness Assessment form
Independent study, 25
Individualized instruction, 26
Informative feedback, 6
Institutional culture, and personal values, 3
Instructional Assessment System (IAS), at University of Washington, 53–54, 179–180
Instructional Development and Effectiveness Assessment (IDEA) form, 53, 67, 68, 71, 91, 182–187

Instructor and Course Evaluation (ICE), 180–181
Instructor and Course Evaluation System (ICES), 53, 181–182
Intrinsic motivation, 12–14

J

Jauch, L. R., 140
Jesus, as teacher, 20, 21
Johnson Foundation, Inc., 25

K

Kane, J. S., 116, 117
Kane, M. T., 58, 60
Kansas State University, Center for Faculty Evaluation and Development at, 53
Kaplin, W. A., 160, 161, 162, 163, 167, 169, 170, 171
Kaschak, E., 75
Katz, J., 122–124
Keith-Spiegel, P., 36
Keller method. *See* Personalized system of instruction (PSI)
Kemerer, F., 162
Koocher, G. P., 36
Kremer, J., 119
Krotkoff v. Goucher College, 163
Kulik, C.L.C., 33
Kulik, J. A., 33

L

Laboratory, as active teaching practice, 23
Lambert, L. M., 42, 43, 131, 132, 207
Lane, D. M., 40
LaNoue, G. R., 169
Lawler, E. E., 12, 116, 117
Learning, types of: active, 23, 24–28, 33; collaborative, 29–32, 44; cooperative, 29; passive, 25
LeCount, J., 96
Lecture method: active modifications to, 28–29; alternatives to, 24–26; behaviorist approach in,

44; history of, 21; limitations of, 23

Lee, B. A., 159, 169, 170, 171

Legal guidelines for institutions, 171–172

Lepper, M. R., 13

Leventhal, L., 76, 77, 88

Levinson, D. J., 121, 122

Lewin, Kurt, 29

L'Hommedieu, R., 83

Lichtenstein, S., 95

Lilly Endowment, 151

Lin, Y., 28, 32, 64

Lin, Y. G., 88

Linn, R. L., 54

Lloyd, K. E., 33

Lloyd, M. E., 33

Lombardo, J., 75

Loretto Heights College v. *NLRB*, 162

Love, K. G., 116

Lowman, J., 40, 41

Lynton, E. A., 2, 147, 153, 156

M

Master Faculty Program, 122–124

Mentoring, faculty, 121–122

Merit increases, 120; and faculty-performance ratings, 8–9; and merit ratings, adverse effects of, 7–8; symbolic value of, 13

Motivation, extrinsic versus intrinsic, 82; and student evaluations, 82–83

N

National Labor Relations Board (NLRB): jurisdiction of, 161–162; and *Yeshiva* decision, 161

New Directions for Teaching and Learning series, 112

New Jersey Department of Higher Education, 123

New Jersey Institute on Collegiate Teaching and Learning, 123

NLRB. *See* National Labor Relations Board

Norms, academic, 34

NVHM model for change, 9–14, 15

O

Oakland University, 163

One-minute papers, 111

P

Perry v. *Sindermann*, 164, 165, 166

Personalized system of instruction (PSI), 32–33

Pew Charitable Trust, 110

Piaget, J., 29

Portfolio. *See* Teaching portfolio

PSI. *See* Personalized system of instruction

Public service: evaluation and documentation of, 154–156; and scholarship of application, 149–150, 153

Purdue's Cafeteria System, 198–199

Q

Quality-management principles, in academic environment, 7–8

R

Racial discrimination, 168–169

Rashdall, H., 49

Rees, A., 136

Reflection-in-action, 11, 112, 177–178

Reflective evaluation, and reflective thinking, 177

Rehabilitation Act of 1973, 168

Relative judgments, adverse effects of, 7

Remmers, H. H., 49, 64

Research: citation counts, use of, 138–139; defined, 135; and effective teaching, 139–43; ethics in, 145–147; evaluation criteria and standards for, 6–9; and faculty advancement, 4; productivity in,

143–145; publication of, 136–
139; versus teaching, 3, 136
Richardson, L., 75
Robinson, J., 101
Root, L. S., 107, 109, 120
Roth case. See Board of Regents v.
Roth
Roueche, J., 102, 132
Rudolph, F., 22
Rudy, W., 21, 22, 23
Rushton, J. P., 140
Ruston, P. J., 59
Rutherford, R.J.D., 23
Ryan, R. M., 11, 12

S

Salthouse, T., 88
Sands, R. G., 121, 122
Scholarship: integrative forms of,
148–149, 153; redefinition of,
147–154
Schön, D. A., 10, 11, 100, 110, 112,
177
Schrader, W. B., 138
Schurr, G. M., 34
Schuster, J. H., 135, 155
Scriven, M., 34
Seattle Community College, 125
SEEQ. See Students' Evaluation of
Educational Quality form
Seldin and Associates, 4
Self-evaluations: and new informa-
tion, 10; and NVHM model, 15;
research evidence on, 95–97; for
summative purposes, 97, 113
Self-improvement: and classroom
research, 111–113
Self-initiated learning, 44
Self-report, 97–99. See also Teach-
ing portfolio
Seminar, as active teaching, 23
Sexual discrimination, 167, 169
SGID. See Small Group Instruc-
tional Diagnosis
Shore, B. M., 99
Shulman, L. S., 41, 110, 122
Silberg, N. T., 75

SIR. See Student Instructional
Report
SIRS. See Student Instructional
Rating System
Sisco, B., 26
Small Group Instructional Diagno-
sis (SGID), 125–126
Smith, D.A.F., 28, 32
Smith, S. P., 136
Smith v. Losee, 167
Smock, S., 153, 155, 156
Socrates, 20–21
Sola v. Lafayette College, 163
Solem, A. R., 127
Stanford Teacher Assessment Proj-
ect, 100
Statement on Academic Freedom
and Tenure, 33
Statement of Principles on Aca-
demic Freedom and Tenure, 163
Statement on Professional Ethics,
33–34
Stearns, J., 17
Stevens, E., 11
Stratham, A., 75
Stuart, J., 23
Student culture, and institutional
culture, 4
Student evaluation(s), 5, 6: versus
alumni ratings, 64–65; background of, 49–51; bias in, 77–78;
and colleague evaluations, similarities in, 119; computer-aided
communications in, 86–88;
course characteristic variables
in, 66–67, 71–72; forms of, 11,
47–48, 52–58; gender and racial
factors in, 75–76; guidelines for
use of, 89–93; and instructor
characteristics, 73–77; and method of teaching, 65–66; misuse of,
48; as new knowledge, 81;
NVHM model in, 15; reliability
and validity of, 60–63; and student characteristics, 72–73; and
subject matter or discipline, 67–
71; and teacher improvement
and motivation, 82–84; teacher
utilization of, 80–88; and tenure

and promotion, 58–59, 80–81,
88–89; versus trained observers'
ratings, 63; and type of course,
59–60; usefulness of, 10, 11; written comments in, 85–86
Student Instructional Rating System (SIRS), 194–197
Student Instructional Report (SIR),
53–55, 67, 68, 71, 91, 106–107,
188–193
Student learning, measures of, 173–
175
Student rating instruments, 179–
202
Students' Evaluation of Educational Quality (SEEQ) form, 58,
200–204
Study Group on the Conditions of
Excellence in American Higher
Education, 18, 24
Summative evaluation, 5–6, 128–
133
Swazey, J., 145
Syllogistic disputation, 21–22
Syracuse University: Center for In-
structional Development at, 151;
Teacher-of-the-year awards at,
13
Szego, K., 17

T

Tarule, J. M., 25
Teacher-as-performer skills, 40
Teacher-of-the-year awards, 6, 13
Teaching: active approaches to, 23;
as art versus science, 37–39; behaviorist approach to, 43; behavior patterns in, 34–36, 63; and
cognitive theories of learning, 44;
collaborative, Master Faculty Program in, 122–124; collaborative,
mentoring in, 121–122; and
course-level assessment, 175–176;
cross-disciplinary experiment in,
126–127; ethics and norms of, 33–
37; historical perspective on, 20–
24; humanistic approach to, 44;
improvement in, and student
evaluations, 83–84; improvement

guidelines for, 36–37; instructor-
centered, 42, 44; method of, and
level of learning, 27–28; performance evaluation criteria for, 6–9;
versus research, 3, 136; scholarship of, 150, 153–154; and self-
evaluation, 96–97; two-dimensional model of, 40–41; undergraduate, normative structure of,
34–35. See also Teaching, effective
Teaching, effective: and academic
discipline, 41–42; definitions of,
42–45; qualities of, 39–45; and
research productivity, 74, 139–
143
Teaching assistantship, evaluation
in, 15–16
Teaching dossier, 99
Teaching portfolio, 94, 99–107;
criteria and standards for, 7; formative versus summative purposes of, 101, 102; for graduate
students, 110–111; and student
evaluations, 106; for summative
purposes, 107–109
Tenure, formal and implied, 165–
166
Tenure and promotion: ad hoc
committee role in, 129–131; and
colleague and chair evaluations,
120–121; and confidential peer
evaluations, 128; and constitutional rights, 158–160; and factor
analysis, 57; and publishing, 3,
136–39; and student evaluations,
80–81, 88–89; and summative
evaluation, 8
Theall, M., 48, 65
Thielens, W., Jr., 23
Title IV of the Education Amendments Act of 1972, 167
Title VII of the Civil Rights Act of
1964, 159, 167, 168; and peer
evaluation, 170
Tobias, S., 126–127
Tocci, M., 75
Total Quality Management
(TQM), 7–8
Training sessions, and formative
evaluations, 14

Treatment law, versus preventive
   law, 160–161
Treisman, U., 31
Tucker, D. G., 88
Tucker, L., 54
Tung, R., 170

U

Universities, land-grant, 155
University of Chicago's Graduate
   School of Business, 124
University of Georgia, 170–171
University of Illinois, 132; Office of
   Instruction Resources at, 53
University of Pennsylvania v.
   EEOC, 128, 170, 171
University of Washington, 125

V

Verner, C., 23
Vygotsky, L. S., 29

W

Webber, P. L., 96
Weimer, M., 4, 12, 28

Weiner, H. S., 31
Weston, C., 27
Whiting v. Jackson State Univer-
   sity, 168–169
Williams, R. C., 181
Wilson, R. C., 84, 86
Wilson, T., 17
Winer, B. J., 58
Winkler, A. M., 140
Wisconsin State University, Osh-
   kosh, 164
Wolf, K., 100
Wood, R. V., 139
Workshops, and formative evalua-
   tions, 14
Wulff, D. H., 17

Y

Yale Report of 1828, 22–23, 24
Yeshiva decision. See National Labor Relations Board

Z

Zuckerman, H. A., 145, 146